THE AMERICAN BAR ASSOCIATION

THE
LEGAL GUIDE
FOR MILITARY
FAMILIES

Everything you need to know about
Family Law, Estate Planning, and
the Servicemembers Civil Relief Act

RANDOM HOUSE
REFERENCE

NEW YORK TORONTO LONDON SYDNEY AUCKLAND

Copyright © 2013 by The American Bar Association

All rights reserved. Published in the United States by Random House Reference, an imprint of The Random House Audio Publishing Group, a division of Random House, Inc., New York, and in Canada by Random House of Canada Limited, Toronto.

RANDOM HOUSE is a registered trademark of Random House, Inc.

Please address inquiries about electronic licensing of any products for use on a network, in software, or on CD-ROM to the Subsidiary Rights Department, Random House Information Group, fax 212-572-6003.

This book is available at special discounts for bulk purchases for sales promotions or premiums. Special editions, including personalized covers, excerpts of existing books, and corporate imprints, can be created in large quantities for special needs. For more information, write to Random House, Inc., Special Markets/Premium Sales, 1745 Broadway, MD 3-1, New York, NY, 10019 or e-mail specialmarkets@randomhouse.com.

Visit the Random House Web site: www.randomhouse.com

Library of Congress Cataloging-in-Publication Data

The American Bar Association legal guide for military families : everything you need to know about family law, estate planning, and the Service-Members Civil Relief Act.
    pages cm.
  Includes index.
  ISBN 978-0-375-72384-1
  1. Families of military personnel—Legal status, laws, etc.—United States—Popular works.
  KF390.M55A58 2013
  349.73088'355—dc23

                          2013010394

ISBN: 978-0-375-72384-1

Printed in the United States of America

10 9 8 7 6 5 4 3 2 1

First Edition

American Bar Association

Kevin Patrick Flood
Jacksonville, FL

Charlene Foss
Chicago, IL

Julie A. Govreau
Chicago, IL

Jaye Richard Lindsay
Chicago, IL

Kenyon Luce
Tacoma, WA

Anthony R. McGee
Chicago, IL

Steven M. Novak
Chicago, IL

Hilary Phillips
Chicago, IL

Lyndsey MD Olson
St. Paul, MN

Robert Olson
Park Ridge, IL

John B. Oldershaw
Burr Ridge, IL

Zenia Salles
Chicago, IL

Samuel F. Wright
Washington, DC

C O N T E N T S

FOREWORD

Jack L. Rives
Executive Director, American Bar Association

Our nation owes a real debt of gratitude to military families. Servicemembers willingly put themselves in harm's way to protect the freedoms that we hold so dear. Too often, we do not also think of their spouses and children, who endure frequent moves, prolonged separations, and financial sacrifices so that their loved one may serve. Our nation's security depends upon the commitment and dedication of these families.

The heavy costs borne by members of the military and their families often include facing a variety of legal concerns. The servicemember who is transferred to a new location may face difficulty getting out of her lease. The servicemember returning from a lengthy deployment in a high-risk location may find his spouse wants a divorce. The reservist who is called up to active service from a lucrative civilian position may worry what will happen to her position upon her return from serving. It is essential that military families, who sacrifice so much for all of us, be aware of the legal protections to which they are entitled.

The Legal Guide for Military Families is a comprehensive resource, providing military families with a practical understanding of the legal issues they frequently encounter. The authors of this Guide are attorneys with years of experience dealing with servicemembers and their families. They are well versed in the relevant legal subject areas, including the special legal protections available only to military families. The legal information and practical tips contained in this book are presented in a user-friendly, plain-language format. In addition to reading this book, I encourage you to visit ABA Homefront (www.abahomefront .org). That site has a wealth of information about the legal resources available for veterans, servicemembers, and military families, including how to find an attorney.

The Legal Guide for Military Families is one of a series of legal guide books published under the auspices of the American Bar Association's Standing Committee on Public Education. This book was designed to provide you with knowledge of the law and the legal framework of issues impacting military families. It is *not* intended as legal advice. You should always consult an attorney licensed in your state to help you with your specific legal needs.

With nearly 400,000 members, the ABA is one of the largest voluntary professional associations in the world. Its members represent every legal specialty. Public service and public education are among the ABA's most important goals. The ABA educates the public through publications such as this book, online initiatives, programs, collaborations and partnerships with other organizations, and public outreach. Making the public knowledgeable about legal rights is an important cornerstone of a free society.

For more information about the many services and resources the ABA makes available to the public, please visit the ABA's website, www.americanbar.org. Information specific to public education is available on the Division for Public Education's website, www.americanbar.org/publiced.

Jack L. Rives, Lieutenant General, USAF (Retired), is the executive director of the American Bar Association. He formerly served as The Judge Advocate General of the United States Air Force.

INTRODUCTION

Kim Askew, *Chair*
Standing Committee on Public Education

The United States Department of Veterans Affairs reports there are over 23 million veterans in the United States. After more than a decade of repeated and often extended deployments, the legal issues of our nation's servicemembers, veterans and their families are increasing and will continue to do so for years to come. The news media are replete with stories of credit card debt, foreclosures, and other recession related financial issues affecting all families, but for military families, there are added stresses.

Many of the issues servicemembers and their families face require legal assistance and guidance. This book is intended to help servicemembers and their families make sense of complex legal issues, understand the options available to them, and access appropriate resources to resolve their legal concerns. This practical guide focuses on problems and resolutions, not legal jargon or obscure legal principles. Each chapter is framed by a real-life problem and concludes with additional resources, both in print and online, to help the user understand the legal issues they face and options for resolving them. Like many things in life, knowledge is power when it comes to resolving legal issues.

We also encourage servicemembers and their families to go online to ABA Homefront (www.abahomefront.org). In addition to legal information, the site provides an online database of legal referral services, agencies, and organizations that provide low-cost or free legal services to servicemembers and their families. The database features a state-by-state directory to assist in finding a legal professional in a community. One note of caution: when reading this book, or any other source of legal information, keep in mind that it is intended to provide general background knowledge on the legal issues involved; it is not legal advice. Only a lawyer who understands the facts of a particular case can do that. Although every effort has been made to present information that is current, laws can and do change, and may vary widely from one jurisdiction to the next. Consulting with a lawyer is always recommended before pursuing legal action. To find a lawyer, contact the local military installation or local or state bar association.

This book can help readers make informed decisions about a wide range of problems and options. Armed with the knowledge and insight this book provides, servicemembers, veterans and their families can make informed decisions.

Thank you for your service to our country.

Kim J. Askew is the chair of the ABA's Standing Committee on Public Education and an attorney in Dallas, Texas. Ms. Askew represents clients in complex commercial and employment litigation. She has successfully tried cases to jury verdicts in state and federal district courts around the country, and handled appeals before the Texas Courts of Appeals and the Fourth, Fifth, and Eighth Circuit Courts of Appeals.

CHAPTER 1

Working with a Lawyer

John, an airman at Maxwell Air Force Base in Alabama, has two kids with his former girlfriend. John and his former girlfriend are having problems working out a custody agreement. John's girlfriend is threatening to take him to court if he doesn't sign the forms her lawyer has drafted. John thinks he should have a lawyer review the forms first, but he doesn't have one and isn't sure where to find one. Is this something he can do on his own? Where can he find a lawyer to help him? How much will it cost?

Almost everything we do—from making a purchase to driving a car to interacting with others—is affected by the law in some way. But clearly we don't need a lawyer for all of these everyday interactions. So when do you need a lawyer? When can (or should) you handle a matter on your own? This chapter outlines those times when you need the help of a legal professional and details how to find the right one for you.

WHEN DO YOU NEED A LAWYER?

Some problems are not really legal—or are not *exclusively* legal—and can be handled, at least in part, with the help of other professionals such as accountants, doctors, psychologists, the clergy, or other counselors. But many problems do have a legal dimension and require a lawyer's help.

Simply put: Some matters are best handled by a lawyer. Nearly everyone agrees that you should talk with a lawyer about major life events or changes. Some examples include:

- **being arrested for a crime;**
- **being served with documents related to a legal proceeding or lawsuit;**

- being involved in a serious accident causing personal injury or property damage;
- a change or pending change in family status such as divorce, birth, child custody, adoption, or death; or
- a change or pending change in financial status such as filing for bankruptcy or getting or losing valuable personal property or real estate.

When it comes to these types of issues, an ounce of prevention is worth many dollars and anxious hours of cure. When in doubt, it is best to at least pick up the phone and consult with a lawyer briefly. In addition to obviously legal disputes, there are many other issues a lawyer can help you with, including starting a small business, buying or selling a home, and estate planning.

Once you have determined that you need professional legal help, get it promptly. You can get the most help if you are in touch with a lawyer as soon as possible. Failing to contact a lawyer early may mean that you lose important rights or opportunities.

Of course, you can represent yourself during legal proceedings. People without legal training may be able to handle some simple matters—this is called proceeding **pro se** or **pro per**. Taking on a legal matter yourself, however, is extremely risky because each step may involve consequences you may not think about in advance. Doing it yourself also requires a lot of time and

▶ **START EARLY**

Don't just ignore documents or letters detailing a legal action. Contacting a lawyer after a legal problem has escalated to crisis proportions can lead to unnecessary anxiety and may make resolving the problem more difficult and any solutions more expensive. A lawyer may not be able to help you protect rights you have already lost.

energy. If you choose to proceed pro se, a number of local courts or nonprofit organizations provide guidance to people who want to handle legal matters pro se. They assist you in selecting and completing court forms, understanding court procedures, and filing cases.

A lawyer (also called attorney, counsel, counselor, barrister, or solicitor) is a licensed professional who advises and represents others in legal matters. Lawyers practice in the military (Judge Advocate General, or JAG) and in civilian communities. Lawyers must go through special schooling. Before being allowed to practice law in most states, a person must:

- have a bachelor's degree or its equivalent;
- complete three years of education at an accredited law school;
- pass a state bar examination, which usually lasts for two or three days and tests knowledge in selected areas of law;
- pass a national or state examination on professional ethics and responsibility;
- pass a character and fitness review by a committee that investigates his or her character and background;
- take an oath swearing to uphold the state and federal constitutions and the state laws where the person is sworn in;
- receive a license from the state supreme court;
- and in rare instances, complete an internship in a private or public legal or law office.

When looking to hire an attorney for any matter, it is important to find someone who is experienced (done it before), successful (done it well), current (done it well recently), affordable (charges a rate within your budget), reliable (does what is promised), and trustworthy (keeps confidences).

When looking to hire an attorney for military proceedings (be it a court-martial or a discharge board), it is helpful if the attorney has experience with the proceedings for the military service in question—the more successful experience, the better.

For a military proceeding, it is best if the attorney has served on active duty as a JAG and participated successfully in the proceedings as a JAG. It is also helpful if the civilian attorney has recent experience with the proceedings as a civilian counsel because military boards and panels sometimes view civilian counsel differently than JAG attorneys.

Another consideration is if the civilian attorney has actually litigated military cases, as opposed to simply negotiating a plea or administrative separation agreement. While the vast majority of courts-martial are resolved by plea agreements, if you do not wish to plead out, you will want to hire an experienced litigator.

Certain veteran matters may not require prior military experience, but do require special knowledge of veterans law. As a rule, military proceedings do not impose special certification requirements, but it never hurts to ask.

Finding, assessing, and hiring civilian lawyers are dealt with on page 9.

MILITARY LEGAL REPRESENTATION

For military members facing legal issues, you may be able to find legal assistance at no expense. Depending on the type of issue, there may be attorneys associated with the military, or with non-profit organizations, available to help you.

Before getting into the details of when you should seek military legal assistance or not, it is first necessary to look at the difference between *criminal* and *civil* cases.

Criminal cases involve wrongs against the public. Although a criminal defendant may have injured only one victim, any violation of criminal law harms society. Criminal cases are always started by the government. Although victims of crimes may be consulted, they have no power to make a prosecutor bring charges or to prevent the prosecutor from dropping charges. A convicted defendant in a criminal case may be ordered to pay a

	CRIMINAL TRIALS	CIVIL TRIALS
How the trial is commenced	The government brings charges through its prosecutors.	One or more private citizen or corporation brings a complaint against one or more other private citizens or corporations. (Note that sometimes the government can be a party in a civil trial.)
Parties involved	Government v. defendant	Plaintiff v. defendant
Burden of proof	Beyond a reasonable doubt	Preponderance of the evidence
Possible results	Jail time, fines, community service	Paying or recovering damages, restoring the wronged party to the position he or she would have occupied were it not for the wrong committed by the defendant.

fine or may be sentenced to probation, community service, jail, prison, or even death.

Civil cases are private matters, which typically involve one person suing another person for a money award to compensate him or her for an injury to people or property or a court order to make the other party do (or stop doing) a particular act.

Military Legal Representation for Criminal Matters

Military members facing discharge from the military or criminal prosecution by the military (court-martial) should seek help from a JAG known as trial defense or defense counsel, and *not*

> ## FINDING TRIAL DEFENSE/AREA DEFENSE COUNSEL
>
> The simplest option is to contact the nearest military legal assistance office (using the web-based locator service (http://legalassistance.law.af.mil/content/locator.php) and ask for contact information for the nearest trial defense or area defense counsel office. If that does not work, contact *any* military trial defense or area defense counsel's office and ask if they can provide you with contact information for the office closest to you. Each office should have a list of contact information for every other office in the military legal defense community.

from military legal assistance attorneys. You can also hire civilian criminal defense attorneys to represent you in military proceedings.

If you have a nonmilitary criminal case (for example, a DUI or a domestic violence charge), you should seek help from the local public defender or the local bar associations; these are local organizations formed for and by local attorneys and may be a great resource for locating the help you need. You can find such contact information on the ABA HomeFront Directory of Programs (www.abahomefront.org).

Military Legal Representation for Civil Matters

Military attorneys who provide representation in civil matters are called "legal assistance attorneys." Many civil legal matters can be handled by a military legal assistance attorney at no cost to servicemembers. Civil matters include landlord-tenant disputes, wills and trust, family law (including divorce, separation, custody, and child support), consumer issues (including debt collection, consumer scams, identity theft), powers of attorney, advanced medical directives (living wills), and asserting your rights under the Servicemembers Civil Relief Act or the Uniformed Services Employment and Reemployment Rights Act.

To find the nearest military assistance office, go to the Armed Forces Legal Assistance website, http://legalassistance.law.af.mil/content/locator.php. This site contains a locator based on zip code. Even if you do not live close to military installations, start with the locator. There may be a smaller legal assistance office nearby of which you are unaware.

Servicemembers should start by contacting the nearest military legal assistance office for an appointment. Every military legal assistance office provides free legal assistance to eligible personnel regardless of his or her branch of service. You do not need to seek help from the nearest legal assistance office for your branch of service. For example, a Marine can obtain legal assistance form an Army JAG, just as a Soldier can receive legal assistance from a Marine JAG.

If there are no legal assistance offices near you, consider contacting a local legal clinic, which are often sponsored by law schools and offer free legal services to military personnel. Another option is to contact your local legal aid office and your local bar association to see if either offers free or low-cost services to military personnel. Finally, find out if your state attorney general's office provides free civil legal services to military personnel.

Using Military Legal Assistance

You will not have to pay for the services provided by military legal assistance offices. All services provided by a military legal assistance lawyer are free to eligible personnel. However, know that if your legal problem involves costs or fees (for example, a filing fee to file a case with the court), you will probably have to pay these charges.

Legal assistance attorneys can provide help and advice on a number of topics, such as:

- **Planning your estate and drafting your will;**
- **Drafting appropriate powers of attorney and living wills (advanced medical directives);**

- Helping with your taxes or challenging a tax assessment;
- Assessing family law issues including divorce, child custody, and support;
- Reviewing contracts and leases;
- Advising you on credit and lending issues; and
- Ensuring your rights under various laws aimed at protecting servicemembers (for example, the Servicemembers Civil Relief Act or the Uniformed Services Employment and Reemployment Rights Act).

Know that military legal assistance attorneys may not be able to provide you the full range of legal services. Depending on your issue, a military legal assistance attorney may be limited in how much he or she can do to help you with a legal problem, and the lawyer may need to refer you to a civilian attorney for representation to fully resolve your problem.

There are also legal areas in which a military legal assistance attorney may *not* be able to help you. This includes primarily bringing claims against the government and going to court on your behalf. Military legal assistance attorneys also cannot help you with legal matters on behalf of your privately owned business and likely cannot help you with many criminal matters. For these types of legal matters, you will need to contact a civilian attorney for assistance. See the ABA HomeFront's Directory of Programs, www.abahomefront.org, for programs in your area that can connect you to a civilian attorney or other referral programs in your location.

The ABA provides a resource to military legal assistance lawyers, the ABA Military Pro Bono Project, www.militaryprobono. org, which helps military lawyers easily connect their clients to pro bono attorneys who provide representation for no fee.

Determining Eligibility for Military Legal Assistance

Active-duty servicemembers are eligible for military legal assistance programs, but these programs are not limited to only them, and eligibility and the services provided may differ among the military branches. Military spouses are often eligible too, subject to the availability of legal assistance attorneys. Active-duty personnel, particularly those in the junior enlisted ranks and those preparing for deployment, will have first priority.

Reservists and members of the National Guard who have been activated, are preparing to deploy, or have recently returned from deployment, as well as their family members with Department of Defense (DoD) ID cards are also eligible for legal assistance. Retired military personnel and their dependents with DoD ID cards are also eligible—subject to resource availability.

Individual State National Guard Bureaus (NGB) often have legal assistance offices specifically for that state. If you are a member of the National Guard, ask your chain of command whether your State NGB offers such service. (Although it's always good to keep your chain of command informed, you are not required to tell them the reason you would like to see an attorney. You may simply say it is a private matter.)

Military legal assistance may also be available to survivors of eligible servicemembers and retirees, certain overseas civilian employees and their family members, and Allied Forces service members serving with U.S. Armed Forces in CONUS (contiguous United States) and their family members.

FINDING A LAWYER

Most people don't have a "regular" lawyer, in the sense that they have one or more doctors that they see regularly. So how do you find the lawyer who's right for you? Where do you turn for recommendations? What about military families?

On Base

As described earlier, military families may be eligible to obtain free legal services through their base military legal assistance office. Even if you do not live on base, or if your particular base does not have a legal assistance office, you can contact your nearest base legal office for an appointment—and remember, it doesn't matter if the nearest base is for a different service branch (e.g., you are in the Army Reserves and the nearest installation is a Navy base). To find your nearest legal assistance office, use the Armed Forces Legal Assistance locator at http://legalassistance. law.af.mil/content/locator.php.

Off Base

Finding a civilian lawyer may seem daunting, but if you need legal help, it is process you must undertake carefully and thoughtfully. One way to find a lawyer is to start by getting recommendations from the local military legal assistance office. Another is to get recommendations from a trusted friend, relative, or business associate. Be aware that each legal case is different and that a lawyer who did a great job handling a friend's divorce case might not be the right person to handle your landlord-tenant dispute. You may also want to consider reaching out to local legal aid clinics, law school legal clinics, or pro bono networks. A simple Internet search can help you find such programs in your community, particularly if you live near a big city.

Check with your state and local bar association, many of which have programs for military and veteran representation. You may also want to consider contacting a local referral program. Most communities have referral services to help the public find lawyers. These services usually recommend a lawyer in the area—sometimes at a reduced cost. Many services offer help to groups with unique characteristics, such as the elderly, immigrants, victims of domestic violence, or people with disabilities. These services usually make referrals according to

▶ **SPECIAL CONSIDERATIONS: LAWYERS DURING CRIMINAL TRIALS**

If the government accuses you of committing a crime, the U.S. Constitution guarantees you the right to be represented by a lawyer in any case in which you could be incarcerated for six months or more. If you cannot afford a lawyer, the judge handling the case will appoint a private lawyer to represent you free of charge or the government's public defender will handle your case, also at no charge.

Military members facing discharge from the military and criminal prosecution by the military (court-martial) should seek assistance from military attorneys known as trial defense or area defense counsels, and *not* from military legal assistance attorneys. You can also hire a civilian defense counsel to represent you during your military proceeding. More information on these types of lawyers can be found on page 5.

specific areas of law, helping you find a lawyer with the right concentration. Many referral services also have competency requirements for lawyers who wish to have referrals in a particular area of law.

Visit the ABA's Referral Directory, http://apps.americanbar.org/legalservices/lris/directory/, for a list of 300 lawyer-referral services across the country.

There are a number of factors to consider when deciding which lawyer to hire; of course, the lawyer's area of expertise and prior experience are important. A number of states have specialization programs that certify lawyers as specialists in certain stated types of law. The ABA's Standing Committee on Specialization also offers a searchable map, http://apps.americanbar.org/legalservices/specialization/directory/home.html, to determine whether your state has certification. In states without certification programs, you may want to ask about your lawyer's focus areas. You also may wish to ask about the type of cases your lawyer generally handles.

Questions to Ask When Talking To A Lawyer

Don't be intimidated when meeting with a lawyer. Remember, you are the client, which means you are the boss and the lawyer is your employee. By asking the right questions, you can help yourself find the right lawyer.

A lawyer will usually meet with you briefly or talk with you by phone so the two of you can get acquainted. This meeting is a chance to talk before making a final hiring decision. In many cases, there is no fee charged for an initial meeting. However, to be on the safe side, ask about fees before setting up your first appointment.

During this first meeting, ask about the lawyer's experience and areas of practice. How long has the lawyer been practicing law? How long has the person's law firm been open? What kinds of legal problems does the lawyer handle most often?

You should also ask if non-lawyers, such as paralegals or law clerks, will be used to research or prepare your case. If so, find out if there will be separate charges for their services. Who will be consulted if the lawyer is unsure about some aspect of your case? Will the lawyer recommend another attorney or firm if this one is unable to handle your case?

You can ask the lawyer about what he or she thinks the outcome of the case will be, but beware of any lawyer who guarantees a big settlement or assures a victory in court. Remember that there are at least two sides to every legal issue and many factors can affect its resolution. Ask for the lawyer's opinion of your case's strengths and weaknesses. Will the lawyer most likely settle your case out of court or is it likely that the case will go to trial? What are the advantages and disadvantages of settlement? Going to trial? What kind of experience does the lawyer have in trial work?

LEGAL FEES AND EXPENSES

If you need assistance outside of the services offered by your military legal assistance office and cannot get a civilian attorney to handle your matter pro bono (free of charge), you may have to hire a lawyer who will charge attorney's fees. Lawyers are ethically obligated to charge only "reasonable"—and not excessive—fees. The method used to charge fees is one of the things to consider in deciding if a fee is reasonable. You should understand the different charging methods before you make any hiring decision. At your first meeting, the lawyer should estimate how much the total case will cost and inform you of the method he or she will use to charge for the work. As with any bill, you should not pay without first getting an explanation for any charges you do not understand.

The most common billing method is to charge a set amount for each hour of time the lawyer works on your case. More experienced lawyers tend to charge more per hour than those with less experience—but they also may take less time to do the same legal work. In addition to hourly rates, attorneys may bill separately for copying costs, mileage, court fees, witness fees, expert fees, legal research services, and other expenses. These additional fees should all be spelled out in the engagement agreement—the agreement you and your lawyer make when he or she agrees to take your case.

Lawyers may use a flat fee in handling certain cases where the work involved is usually straightforward, predictable, and routine. Thus, some lawyers may use flat fees or set rates in uncontested divorces, simple wills, traffic tickets and misdemeanors, adoptions, and name changes. A flat fee is usually paid ahead of time and does not vary depending on the amount of time or work involved. No refund is due if the work takes less time than expected and no additional charge is made if the case is longer or more complex than usual.

Contingent Fees

A different type of billing method is a contingent fee. A client pays the contingent fee to a lawyer only if the lawyer handles a case successfully. Lawyers and clients use this arrangement only in cases where money is being claimed—most often in cases involving personal injury or workers' compensation.

In a contingent fee arrangement, the lawyer agrees to accept a fixed percentage (often 33⅓ to 40 percent) of the recovery, which is the amount finally paid to the client. If you win the case, the lawyer's fee comes out of the money awarded to you. If you lose, neither you nor the lawyer will get any money, but you will not be required to pay your attorney for the work done on the case.

On the other hand, win or lose, you probably will have to pay court filing fees, the costs related to deposing witnesses, retaining experts, and similar charges.

Reducing Legal Fees

There are several cost-cutting methods available to you. First, answer all your lawyer's questions fully and honestly. It will save time and help your lawyer do a better job.

Remember that the ethics of the profession bind your lawyer to maintain in the strictest confidence almost anything you reveal during your private discussions. It is particularly important to tell your lawyer both the good and bad facts of your case. These will almost certainly come out as your case moves forward.

Stay informed and ask for copies of important documents related to your case. Let your lawyer know if you are willing to help out, such as by picking up or delivering documents or by making a few telephone calls.

You should feel free to compare various attorneys, but don't just shop for the lowest fee. The cheapest lawyer is not necessarily the worst or the best, and the most expensive one may not be the right one for you. Be sure to consider factors such as location, accessibility, personality, time available, and experience in your problem area.

WHEN THINGS GO WRONG

When you agree to hire a lawyer and that lawyer agrees to represent you, a two-way relationship begins in which you both have the same goal: to achieve a satisfactory resolution of your legal matter.

You have the right to expect competent representation from your lawyer. However, every case has at least two sides. You cannot always blame your lawyer if the case does not turn out the way you thought it would. If you are unhappy with your lawyer, it is important to determine the reasons. If you believe you have a genuine complaint about your legal representation, there are several things you can do.

If you believe you have a valid complaint about how your lawyer has handled your case, inform the organization that grants or withholds licenses to practice law in your state. Usually this is the disciplinary board of the state supreme court. You may find the board's contact information under the government listings for your state. You can also obtain its location from the local bar association. Finally, you can access the ABA's Center for Professional Responsibility's listing, www.americanbar.org/content/dam/aba/migrated/cpr/regulation/directory.pdf, of lawyer disciplinary agencies to find the agency in your state.

If your complaint is against a military legal assistance attorney, you can also file it with the attorney's military supervisor or with the Judge Advocate General (the senior military attorney) for the appropriate branch of service.

Making a complaint of this sort may result in a disciplinary action against the lawyer for misconduct, but it will probably not help you recover any money.

In order to get any monetary compensation for your lawyer's misconduct, you may have to file a malpractice suit against your lawyer. You may also have the right to receive compensation from a client security fund. These funds may reimburse clients if a court finds that their lawyer has defrauded them. Lawyers pay fees to maintain such funds. Your local bar association or the state disciplinary board can tell you how to contact the correct client security fund for your claim. Be aware, however, that most state client security funds divide the money that is available in a given period of time among all the clients who have valid claims. As a result, there is rarely enough money to pay 100 percent of every claim.

RESOURCES

- **Stateside Legal** (http://statesidelegal.org): Online legal web portal for military members, veterans, and their families; includes summaries of federal laws and information on finding legal help in your area.

- **ABA Homefront** (www.abahomefront.org): Includes three sections: Information Center, Directory of Programs, and Pro Bono Center for attorneys interested in helping servicemembers.

- **Military One Source** (www.militaryonesource.mil): free web-based service provided by the DoD for servicemembers and their families; provides information about a broad range of topics including legal issues.

- **Armed Forces Legal Assistance** (http://legalassistance.law.af.mil/content/locator.php): Web-based database to locate local military legal assistance offices.

- **ABA Lawyer Referral Database** (http://apps.americanbar.org/legalservices/lris/directory/): A state-by-state listing of 300 lawyer-referral services across the country.

- **Martindale-Hubbell** (www.lawyers.com): A leading source for information on lawyers practicing in the United States and abroad; the site provides profiles of more than 440,000 lawyers and law firms and a "Find a Lawyer" service.

- **Department of Veterans Affairs** (www.va.gov): Includes information on working with a legal advocate during VA procedures; your State Veteran's Affair Office can also be accessed from the VA's site (www.va.gov/statedva.htm).

CHAPTER 2

Family Law and the Military

Sean, a nineteen-year-old Private First Class in the U.S. Army, met eighteen-year-old Jessica while he was stationed at Fort Benning, Georgia, for his infantry training. Sean and Jessica are young, very much in love, and thinking about getting married, but there are limitations on their time and circumstances. Sean has received orders for his first permanent duty station in Germany. Sean is likely to deploy to Afghanistan shortly after arriving at his unit in Germany. Sean and Jessica are thinking about getting married in Georgia, but if they wait, can they get married in Germany? What are the options?

For military members, being married isn't always easy. Military members move frequently and may be deployed in a combat zone or other danger area, but that doesn't stop love from blooming. The rate of married military members has steadily increased over the last two decades from around fifty percent to nearly sixty percent. Among career and senior personnel, the married rate is around ninety-three percent. However, in the last decade or so, the divorce rate among military members has also increased. The likelihood that a military member will marry or divorce at least once within his or her military career is high. And of course, family issues don't just involve marriage and divorce—what happens if Sean and Jessica decide they want to adopt a child? What about if they do marry and divorce, how are their assets to be split? This chapter discusses marriage options and military benefits, custody of children, care of dependents, separation, and divorce.

MARRIAGE

The decision to get married is a serious personal and legal decision. For this reason, premarital counseling may be recommended or required before marriage by certain religions or by the laws of the state in which you are marrying. As a practical matter, timing is often an issue for marriages involving military members, and this may affect the decision of where to marry. A religious ceremony may join two people together in marriage according to a specific religion, but to be legally married requires a license and the filing of paperwork according to the laws of the state where the marriage will take place. The military has no specific pre-marriage requirements for marriages that take place in the United States. However, a copy of your marriage license properly signed and certified by the state where you got married is needed after your marriage to qualify for military benefits. Marriage license requirements vary from state to state, so it is important to understand the state's requirements before committing to a wedding in a specific location. Depending on your

CHECKLIST FOR COMMON MARRIAGE LICENSE REQUIREMENTS

☐ Are we required to be residents of the state?

☐ Are we both required to appear in person to apply for the marriage license? Is there a waiver?

☐ What are the ID requirements?

☐ If previously divorced, is proof of divorce required?

☐ Does the marriage license expire?

☐ Is a blood test required?

☐ What are the fees? Can they be waived?

☐ Is there a waiting period for the license after application? Can this be waived?

☐ Who can marry us? (ordained ministers, justices of the peace, judges, etc.)

☐ Do we both need to be present in the state for the marriage? (see Proxy Marriages, on page 19)

circumstances and whom you want to marry, state requirements can make or break the wedding plans.

Requirements for marriage licenses can be found at county and city government centers or at clerk of court offices in any county or city. Most counties and cities also have websites with downloadable forms for marriage license application. These forms will list the requirements to obtain the license.

This section looks at some of the possible types of marriage, as well as the special considerations for those who are marrying in a foreign country.

Proxy Marriages

Even in the event of a deployment or a permanent change of station (PCS), marriage is possible in some states, even with the bride or groom absent! Proxy marriages are those marriages where either the bride or the groom is not physically present in the state where the marriage is taking place. Someone else usually represents the person who is not present. Proxy marriages are legally recognized only in the states of Colorado, Missouri, Texas, and California. In California, proxy marriages are limited to military members who are stationed overseas serving in a conflict or war. Marriages where neither the bride nor the groom is present in the state are called double-proxy marriages. Montana is the only state that allows double-proxy marriage. Some foreign countries may also offer proxy marriages. Due to deployments, PCS, or temporary remote location duty assignments, a proxy marriage may be a convenient option for military members.

Covenant Marriages

For those looking for extra commitment, not extra convenience, there are three states that have adopted covenant marriage laws: Arkansas, Louisiana, and Arizona (though at least 20 other states have considered adding this marriage option). A covenant marriage is a marriage that is legally harder to dissolve. Covenant marriage requires premarital counseling and marriage education. Divorce is allowed only in limited circumstances, and the divorce must be a fault divorce, meaning there must be a reason for the divorce, such as abuse, adultery, addiction, etc. Normally divorce in a covenant marriage is not granted without a substantial separation period and marital counseling.

Common Law Marriage

Currently only nine states recognize common law marriages (Alabama, Colorado, Kansas, Rhode Island, South Carolina, Iowa, Montana, Oklahoma, and Texas). Five additional states (Georgia, Idaho, Ohio, Oklahoma, and Pennsylvania) have grandfathered in certain relationships beginning before a certain date, which may vary by state. Before modern marriage laws, people sometimes became married through conduct rather than by a ceremony. Common law marriages may occur under the laws of states that recognize it if a couple agrees that they are married, lives together, and publicly presents themselves as husband and wife, though there is no specific formula. However, merely living together is not enough to constitute a common law marriage. Further, because there is no paperwork showing a valid marriage and the marriage is largely established through consent and perception, the existence of a common law marriage is easily subject to challenge. Therefore, common law marriage is generally not a substitute for people who intend to enter into a licensed marriage recognized by states and religious communities.

It is also important to note that the military will recognize a common law marriage if it is legally recognized in the state where it took place. A written statement from the military legal office confirming the validity of a common law marriage will allow a common law spouse to be considered a military spouse. Common law marriage cannot be a sham to collect benefits. The marriage may be scrutinized if it appears not to be valid. Military benefits collected based on a sham marriage may be subject to recoupment, and the servicemember involved may be subject to adverse administrative or criminal action.

Same-Sex Marriage

On September 20, 2011, the repeal of "Don't Ask, Don't Tell" took effect. Openly gay and lesbian individuals are now allowed to be members of the military and engage in same-sex relationships, including marriage. So although the military does not place limits on a servicemember's ability to enter into a same-sex marriage, the state where the couple intends to marry may. At the time this chapter was written, six states (Massachusetts, Vermont, Connecticut, New Hampshire, Iowa, and New York) and the District of Columbia currently grant marriage licenses to same-sex couples. New laws passed in Maryland and Washington will recognize same-sex marriage in those states when the

▶ FEDERAL BENEFITS DENIED TO SAME-SEX SPOUSES

The following benefits and privileges may be denied to same-sex spouses under DoD regulations or the Federal Defense of Marriage Act:

- Housing allowance at the "with dependent" rate
- Coverage under military Medical and Dental Insurance and TRICARE
- Access to morale, welfare, and recreation programs
- Family relocation and transportation benefits for PCS
- Family separation allowance
- Surviving spouse benefits
- Family advocacy services
- Joint duty assignment
- JAG legal services
- BX, PX, Commissary privileges
- "Command sponsored" status for overseas assignments

> ### BENEFITS AVAILABLE TO SAME-SEX SPOUSES
>
> The following federal benefits are available to same-sex spouses:
>
> - Servicemembers Group Life Insurance (SGLI) payments
> - Montgomery G.I. Bill Death Benefit (if person is designated as SGLI beneficiary)
> - Beneficiary of Thrift Savings Plan (TSP)
> - Designation of Survivor Benefit Plan (SBP) if no dependent child
> - Appointment as the designated care giver of a wounded servicemember under the Wounded Warrior Act
> - Appointment as a caregiver to a servicemember's children under a Family Care Plan
> - Designation on a DD-93 Record of Emergency Data as a "designated person," but cannot be designated as "next of kin" (DOMA prohibits this at the time this was written)

laws, passed in 2012, take effect. California granted marriage licenses to same-sex couples for several months in 2008. (The marriages that occurred during that time are still valid.) Several other states grant civil unions or domestic partnerships, granting various levels of state spousal rights.

For servicemembers who are considering a same-sex marriage, it is important to understand the impact of the Defense of Marriage Act (DOMA). DOMA is a federal law that defines marriage as a legal union between a man and a woman and prohibits receipt of many federal benefits to same-sex partners. Under DOMA, many military benefits available to dependents are not available to same-sex couples, even if they are legally married under the laws of a state. Children of gay and lesbian servicemembers receive all the same benefits and privileges any other dependent child receives. (Note that at the time this book was going to print, parts of DOMA were being challenged in court.

Talk to a trusted legal advisor for the most up-to-date information on this rapidly changing legal field.)

Marriage in a Foreign Country

Destination weddings are a popular option for many people, especially servicemembers who are already stationed in a foreign country. In general, marriages performed abroad under the laws of another country are valid in the United States. Foreign marriages of U.S. citizens are subject to the laws of the country where the marriage is performed and are often subject to lengthy waiting periods, so plan ahead! Foreign countries often require presentation of U.S. passports for the couple, may require blood tests and may require other documents too, such as birth certificates, divorce decrees, or death certificates (for people previously married). Additionally, some countries require that these be officiated in the United States by a consular official for the country where the marriage will be performed.

Before planning a marriage under the laws of a foreign country, it is best to contact the consulate or embassy for the country you wish to marry in to inquire about the requirements. General information on marriage in some countries can be obtained from Overseas Citizens Services, Room 4811, Department of State, Washington, D.C. 20520. As an alternative, American embassies and consulates abroad frequently have information about marriage in that country. A listing of foreign embassies and consulates in the United States is available on the Department of State's website at www.state.gov/s/cpr/rls/dpl/32122.htm. It is also wise to contact the state attorney general's office in the state of your residence to ensure the marriage will be recognized in the United States. Once you are married abroad, U.S. consular officers can authenticate your foreign marriage document. Note: This authentication simply signifies that your foreign marriage documents are real; it does not necessarily mean that your marriage will be recognized by your home state.

▶ MARRIAGE TO A FOREIGN NATIONAL OUTSIDE THE UNITED STATES

For servicemembers, marriage to a foreign national can present special challenges or even be forbidden. If you would like to marry a foreign national, the first step is to get military service approval. The approval authority is your area commander. You should begin by informing your chain of command and making a legal assistance appointment at the base or post legal assistance office. Each military service has a regulation that governs this request. A visit to the legal assistance office to see a judge advocate will help you identify the requirements for the marriage application under the appropriate service regulation. The application for permission to marry a foreign national is required regardless of whether you are stationed overseas or just traveling to another country to marry a foreign national. The application process requires a medical screening and background investigation of the foreign spouse.

Once married, you probably have questions about immigration and naturalization of your spouse. There is no legal provision for expedited naturalization processing for dependents of servicemembers. For assistance with naturalization and immigration for military dependents, make an appointment with a judge advocate at your post or base legal office.

I'M MARRIED—NOW WHAT?

Congratulations! You're married. Now, as a servicemember, there are a few things you should do to ensure your new spouse and any children are properly registered for military benefits. The very first thing to do is go to your unit's personnel office with a certified copy (that's a copy with an official stamp from the court) of your marriage certificate to register in the Defense Enrollment Eligibility Reporting System (DEERS) system. DEERS is a database that the military services use to validate eligibility for TRICARE medical benefits. Servicemembers are automatically enrolled, but servicemembers must take action to enroll their dependents. Dependents need DEERS enrollment to receive a dependent military ID card. You can find the nearest uniformed services personnel office at www.dmdc.osd.mil/rsl/.

Protecting Your Dependents

Beyond registration for DEERS, the military offers other benefits for military family members, such as wills for both servicemembers and their spouses, servicemembers group life insurance (SGLI) and family SGLI. SGLI benefits are designated by filling out form SGLV 8286. Your military unit's personnel office can provide you with this form and ensure that an executed copy of the form is filed in your official military personnel file.

Do I Need A Will?

A will is a legal document that designates who will receive your property when you die. This situation is not one people want to think about, but the decision to create or update a will is an important one that will ensure your assets are divided and your family is cared for the way you intend. Creation of a will is a free service offered by the Judge Advocate General's Corps of each military service. The military member and spouse each can sit down with a licensed attorney who works for the military and have a will, and possibly a simple trust, drafted for free. This is a valuable service that can save you several hundred to several thousand dollars. Even single servicemembers should consider having a will drafted, but married servicemembers, particularly those with children, are highly encouraged to create a will. Single servicemembers who created a will prior to marriage should consider creating a new will that includes their spouse as a beneficiary. Chapter 6 explains more about wills and estate planning generally.

RESOURCES

- All of the military services have chaplain corps websites. Chaplains are ordained clergy in the military services who represent a variety of different religions. Chaplain corps websites offer resources and chaplain services for military members and their families. Chaplains mainly perform marriages, and other services may include religious education, couple counseling, premarital counseling, and crisis counseling. Some of the military services even have chaplain services online. The Navy Chaplain Corps website (http://www.chaplaincare.navy.mil/) provides contact information for chaplain's service via phone or email.

- **The American Military Partner Association** (http://militarypartners.org/) is a nationwide support organization for gay and lesbian military members. The website provides information on current military benefits for partners as well as a resource page with links to other organizations providing support and services for LGBT military members.

- *The Military Marriage Manual: Tactics for Successful Relationships,* by Janelle Hill, Cheryl Lawhorne, Don Philpott (Government Institutes 2011). This book offers advice and resources for military spouses on all aspects of marrying into the military.

FAMILY CARE PLANS AND FAMILY SUPPORT

Military service regulations require servicemembers to provide support and care to their dependent family members. Although military service may require a servicemember to move around a lot, such moves do not relieve a servicemember from responsibility to abide by court orders; the military will assist courts in enforcing support orders if servicemembers do not properly handle their legal responsibilities. The Department of Defense (DoD) requires both active and reserve servicemembers to plan for the care of their dependent family members in certain circumstances. This section outlines two obligations faced by many servicemembers: family care plans and family support requirements.

Defining a "Family Member" and Do These Requirements Apply to Me?

According to the DoD, a servicemember may have the obligation to create a family care plan for the following categories of "dependent family members":

- A servicemember's spouse;
- Children who are younger than 19 and unmarried;
- Children of any age who are physically or mentally incapable of self-support;
- Other family members such as brothers and sisters or parents of the servicemember or spouse who are physically or mentally incapable of self-support that are dependent on the servicemember for financial, medical or other support; and
- Family members without the basic English skills needed to access basic needs (e.g.: food, shelter, or medical care).

For the purposes of family support requirements, family members may include:

- A servicemember's current spouse (a former spouse is not considered a family member);
- A servicemember's minor children from a current marriage;
- A servicemember's children from a previous marriage if the servicemember has a current legal obligation to support that child;
- Children legally adopted by the servicemember;

- Children born outside of a marriage to:
  - A female servicemember; or
  - A male servicemember if a court order or comparable legal document exists identifying the servicemember as the father (evidence of a legal obligation to support a child may include a child support order, a signed recognition of parentage filed with a court, a birth certificate, or a determination of paternity depending on applicable state laws); and
- Another person (such as a parent, stepchild, or sibling) that the servicemember has a legal obligation to support under a court order.

Family Care Plans

Family care plans are planning tools that assist commanders in ensuring that military members in their command have an approved plan for the financial, medical, educational, and logistical care for their minor children or other vulnerable adult dependents in the event that military duty prevents servicemembers from caring for their own dependents. Family care plans are required for servicemembers who are single parents, dual military couples with children, married with primary or joint custody of a child from a prior relationship, or primarily responsible for another dependent family member. The DoD requires that servicemembers in these categories complete dependent care plan paperwork and have this plan approved by their commander. If a servicemember does not create an approved dependent care plan, he or she may face disciplinary or administrative action that can lead to separation from the military.

Selecting a Caregiver

Determining whom to select as a caregiver is possibly the most important part of creating a family care plan. This is the person who will step into your role as a parent if your military absence

▶ SOME FACTORS TO CONSIDER IN SELECTING A CAREGIVER

- Select someone you and your child know well and trust. Designating a relative or close family friend your child sees often and has a relationship with will help your child's transition while you are gone.

- Select someone who lives in the same general area in which you live. Your child may feel less disruption with your absence if he or she can continue to attend the same school, see his or her current friends and family members, and continue with the same activities.

- Select someone who is physically capable of caring for your child. Consider a possible caregiver's health concerns. Is the person elderly or in bad health? If so, what effect might this have on your child?

- Select someone who will and can facilitate communication between you and your child while you are absent.

makes it so you are unable to care for your child or other dependents. The biological or legal parents of a child are normally considered a child's best caregivers. If possible, both parents should attempt to agree on an arrangement that is in the best interests of the child. If there is no other parent, or the other parent of your child is not willing to, or cannot, take care of your child during your military absence, you should consider a third party who can provide a safe, nurturing environment that involves the least amount of disruption to the child's normal routines during your military absence.

You can, however, designate whomever you want as a caregiver on the family care plan, if that person is available and agrees to care for your dependents. Be aware: The DoD encourages you to try to the greatest extent possible to come to an agreement with the other legal parent of your child about the care of your child during your absence for military duty. Designating a third party (that includes your current spouse or your parents) as a caretaker on your dependent care plan does not take the place of a custody agreement from a court. So, if the other legal parent does not agree to the designation of someone else, the person you designated will not be able to legally enforce your designation using the dependent care plan paperwork.

Care Plans vs. Custody Agreements vs. Powers of Attorney

Perhaps you are thinking that if you have a dependent care plan, you don't need a custody agreement. Wrong! A dependent care plan does not grant any legal custody rights; you need a custody agreement from a court in order to give another person legal custody of a dependent. Dependent care plans may include a document that designates someone rights under a power of attorney. These rights are granted to either the other parent or a third person, to assume guardianship and care for the child in his or her absence. Many people confuse the power of attorney document with a custody agreement since it is a signed and notarized document. A power of attorney for guardianship does grant another person some of your parental rights temporarily, but neither the power of attorney nor the dependent care plan documents replace or modify court-issued custody agreements. In certain circumstances, some state courts have recognized dependent care plans signed by both parents as evidence of an existing agreement for custody purposes, but the document itself is *not* a legally binding custody arrangement. It is also important to understand that you are not giving up the parental rights that you have by filling out a dependent care plan or a power of attorney for guardianship.

A power of attorney for guardianship gives the person (or people) you designate temporary guardianship of your dependents, but does not revoke or replace your custody or parental rights. A person designated as a guardian by power of attorney will be able to take many of the actions for a child that a parent does. Depending on the state, these actions may include medical and dental decisions (like admission to the hospital, immunizations, and dental cleanings), enrollment of your child in school, traveling with your child, and granting permission for your child to participate in school or organizational activities. This document should include an expiration date, but may also be revoked at any time by you as the parent. A power of attorney for guardianship will expire upon the parent's death.

Family Support Requirements

A servicemember may be required to support family members under a civilian or military obligation or both. Any court-ordered support obligations or those that come from a formalized agreement like a contract, trump service-related support obligations. Service regulations that provide for family support are meant to be temporary in order to allow the family members to seek court-ordered support.

Servicemembers are expected to handle their personal affairs and pay their financial obligations. Active-duty servicemembers may set up voluntary allotments from their military pay for direct payment of family support or other financial obligations by filling out a DD Form 2558 (Authorization to Start, Stop or Change an Allotment) and submitting the completed form to the finance office. When necessary, the military will take an active role in ensuring that servicemembers meet their financial obligations. The military can garnish a servicemember's paycheck if that member fails to follow a court order for family support. If there is evidence of a legal obligation for a servicemember to support his or her family members, the military will assist in enforcing these orders if necessary. In instances where there is no formalized agreement for support, each military service has a regulation that outlines how that service will determine family support obligations. These regulations also provide a process for making a complaint that a servicemember is not meeting support requirements. If you are a family member or the parent of a dependent child of a servicemember and you need to make a non-support allegation, you will need to go through the servicemember's commander. You may contact the servicemember's command to make the complaint or you may seek assistance in making this complaint from a civilian attorney; if you are eligible for legal assistance, you may receive help in making such a complaint from a military legal assistance office at the nearest military installation. Family advocacy, family support centers, or family assistance centers may also provide assistance.

Custody Arrangements and Family Care Plans

Placing your children with the other parent or a third party during your absence for military leave may affect your custody rights! If you have a current custody agreement through a court and that agreement does not discuss temporary custody arrangements for your child(ren) during an absence for military duty (or have no custody agreement at all), you should discuss your upcoming military absence and the effect of any temporary arrangement for your child(ren) with a family law attorney as soon as possible before you leave. In some circumstances, your absence for military duty may affect your legal custody rights if the other parent or a third party attempts to change the custody agreement during your absence. An attorney can discuss options with you for properly protecting your custody rights while you are absent for military duty.

Support Obligations by Branch

Army

Without a court order or another formal agreement for support, the Army Regulation (AR 608–99) states that family support requirements are based on basic allowance for housing (BAH). A soldier may also be entitled to specific BAH rates based on family support requirements. The Army regulation for support is complex and the amount of support available to family members varies depending on the family situation and the soldier's rank. If you are a soldier or family member and need to determine what family support is available to you under the Army Regulation, it is best to see a legal assistance attorney located at your local Army installation. These attorneys will be able to review your situation and assist you in understanding the amount of support available in your situation.

While the legal assistance office may give you legal advice and information on the support requirement, enforcing the support obligation of soldiers is a function of the commander. AR 608–99 is a punitive regulation, meaning soldiers may be punished under the Uniform Code of Military Justice (UCMJ) or receive adverse administrative action if they fail to fulfill their support requirements under court order, agreement, or the requirements in the Army regulation. The Army Regulation applies to all active Army members and to reserve component soldiers on military orders for 30 days or more. The legal assistance office can assist family members in contacting a soldier's commander to request assistance in receiving required support.

Navy

The Navy's support requirement comes from Military Personnel Manual (MILPERSMAN) 1754–030. In the absence of a court order or another agreement, this manual requires a percentage of gross military pay to be paid in support of family members. If you are a sailor or family member and need to understand what family support is available to you under the MILPERSMAN, it is best to see a legal assistance attorney located at the JAG office of your local Navy base. While the JAG office may give you legal advice and information on the support requirement, enforcing the support obligation of sailors is a function of the commander. The manual is punitive, meaning a sailor may be punished under the UCMJ or receive adverse administrative action if he or she fails to fulfill support requirements under court order, agreement, or the requirements in the MILPERSMAN. The JAG office can assist family members in contacting a sailor's commander to request assistance in receiving required support.

Air Force

In the Air Force, there are no specific temporary support measures or guidelines in effect. The Air Force Instruction 36–2906 does require airmen to "provide adequate financial support." Airmen are also required to comply with family support required court order or another written agreement. If Airmen are receiving a basic allowance for quarters (BAQ) at the "with dependent" rate, refusal to provide adequate support will result in cancellation of BAQ and may result in recoupment of BAQ from the airmen. An airman's noncompliance with financial obligations, including family support obligations, may result in disciplinary or administrative action. Family members and airmen seeking further information on family support requirements in the Air Force may visit their base JAG office or Family Support Center.

Marines

The Marine Corps has established family member support requirements in Marine Corps Order P5800.16 (LEGADMIN), Chapter 15. This document makes a Marine's failure to sup-

TYPE OF DEPENDENT	LEVEL OF SUPPORT
Spouse only	BAH difference plus 20 percent of basic pay
Spouse and one minor or handicapped child	BAH difference plus 25 percent of basic pay
Spouse and two or more minor or handicapped children	BAH difference plus 30 percent of basic pay
One minor or handicapped child	16.7 percent (⅙) of basic pay
Two minor or handicapped children	25 percent (¼) of basic pay
Three or more minor or handicapped children	33 percent (⅓) of basic pay

> ## GARNISHING SERVICEMEMBER PAY THROUGH
> ## THE DEFENSE FINANCE ACCOUNTING SERVICE
>
> The pay of servicemembers, both active-duty and reserve, may be garnished through the Defense Finance Accounting Service (DFAS). Garnishments are an involuntary direct payment of a debt to the person to whom the debt is owed. Garnishment may be an option for enforcing family support obligations ordered by a court (such as child support, alimony, or division of military retirement pay). In order for DFAS to garnish a servicemember's military pay, there must be an order from a judge ordering the income withholding. If you are trying to enforce a family support obligation, it is a good idea to talk to a lawyer at your installation legal office or a civilian attorney. You can find more information on the garnishment process at www. dfas.mil/dfas/garnishment.html. You may also call DFAS directly at 1-888-332-7411 for general information on the process. Be aware though that DFAS does not provide legal advice.

port family members punitive upon violation of a court order or upon a verified non-support allegation made to the command. Marines may be punished under UCMJ or be subject to adverse administrative action for failure to comply with family support obligations. In the absence of a court order or other written agreement, the Marine Corps has established minimum support at the greater of a set dollar amount ($350/month) for one child *or* one half of the monthly BAH/OHA (Overseas Housing Allowance), up to one third of the member's gross pay.

Coast Guard

The Coast Guard's requirement is found in Coast Guard Personnel Manual (PERSMAN) Chapter 8M. Enforcing the support obligations of members of the Coast Guard is a function of the commander. The PERSMAN is a punitive manual, meaning Coast Guard members may be punished under the UCMJ or receive adverse administrative action if they fail to fulfill their support requirements under court order, a separate agreement, or the requirements in the PERSMAN. In the absence of a court order for support or other written agreement, the PERSMAN provides for the following:

DIVORCE

Sergeant First Class (SFC) Frank Smith has been in the Army for 15 years. He just returned to Minnesota from an unaccompanied tour in Korea to see his wife and children. Carol and SFC Smith have been married for 12 years. Carol is a resident of Minnesota and has been renting a house near her parents and sister during SFC Smith's Korea tour. Things have not been going well between SFC Smith and Carol. Their troubles began right before SFC Smith left for Korea and things have only gotten worse during the unaccompanied tour. SFC Smith's next duty station is Germany. Carol does not want to move to Germany. She is particularly concerned about moving the kids, who have become very close to their grandparents and cousins in Minnesota. Carol is thinking about divorce but is not sure what her next step should be. SFC Smith is also thinking about divorce; in fact, he found some divorce forms online and all he had to do was fill in the blanks. He plans to "hand Carol divorce papers" when he arrives in Minnesota.

SFC Smith and Carol actually have a complicated situation on their hands. Some military members or military spouses want to find the cheapest or fastest way to get a divorce, but shortcuts in a divorce proceeding can lead to errors and oversights that can be costly to fix legally—that is, if the issue is fixable. If divorce papers are filed incorrectly, a court may later reject the documents or the divorce may later be found to be invalid. Divorce and custody documents that are incomplete or incorrect may result in a military parent losing custody during a future deployment, or a military spouse unknowingly giving up hundreds of thousands of dollars in military pension. Hiring a family law attorney who is familiar with the unique issues of military divorces is highly recommended to ensure your rights are protected.

Separation vs. Legal Separation

Military members often think that as long as they are "separated" from their spouses they are single. This is simply not true, and because adultery and other types of inappropriate relationships are against military law and regulation, it is important to understand your legal situation. Sometimes military members make the mistake of beginning a new relationship with someone else before they are divorced. The military does not consider a military member to be single unless a divorce action is completed, even if you are "legally separated." It is not enough to simply file the paperwork; all the legal steps must be final before the military considers the servicemember's legal status changed.

Some states offer the option of obtaining a legal marital separation. Separation simply means living apart. A legal marital separation is different; it requires the filing of an agreement with the civilian family court and can change the legal status of your marriage to a "separated" status. Some states require a legal separation period before a divorce can be granted. However, in most states, a legal separation is optional and is a completely separate process from divorce. A legal separation is like a divorce in a number of ways, but during legal separation you remain legally married. Many of the same issues that may be addressed in a divorce will often be addressed in marital separation, for example, division of assets, debts, custody, and child support. The court will approve the terms of an agreement that outlines the responsibilities of each spouse during the separation period. The terms of a separation agreement may not be the final terms of the divorce once settled, but they may impact the negotiation process. You should consult your attorney on what effect the terms of separation may have on your divorce according to state law. It is also important to realize that a legal separation can often take as long and be as expensive as a divorce. Therefore, you and your attorney should discuss whether a legal separation makes sense for your situation.

Annulment vs. Divorce

When weighing options for divorce, many servicemembers and spouses wonder whether an annulment is an option. An annulment is a legal action or an action by church authorities, which treats the marriage as though it never happened. Religious annulments are different from legal annulments, which are legal steps taken by the state. Religious annulments may be preferred or required in some religions but do not change the legal status of a marriage with state authorities. Some states allow annulments under very narrow circumstances. For this reason, most people will not qualify for an annulment and will have to pursue a divorce, even if the marriage was very short. The basis for an annulment will vary by state law so be sure to discuss your situation with an attorney. In general, the following circumstances may qualify a couple for an annulment:

- One party's inability to legally consent to the marriage;
- One of the parties was under the legal age for marriage;
- One party could not "consummate" the marriage by sexual intercourse and this fact was unknown to the other party at the time of the marriage;
- One or both parties were under the influence of alcohol or drugs or other substance at the time of the marriage;
- The marriage was obtained by fraud or force; or
- One party had a mental illness, mental incapacity, or insanity at the time of the marriage.

Common Law Divorce?

There is no common law divorce. As mentioned on page 20, a limited number of states recognize common law marriages, that is, marriages in which the couple never went through a formal ceremony but are considered married based on their conduct. Common law marriages may occur under the laws of states that

> ### DIVORCE AND CUSTODY—THE RESERVE COMPONENT
>
> The issues covered in this section on divorce and the following section on custody has equally serious implications on military members who serve in reserve components of the military (Reserve or National Guard). Divorce decrees of reserve component members should address disposition of military retirement and custody of child(ren) during military duty and deployment. Reserve component members should also consider the effect certain personal conduct, such as extramarital relationships and family violence, may have on their military careers; reserve component servicemembers may face the same or similar consequences for these actions as their active-duty counterparts either under the UCMJ or under the military code of the state (if National Guard).

allow it if a couple agrees that they are married, live together, and publicly present themselves as husband and wife. For parties in a common law marriage, divorce may be accomplished only through a court order. If you believe you may be in a common law marriage and are separating from your partner, you need to consult an attorney licensed in the state you reside in to determine what rights and benefits you may be entitled to under law and whether your situation requires a divorce action through a court order.

So, You Want to File for Divorce?

Many people who are ready to divorce simply want to find the fastest, easiest, and cheapest way to complete their divorce. If this is you, stop for a second and consider that what is fast, easy, and cheap on the front end may be incomplete, expensive, and just plain legally wrong. Some divorce actions may be very simple if a marriage is short and does not involve children or significant debts and assets. However, many are complicated, time consuming, and require considerable legal expertise. Regardless

▶ **A LEGAL SEPARATION MAY NOT PROTECT MILITARY MEMBERS FROM ADULTERY CHARGES**

Legal Assistance attorneys often receive the question, "If I get a 'legal separation' and start dating can I get in trouble in the military for adultery?" Unfortunately the answer is not just a simple "yes" or "no." There are many types of prohibited relationships between servicemembers in the military. Receiving a "legal separation" may help protect a servicemember in some circumstances where they enter into another relationship before a final divorce, however, this protection is not absolute. The UCMJ crime of adultery contains three elements: one, a servicemember must have had sexual intercourse with someone; two, the servicemember or their sexual partner was married to someone else at the time; and three, that under the circumstances, the conduct of the servicemember was to the prejudice of good order and discipline in the armed forces or was of a nature to bring discredit upon the armed forces. Under the UCMJ, a "legally separated" servicemember is still considered married. A servicemember's "legal separation" will be considered as part of the command's analysis of whether the relationship was prejudicial to good order and discipline or of a nature to bring discredit upon the armed forces. Servicemembers should also know that if the relationship involves two servicemembers, both servicemembers may face adverse action for any prohibited relationship; however, in most situations, the senior member may face more serious consequences.

(sidebar continued on next page)

of complexity, all divorces will take an emotional toll on everyone involved. Personal counseling for all parties is highly recommended in connection with any divorce. The stigma formerly associated with personal counseling has diminished significantly within the DoD as the military components have begun to focus more on the mental and emotional health of their members

Of course, exactly what will happen to any given member is dependent on the specific circumstances. Here are examples to clarify the possible difference in outcome.

- Example 1: *A legally separated officer begins dating an enlisted service member.* Personal and sexual relationships between officers and enlisted members are generally prohibited. A legal separation will not protect the officer from UCMJ action for this relationship. This relationship is therefore against the good order and discipline of the armed forces, and the crime of adultery might be prosecuted in addition to other crimes such as fraternization or conduct unbecoming to an officer.

- Example 2: *A legally separated enlisted servicemember begins dating another single enlisted servicemember of the same rank who works at the same military installation, but in a different command.* This relationship is probably not prohibited unless the actions of the servicemembers in the relationship become a concern for the command and has an effect on good order and discipline or bring discredit to the armed forces.

- Example 3: *A legally separated non-commissioned officer (NCO) begins dating a junior enlisted servicemember.* This relationship may raise concern with the command depending on the rank and position of each of the servicemembers. This type of relationship may have a specific effect on good order and discipline if the NCO is a senior NCO (like an E8) and the junior enlisted is very junior (like an E2). Further, if the NCO and the junior enlisted member are within the same unit or chain of supervision, this will most likely be a prohibited relationship based on the perception created by the relationship.

and families. Many free and low-cost confidential counseling resources are available for military members.

Legal representation is essential in divorce actions, especially those that involve child custody, child support, and division of significant assets such as real estate, military retirement, and other retirement accounts. The level of legal assistance you may need will vary depending on your situation. The Legal Assistance Office of the nearest military installation is often a good starting point for servicemembers and spouses seeking general information on free or low-cost legal assistance for divorce and custody or referrals to civilian attorneys. Some military legal assistance offices may be able to represent you with your divorce action through the Expanded Legal Assistance Program (ELAP). Otherwise, military legal assistance attorneys can give general legal advice about your situation and provide you with a referral to an attorney who can represent you. Programs for legal referrals for servicemembers exist through the American Bar Association's Legal Assistance for Military Personnel (ABA LAMP) Committee and through state bar associations in most states around the country. For more information on finding an attorney or legal referral service in your area, visit www.abahomefront.org and click on "Directory of Programs." If you need a referral to an attorney in an international location, ABA LAMP may also assist with this through your military legal assistance office. Additional information on finding and hiring an attorney can be found in Chapter 1.

Got Served?

Let's go back to SFC Smith and his wife's situation. What if he does "hand Carol divorce papers"? What if Carol mails SFC Smith divorce papers first?

Divorces take place in state courts. There are no federal divorces—even for servicemembers. The serving process, defined as the formal notification to another party in a legal action as required by law, is one of the first steps in a divorce action, even before filing with the court. States have various requirements for serving the other party in a divorce case. Depending on the laws of the state, this may be done in person by handing the paperwork to the person or leaving the paperwork with an adult at the person's residence. Many states also allow service by mail, in some cases only if the other party is willing to accept service, meaning the person is willing to sign and return paper-

▶ **DIVORCE BY DEFAULT**

Divorce by default occurs when a party to a lawsuit, usually the defendant/respondent, does not respond to legal deadlines for the lawsuit. In a divorce, this can occur if the respondent fails to file a response to the petition for divorce and fails to file a response after being served with a motion for default. Sometimes default can occur if one party cannot be located after a legally specified period has passed and the party filing the lawsuit has complied with service of process requirements by delivering service or by publication.

However, a note of caution: a default divorce involving a service-member may be reopened under the Servicemember's Civil Relief Act (SCRA) in certain circumstances. The SCRA will also allow the servicemember to stay the action for divorce, even if service of process has been accomplished. (SCRA stays are discussed in greater detail on page 47.) Again, such a stay is not an indefinite suspension of the divorce action. It is a temporary stay to allow the service-member an opportunity to prepare and appear for the action after the completion of his or her military duty.

work showing they have consented to receiving the paperwork. The person serving the notice must be a third party. The third party serving the process will sign a document verifying the service. This verification usually will be notarized and filed with the court when the divorce case is filed.

If you are being served with notice of a divorce case, don't worry: Accepting service does not mean you agree with the information contained in the paperwork, only that you acknowledge receipt of the documents. Accepting service allows the divorce to move forward. There may be some situations where accepting service is not in your best interest; you probably want to talk to your attorney to determine whether to accept service of process from the other party. However, simply refusing to accept service will not put off the divorce indefinitely. Eventually most people can be personally served if they refuse to accept service. Personal service cannot be turned down. If one party to a divorce is unable to be located even after reasonable efforts have been made over a required time, service may be accomplished by publication in local newspapers; if a party to a divorce never accepts service or responds, the divorce still may occur by default.

Service of Process Overseas

Serving process on a servicemember or family member stationed or deployed overseas can be expensive and legally difficult. As previously outlined, if the other party will accept service by mail, this is the easiest way to satisfy the service of process requirement. If the other party will not accept service by mail, there are a couple of options. First, you may choose to wait until the individual returns to the United States, or you can attempt personal service overseas through a process server. This is normally extremely expensive and may be nearly impossible to accomplish in some remote and dangerous duty locations. If you are considering overseas service of process, talk to your attorney to find out how much this will cost and what the laws of the country the servicemember is located in may require.

Self-Help (Pro Se) Divorce: Should You or Shouldn't You?

In the example at the beginning of this section, SFC Smith found some "fill in the blank" forms online and was contemplating using these forms to complete his divorce through "self-help" or *pro se,* that is, representing himself, instead of hiring a family law attorney. To many, this may seem like a cost-saving measure, and for couples who have an uncomplicated divorce (normally a short marriage, no children, little to no debt, and little to no assets) this option can be quick and cost effective. However, beware websites selling divorce kits and premade forms for a fee. A quick Internet search reveals dozens of legal form websites offering divorce at bargain prices. Don't waste your money!

These sites offer quick and cheap divorces that seem too good to be true. This means they are. Often the forms on these sites are not drafted by attorneys and they may not conform to the legal requirements for divorce in your state. Many people find they pay money to a website and then later to an attorney to fix or finish the divorce they thought they got for a "bargain." In this case, the bargain is more than you bargained for.

If you feel you may be a candidate for a "self-help" divorce, you should stick to forms provided by the state court system. Many county courts have self-help centers and court forms for divorce on their websites. Self-help centers at the court do not provide legal advice or assistance filling out these forms. These forms normally contain language and provisions that will satisfy only the minimum legal requirements for divorce. These forms do not address military-specific circumstances, such as division of military retirement or other military benefits, or provisions specific to military members for child custody. You should visit your base or post legal assistance office and meet with a legal assistance attorney to seek help determining if the forms provided will work for your circumstances.

Getting Started—Where To File

Military members and their families tend to be a mobile population, and often families find themselves geographically separated due to military duty. As a result, deciding where to file for divorce may be a question for one or both parties and many factors may be taken into consideration. Most states have a residency requirement for filing for divorce. Under federal law, military members and their spouses do not lose or gain residency due to military assignment. Therefore, military members and their spouses may be able to file for divorce in a state in which they are not physically located *if* residency in that state can be proven. For example, let's say SGT Perry and his wife just PCSed to Fort Bragg, North Carolina, a month ago and want to file for divorce. They are both originally from North Dakota, still own a house there and have North Dakota driver's licenses and

> ## ► UNDERSTANDING JURISDICTION
>
> Simply put, the concept of jurisdiction refers to a court's authority under the law to decide legal actions. This authority can be based on one of the parties being located in the jurisdiction (personal jurisdiction) or the ability of the court to decide certain types of actions under certain circumstances (subject matter jurisdiction), for example, specific courts for family law cases; such a court would lack subject matter jurisdiction over any cases that aren't related to family law issues. Jurisdiction can be an extremely complicated concept, even for experienced attorneys. You should not attempt to determine jurisdiction issues for divorce, property division, or child custody without the help of a licensed attorney who practices family law.

voter registrations, and SGT Perry's wife plans to relocate there. They may be able to file a divorce petition in North Dakota as neither of them has lost residency in that state due to military assignment; this is true even though neither of them has physically been located within the state for several years. Additionally, some states with large military populations have specific state laws that allow military members to file for divorce within the state if the servicemember or spouse is located there for military, even if the military member or spouse is not considered a resident of the state.

If there is a choice, what should you consider when deciding where to file? The obvious consideration is physical location; you probably want to pick a location that is convenient. However, physical convenience is not always the only, or most important, consideration. If children are involved, it may be extremely important to evaluate your options when deciding in what state to file in for custody purposes. If there are significant assets in the marriage, the state where you decided to file can make a big difference when it comes to dividing those assets. It is important to understand that while divorce and custody are usually decided together by the same court, it is not required,

▶ **THE MYTH OF THE MEXICAN DIVORCE**

Some military members looking for the easy (or inexpensive) divorce fall victim to advertisements offering cheap and quick divorces in foreign countries, including Mexico, which has become popular. The bottom line? Except in very limited circumstances, foreign divorces normally offer nothing more than a worthless piece of paper that will likely not be recognized as a legitimate, legal divorce by an American court. If you or your spouse is not legally considered a resident in the state or country granting the divorce, the divorce will not be recognized. So, if you see an advertisement online or in the media about a cheap divorce by mail from a foreign country, save your money!

and the basis for a court to be able to decide certain types of cases, called jurisdiction, is different for divorce and custody. To understand how this might work in your case, it is best to talk to a family law attorney who is familiar with the laws of the state in which you are considering filing. In situations where actions are filed in more than one state, it may be necessary to hire a local attorney in each state until the issue of proper filing location is determined by the court or by consent of the parties.

How Does the Servicemembers Civil Relief Act Affect Divorce?

Most servicemembers, and probably most military spouses, are familiar with the Servicemembers Civil Relief Act (SCRA). This law offers legal protections for servicemembers in civil court proceedings and other related legal issues. Many of the SCRA protections are applicable in divorce actions. Here we list some of the SCRA sections that most often apply during divorce actions. An attorney with experience in military family law can help you understand these concepts and how they apply to your situation.

The Stay

A servicemember who has notice of a divorce action may request a stay of that action; if such a request is made, the action will be stayed, or stopped, for up to ninety days. A stay will be granted as long as the member can provide the court with the necessary information. A servicemember may request additional stays, but it is up to the court whether to grant these extensions.

Servicemembers who are deployed or otherwise unavailable due to military service may request the initial ninety-day stay and a stay of additional time based on the period of their unavailability. A servicemember's request for a stay of court proceedings must be in writing to the court and must include the following:

- An explanation of how duty requirements affect the servicemember's ability to appear for the court proceeding, and
- A letter or other communication from the servicemember's commanding officer stating:
  1. that the servicemember's current military duty prevents appearance,
  2. that military leave is not now authorized for the servicemember, and
  3. a date when the servicemember will be available to appear.

If a civil court action is brought against a servicemember and that member has not received notice, the SCRA requires a court to stay an action for at least ninety days if the court finds:

- that there may be a defense to the action, and such defense cannot be presented in the servicemember's absence, or
- reasonable efforts to contact the military member have failed and it cannot be determined whether a meritorious defense to the action exists.

Stay requests are not considered court appearances by the servicemember. This means that if a servicemember submits a request for a stay, the servicemember is not considered to have consented, or agreed, to the jurisdiction of the court over the action. As previously discussed, this fact could be an important one in family law matters.

The Default Judgment

A default judgment is a court decision made in the absence of one party who has failed to respond after reasonable efforts have been made to notify and contact the party and a set amount of time has elapsed. A court must follow the provisions of the SCRA to lawfully enter a default judgment against a servicemember in his or her absence. If the servicemember has not made an appearance in court for a case, the court must first determine whether the member is actually in the military service. The party wanting to proceed (the moving party, normally the plaintiff) must file an affidavit, or an official written statement, to the court, stating whether the other party is in the military service. There are federal criminal penalties for providing a false affidavit to the court. If the affidavit states that the party is a servicemember, the court is required to appoint an attorney to contact the servicemember before the court may proceed with the default judgment. However, even with a signed affidavit, there is still no guarantee that the default will be final. If the attorney appointed by the court cannot contact the servicemember, the attorney will not have authority to bind the servicemember to any action the court may take in the servicemember's absence or waive any defense a servicemember may have. If the court fails to appoint an attorney, then the judgment is voidable.

The court may also require the moving party to post a bond, or monetary promise, as a condition of entry of a default judgment. If the other party is later determined to be in the military service, the money in the bond may be used to cover any loss or damage suffered by the servicemember from the default judgment if it is later set aside.

> ## ▶ VOID VS. VOIDABLE JUDGMENTS
>
> A void judgment is one where the court did not have proper juris-diction to decide a matter, and a voidable judgment is one where the court had proper jurisdiction over the case, but the judgment is erroneous or has a basis for reversal. A judgment that is void is auto-matically turned over, whereas when a judgment is voidable, one of the parties must convince the court that the judgment should be revoked.

Reopening a default divorce judgment under the SCRA requires that:

- **the default judgment was entered when the member was on active duty in the military service or within sixty days after, and**

- **the servicemember applies to reopen the judgment while still on active duty or within ninety days after.**

To get a court to reopen a divorce judgment under the SCRA, the servicemember must prove that:

- **at the time of the judgment by the court, he or she could not defend the court case due to military service, and**

- **that he or she has a legitimate defense to the claims of the other party in the court case.**

The Waiver of Rights

Those who are bringing suits against servicemembers can under-standably be worried about the SCRA protections available for servicemembers, particularly when the parties want to ensure that any legal judgments are final. Therefore, it is common to see language in divorce decrees waiving rights under the SCRA. Servicemembers may waive their rights under the SCRA for a legal proceeding, but the law requires that the waiver be made only when the servicemember is entitled to the rights and protections of the SCRA. This means that for a servicemember in the National Guard or Reserve, if the servicemember is not a member of the military when the waiver is made, the waiver is invalid, as there are no rights to waive. Specifically, the SCRA requires the waiver be done in the following manner:

- **During a valid period of military service;**

- **In a separate document, meaning that the waiver is not a part of the judgment and decree document or combined with any other legal document in a divorce; and**

- **Written in twelve-point font or larger.**

Dividing Property During Divorce

When it comes to divorcing, if possible, the parties should try to agree to as many issues as possible, including dividing property, in order to avoid having a judge make the decisions for them (and dragging the process out longer than needed). If the parties can reach a fair agreement, the court will usually approve it after a short hearing.

If the parties can't agree, the judge will likely have to divide the property for them; the system a judge uses in dividing the property varies by state. To begin with, each party is likely allowed to keep his or her separate (or nonmarital) property. This includes property that a spouse brought into the marriage and kept in his or her own name during the marriage. It can also include inheritances received and kept separate during the marriage. Beyond that, the judge usually divides marital or community property. How this category of property is defined depends on the state, but likely includes property and income acquired during the marriage, wages earned during the marriage, and any home or furniture purchased with marital earnings. And, to further complicate things, how the community property will be divided again varies by state. Some states, such as California, take a rather simple approach: Property should be split equally. In these states, the net value of all marital property and debt will be divided fifty-fifty unless there is a valid premarital agreement stating otherwise.

Most states apply equitable distribution, meaning the court divides the marital property in a way that it deems fair. The division of property may be fifty-fifty, sixty-forty, seventy-thirty, or whatever the court deems appropriate. The court will consider a variety of factors and need not weigh the factors equally, including: each spouse's earning power, services as a homemaker, fault, duration of the marriage, and the age and health of each party. In these situations, it is best to talk to a family law attorney with experience in the state where your divorce action has been filed in order to understand how the property from your marriage might be divided.

There is one asset that is particularly important and valuable for military couples, and seriously complicates the division of assets: the military pension.

Dividing a Military Pension

Military pension is often the largest asset in a servicemember's marriage. For military couples who are divorcing, it is critical that the military pension be addressed in the divorce decree. Military members and spouses should seek legal representation from a family law attorney who has experience with military divorce and pension division. Failure to address pension division in the final divorce judgment and decree document could result in a reopening of the divorce action due to the failure of the parties to divide a marital asset. Military pensions are not like other pensions from private employers; they are federal benefits and are subject to specific federal laws for division. Division of a military pension can be included in the divorce judgment and decree; however, it is recommended that a separate document, normally referred to as a Military Pension Division Order

(MPDO) be drafted to lay out the specifics of the pension division agreement between the parties. Under the provisions of the Uniformed Services Former Spouses' Protection Act, a state court may have legal authority to divide military pension on one of the following bases: if the servicemember consents to jurisdiction, or through domicile of the servicemember (being a resident of a state, not through physical presence but by intending to reside permanently in that state, which can be shown through a variety of factors including payment of tax, owning property, license registration, etc.), or residence (physically living in the state) due to a reason other than military service. While a state has authority to divide military pay, the court cannot dictate a servicemember's retirement.

Is The Pension Divisible?

The Uniformed Services Former Spouses' Protection Act (USFSPA) allows, but does not require, the division of military pension. However, a military pension is considered a marital asset subject to division between the parties in all fifty states and the District of Columbia. Puerto Rico is the only exception, as it does not allow the division of military retired pay. The portion of the pension subject to division is referred to as "disposable retired pay." Disposable retired pay is an amount less than the gross retired pay amount minus the following amounts:

- Amounts owed by the servicemember for government overpayments, recoupments, or forfeitures;
- Any deductions for disability pay benefits; and
- Amounts deducted for Survivor Benefit Plan premiums.

The USFSPA allows military pensions to be divisible by state law regardless of the length of the marriage or military service at the time of the divorce, though some states have vesting requirements for the pension asset before it is considered divisible.

> **WHAT IS VESTING?**
>
> Vesting means that in order to have a definite right to receive the pension benefit, a certain time must pass. For military pensions, servicemembers are vested at twenty years, meaning they have to achieve at least twenty years of service to receive a military pension. Some states divide the military pension as a marital asset even though the servicemember may never receive the pension. If the servicemember never receives the pension, the spouse would normally not be entitled to receive any share.

Many servicemembers misunderstand pension divisibility and believe that military pension is not divisible unless the marriage has lasted for ten years. This is a common misconception, but nevertheless, it is incorrect. The ten-year notion comes from what is commonly referred to as "the 10/10 rule," which is found in the USFSPA.

The 10/10 Rule

The 10/10 Rule refers to the USFSPA provision stating that pension divisions from marriages of ten years or more, which overlap ten years or more of creditable military service, are subject to direct garnishment through the Defense Finance Accounting Service (DFAS). Remember SFC Smith and his wife Carol from the hypothetical in the beginning of this section? In their hypothetical, SFC Smith has been in the military for fifteen years and has been married to Carol for twelve of those years. Therefore, their situation would meet the "10/10 Rule," and any division of SFC Smith's military pension would be eligible for direct payment to Carol by DFAS if the division of the military pension follows the rules of the USFSPA and the divorce decree or MPDO is filed with and accepted by DFAS. For active-duty servicemembers, creditable military service means years of service during which the servicemember was eligible for pay (excluded time may include time during an AWOL status, time incarcerated, or time lost due to an injury sustained from the military member's misconduct). For reserve component servicemembers, creditable service is any year in which the member accrued at least fifty points toward retirement eligibility. If a marriage lasts for ten years or more and overlaps ten years of creditable military service, it does not matter whether those ten years of military service are spent on active duty, reserve duty, or a combination of both. It also does not matter if there are breaks in service, as long as the total service during the course of the marriage adds up to ten overlapping years.

A military pension is still divisible even if the service time and marriage do not meet the "10/10 Rule." In this case, if military pension is divided by a state court but not subject to direct payment to the former spouse by DFAS, the servicemember is required by the terms of the divorce to pay the former spouse directly (for example through direct debit from a bank, check, money order, or other means). Cash is not recommended since it provides no record of payment.

Dividing the Pension: Calculations, Formulas, and the Marital Share

The proper division of military pension can be extremely complex and involve several factors specific to your situation. There is no cookie cutter entitlement for a former spouse to a certain percentage or amount of the retirement. You should discuss division of military pension with your attorney as part of a complete discussion about the division of your marital assets and debts. This section will introduce the components of military pension and the basics as to how a pension may be divided. However, you should not attempt to determine division of your military pension without the assistance of an attorney or a pension division expert.

The USFSPA provides that no more than fifty percent of the disposable retired pay is divisible. However, this does not mean that a former spouse is automatically entitled to fifty percent of a servicemember's military pension. The division of a military pension is normally determined by a formula that calculates the marital share of the military pension to be divided. To understand how the formula works, you must first understand how military retirement benefits are calculated.

Retirement benefits are the same regardless of what branch of the military a servicemember served in and are generally based on rank and number of years of military service, as well as whether the servicemember retired from the active-duty military or a reserve component. If the servicemember retires from active duty, the servicemember is immediately eligible for retirement pay beginning at twenty years of military service, regardless of age. If a servicemember retires from the reserve component (Reserve or Guard), the servicemember is not eligible to receive retirement pay until the age of sixty, no matter how many years of military service a servicemember may have. Note though that there may be exceptions to this general rule for servicemembers who served in a designated combat zone. These servicemembers may be eligible for receipt of retirement pay before age sixty depending on the number of months spent in a combat zone. This determination is made by the military service.

Calculating Military Retirement Pay

The first step to understanding how military retirement pay may be divided is to understand what military pay system applies to the servicemember's military retirement. A servicemember's eligibility for a specific retirement system is based upon when a servicemember entered military service. This date is the date of initial entry into military service, or the servicemember's Date of Initial Entry to Military Service (DIEMS). There are three systems used to calculate military retirement benefits. In all of the systems, a servicemember who stays in military service for twenty years or more is eligible to receive retirement based on a percentage of basic pay.

Final Pay

Servicemembers whose DIEMS is prior to September 8, 1980, fall under the Final Pay retirement system. The Final Pay retirement system bases the amount of the servicemember's pension on the member's last month of pay.

High 36

Servicemembers whose DIEMS is between September 8, 1980, and August 1986 will fall under the High 36 retirement system. Under the High 36 system, a member's pension is based on the average of the highest thirty-six months' base pay. So if the servicemember retires at twenty years, he or she would get a percentage of the average of thirty-six months (three years) of their highest basic pay.

REDUX

Members on active duty or full-time National Guard duty who entered service on or after August 1, 1986, and have completed fifteen years or more of total active federal military service can choose the High 36 (High-3) retirement plan or REDUX.

The REDUX retirement system comes with a career status bonus. The REDUX portion determines monthly retirement income, and the career status bonus provides a one-time $30,000 payment. Members can choose High-3 or REDUX no later than their fifteenth anniversary of active duty, using DD Form 2839.

Although REDUX provides a $30,000 bonus, monthly retirement payments under this system are less than under the other two systems. For twenty years of service, members receive forty percent of the average of their highest thirty-six months of basic pay, rather than fifty percent.

Also, unlike traditional retirement that provides full annual cost-of-living adjustments (COLAs) for inflation, cost-of-living raises for REDUX retirees are one percentage point less than inflation. There is a one-time "catch-up" COLA raise at age sixty-two that puts REDUX retirement pay on par with traditional retirement pay, but after that, annual adjustments under REDUX again begin to lag inflation by one percentage point per year.

The Multiplier

The multiplier is the percentage of the servicemember's base pay he or she receives for each year of service. For the Final Pay and High 36 retirement systems, the servicemember earns 2.5 percent per year of service. That means the servicemember would receive fifty percent of his or her basic pay for twenty years of service, up to a maximum of 100 percent for forty years of service, which is extremely rare. Under the REDUX and REDUX/CSB systems, the multiplier is two percent per year for the first twenty years, but for each additional year past twenty years of service, there is an increase to 3.5 percent. This means that a servicemember receives 40 percent of basic pay for twenty years of service.

Putting It All Together—How the Division Formulas Work

At this point, you're probably thinking this is all just a big jumble of numbers and information, but let's put it all together in some examples that will help clarify how all this works together.

Active-duty example: Senior Master Sergeant Bob Price has a DIEMS of August 8, 1990, and he retired with twenty-one years of service. He did not take a career status bonus, so his retirement pay will be calculated using the High 36 retirement system. Under the High 36 system, the number of years of service (21) is multiplied by the multiplier amount (0.025 or 2.5 percent per year of service if expressed as a percent). That calculation would be $21 \times 0.025 = 0.525$. This number, 0.525, is then multiplied by the average of the thirty-six highest months of active duty base pay, which is, for the sake of this hypothetical, $4,700. So,

> ≣ **CHECKLIST: WHAT TO PROVIDE YOUR ATTORNEY WHEN CALCULATING MILITARY PENSION DIVISION**
>
> ☐ Servicemember's full name and unit of assignment (if still serving)
>
> ☐ Branch of service
>
> ☐ Rank
>
> ☐ Date of initial entry into military service (DIEMS)
>
> ☐ Basic pay entry date
>
> ☐ Leave and earnings statement (LES) for active-duty personnel (DFAS Form 702) available at www.mypay.dfas.mil
>
> ☐ Retirement points Statement for Guard/Reserve personnel
>
> ☐ Retiree account statement for retired personnel (DFAS-CL Form 7220)
>
> ☐ "20-year letter" for Guard/Reserve personnel for survivor benefit plan (SPB) election
>
> ☐ DD Form 2656–1 for SBP election and coverage for retirees
>
> ☐ Letter from branch of service that servicemembers receive upon retirement (when receiving retirement pay) showing expected amount of retired pay and calculations
>
> ☐ Any disability rating awarded, the percentage, and the dollar amount currently being received

$0.525 \times \$4,700 = \$2,467.50$. Senior Master Sergeant Bob Price will receive $2,467.50 in retirement pay each month.

Reserve component example: Remember, the reserve component creditable retirement is based on points. Generally, a reserve servicemember will need to accrue at least fifty points per year for the year to be considered a "good year" for retirement. To determine how many years a reserve servicemember has toward reserve component retirement, you must look at the Retirement Points Annual Statement (RPAS). The RPAS lists the number of points earned each year, and a total number of points is listed at the bottom of the column titled "Total Pts For Ret Pay." Another column to the right titled "Creditable Svc for Ret Pay" shows the number of total years of military membership creditable toward retirement pay. Colonel Jessica Jones has a DIEMS of April 25, 1989, and she retired with twenty creditable years for retirement pay and 4,758 total retirement points under the "Total Pts For Ret Pay" column on her RPAS. Colonel Jones's retirement will be calculated under the High 36 system. Since she is not an active-duty servicemember, she is not entitled to select the Career Status Bonus. To calculate Colonel Jones's retirement amount, the number of points she has earned toward retirement, 4,758, is divided by 360 to convert the number of points into a years number. So, $4758 \div 360 = 13.22$. 13.22 is then multiplied by the multiplier for the High 36 system (2.5 percent or 0.025), $13.22 \times 0.025 = 0.3305$. This number, 0.3305, is then multiplied by the average of the thirty-six highest months of active-duty basic pay for her rank (O6), which for this hypothetical we'll say is \$9,280. The result is $0.3305 \times \$9,280 = \$3,067.04$ in military retirement payments.

Note that because reserve members do not receive their retirement until age sixty, the number \$3,067.04, which represents the value of the military retirement monthly amount now, may change a bit by the time Colonel Jones reaches sixty. If Colonel Jones spends the time between her date of retirement and age sixty in the Ready Reserve, she will receive the benefit of COLAs added to her retirement amount.

Cost of Living Adjustments

A COLA is a pay adjustment provided to military retirees to help maintain purchasing power. In general, unless the pension division order indicates otherwise, either intentionally or unintentionally, both the servicemember and the former spouse will receive the adjustment.

The COLA will vary depending on the retirement pay system the servicemember falls under. For the Final Pay and High

36 systems, the COLA is determined each year by the National Consumer Price Index; the COLA for the CSB/REDUX retirement system is the Consumer Price Index minus 1 percent.

It is important to note that over the time that a servicemember receives retirement payments, the COLA could more than double the amount of those payments. In pension division

> ### HOW CAN I KEEP MY MILITARY PENSION FROM BEING DIVIDED?
>
> Many servicemembers, at least initially, want to find a way to keep their military pension from being divided in a divorce. Often they have heard that if the marriage is less than ten years, there is no requirement for division. This is simply untrue unless you are able to file for divorce in Alabama (the one state that has a requirement of ten years of marital military service for division), or Puerto Rico, which bars division of military pensions entirely. A few states (Indiana, Arkansas, Ohio, and Michigan) also have established certain "vesting" requirements for division of military pension, which may prevent division in short-term marriages or short-term military service. For short-term marriages of two people who are very young, it may be simple and fair to agree that each party be awarded their own retirement accounts and assets and no division is considered. For other longer-term marriages that overlap with military service, division of the military pension in some manner is likely the fairest result for both parties. While there may be several ways for a servicemember to limit the amount of pension division and in some situations avoid it altogether, avoiding division is difficult and often very time-consuming and expensive. Even in situations where servicemembers want to fight the division of a military pension, the additional time and expense may still result in an eventual division. The details of whether and how a military pension is divided are entirely situational. Ensure you have the conversation with your attorney about pension division sooner rather than later.

▶ USING RESERVE POINTS TO CALCULATE THE MARITAL SHARE

For reserve component members, the marital share may also be expressed in terms of points. This calculation involves adding up the number of points earned during the marriage as shown on the RPAS and dividing by the total number of points the servicemember earned. If we use Colonel Jones's example above and assume ten years of marriage overlapping military service and during that ten years, the RPAS shows 1670 "marital" points were earned, the marital share calculation would be:

1670 (the number of "marital points earned during the marriage) ÷ 4758 (the number of total points Colonel Jones earned during her military career) = 35.1%. 35.1 percent of the disposable income is considered part of the marital share. If the court awards fifty percent of the marital share to each party, the former spouse would receive 17.55 percent of Colonel Jones's disposable military retirement pay.

orders, putting in an exact dollar amount has the effect of leaving all of the COLAs to the retired servicemember. In other words, the former spouse would receive none of the annual adjustments for inflation.

The Marital Share

The "Marital Share" of military retirement is simply that portion of the retirement that accrued, or was earned, during the marriage. The marital share is generally calculated as follows:

$$\frac{\text{Months of marriage (by valuation date) overlapping service}}{\text{Total months of military service at retirement}}$$

Let's look at an example: 10 years (or 120 months) ÷ 24 years (or 288 months) = 42%

In this example, the marital share is 42 percent of the disposable retirement pay. If the court chooses to award the non-military spouse 50 percent of the marital share, then the spouse will receive 21 percent of the retirement payments. The service-member receives the other half of the marital share (21 percent) plus any separate property interest from nonmarital military service, in the example above (14 years) for a total of 79 percent.

The marital share can also be calculated as an exact dollar amount. Such a calculation would look like:

number of years of military service ÷ total years of military service × amount of retirement pay = amount of marital pension

Let's look at an example of how this works. If the number of years of military service during the marriage is seven and the total number of years of military service is twenty-five and the amount of disposable retired pay is $2,800, then seven is divided by twenty-five and multiplied by 2,800 for a total of $784 as the marital share dollar amount divided between the parties. If 50 percent of this amount is awarded to the spouse, then the spouse's share of the retirement is $392.

Awarding the Marital Share—Types of Awards

The marital share can be awarded in several ways depending on how the court orders the division. How this is accomplished depends on several factors in any given divorce situation. A military pension is often the largest asset in a marriage, but it may be one of many assets, depending on the marriage. Dividing a military pension should not be done in a vacuum. In order to determine the proper division, all the assets and debts of the marriage should be looked at, as well as where the parties are in their lives and what their needs are, or are likely to be. In situations where there are other retirement accounts, or other large assets, the parties may prefer to do a present value off-set, allowing for a lump-sum payment of the retirement share to the former spouse.

In situations where this offset is not an option, the division order may allow for payments to be made over a set period of time. Normally, the military spouse will begin to make the payments after he or she starts to receive retirement payments from the military. However, courts in a few states have upheld agreements for the payments to begin before the military member retires. If the servicemember is still in military service at the time of divorce and a present value off-set is not an option, the parties may choose to reserve division until the servicemember retires, or use a hypothetical award of the marital share to determine a set of conditions for the division. For example, you could use the number of years of service and the rank of the servicemember.

Below are a number of the common ways the marital share can be divided. What makes sense for you will depend on your particular situation and desires. No matter what type of award is chosen for your situation, the terms must still be consistent with the USFSPA. Working with a qualified family law attorney will help ensure proper division of all debts and assets, including military pension.

Present Value Off-Set

As mentioned earlier, the former spouse's share of military pension may be paid in a lump sum either by cash or other assets as agreed. Normally, the process for finding the present value of a military pension requires an actuary or a certified public accountant who is familiar with pension valuation; the parties can also agree to a valuation amount without an expert. Using present value off-set can be useful for both parties, particularly if one party needs cash or desires a certain asset. Pension division can be used as a bargaining chip to fulfill the needs of both parties. Present value off-set may also make sense if there are multiple retirement or investment accounts. Instead of dividing each account, the present value off-set of each account is determined so that the assets are divided fairly or in exchange for one party taking on marital debts.

Fixed Dollar Amounts

Awarding the marital share through a fixed dollar amount is the most straightforward of type of division: A specific monthly dollar amount is awarded to the former spouse in the court order. For example, the court order may read something along the lines of: "The former spouse is awarded $325.00 per month of the member's military retired pay."

If a fixed dollar amount is awarded, the former spouse will not be entitled to the military member's COLAs. Even when the amount of retired pay goes up for cost of living, the monthly amount awarded will stay the same.

▶ **USING AN OFF-SET**

Some individuals use assets or debts as an off-set during calculations of military pension division. Be careful using percentage awards if an off-set is also done. Doing this may invalidate the pension division award language unless done properly. For example, if the former spouse is awarded real estate with $40,000 in equity and this amount is supposed to offset $40,000 of the former spouse's share of the military retirement, the percentage awarding the former spouse's share of the retirement should be adjusted down to compensate for this amount. So, taking the example above, the former spouse may be entitled to 21 percent of the disposable retired pay, but there is an off-set of that $40,000 for the equity; this is where things can become quite complicated. To avoid provisions in the court documents that are unenforceable, a pension division expert should calculate the total value of the pension and the total value of the former spouse's 21 percent. The amount of the former spouse's percentage would then be decreased by the $40,000 of equity and the new amount of the former spouse's share would then be recalculated as a lower percentage of the military member's disposable retired pay to reflect the $40,000 asset awarded to the former spouse.

Percentage Awards

Awards of a certain percentage of the military pension may be done in two ways: by a formula or by a hypothetical. Most states take the approach that the former spouse should not benefit from any of the military member's post-divorce promotions or pay increases based on length of service after divorce, though the parties may agree to include these if they wish. The language of a percentage award that is determined by formula is very straightforward. A simple example of a percentage award is: "The former spouse is awarded 21 percent of the member's disposable military retired pay." If this type of clause is used, the former spouse will have the benefit of future COLAs.

In the formula, the numerator is the period of the parties' marriage while the military member was performing military service. The numerator must be provided in the court order or the order will be rejected. The denominator covers the military member's total period of military service. The award is normally calculated by multiplying the marital fraction by 50 percent (or half). In situations where parties meet the 10/10 rule and DFAS will pay the former spouse directly, DFAS will supply the denominator that will be the total number of months of the military member's service.

An example of this type of award is: "Effective January 10, 2013, as division of marital property, Husband shall pay Wife 50 percent of the marital share of his disposable retired pay each month. The marital share is a fraction made up of 132 months of marital pension service, divided by the total months of Husband's military service."

For reserve component retirement awards, instead of months, the numerator is expressed in reserve retirement points.

In circumstances where a divorce occurs in the middle of a servicemember's military service and the terms of military pension division must be agreed upon, hypothetical awards can be useful even when the circumstances of a servicemember's actual retirement are not known. A hypothetical award is computed the same way a military member's actual military retirement pay is calculated, but it uses variables that apply to a hypothetical situation agreed upon by the parties. In these types of awards, all the variables must be outlined in the court order. When these awards are used, the court order may figure the award as though the military member had retired on the date of the separation or divorce, and the former spouse is not given the benefit of the military member's pay increases due to promotions or increased military service time occurring after the divorce. On the other hand, some states mandate that such an award take into account increases in rank and time in service achieved in part by the support the marriage provided. An example of a hypothetical award fixing grade and years of service is: "Wife is granted 21 percent of what a Captain would earn if he were to retire with eighteen years of military service."

Once the marital fraction is determined and method of dividing the military pension is selected, it is important to consider other factors that may influence the amount of military pension actually received by the former spouse. Disability pay is one such factor.

Military Retirement and Disability Pay

Servicemembers with a disability connected to their military service may be eligible for disability retired pay from the military or disability benefits from the Department of Veterans Affairs (VA). If a servicemember receives disability pay from the military or the VA, that money is not taxable and is not divisible marital property in divorce. This means that the amount of disposable retirement pay available to the former spouse may be significantly decreased in some cases. The important thing to understand in a divorce situation is the receipt of disability pay can impact the amount of retirement pay to which the former spouse is entitled. Remember the Uniform Services Former Spouses' Protection Act (USFSPA) mentioned in the last section? This law gives a court the power to divide a military retirement. The retirement amount that can be divided under the law, the "disposable retired pay," does not include disability compensation,

▶ **CONFUSED?**

The dividing of military pension and various benefits is incredibly complex and complicated; and on top of that, if things are not done correctly (for example, if the court order doesn't spell out the division of a certain benefit in a required way), benefits can be lost or waived. Consequently, this is one of those areas where having a qualified, experienced legal adviser help you work through these issues and all the variables is really the best way to make sure your rights are protected and that you fully understand your obligations.

only military retirement pay based on years of service. So, if a servicemember is receiving military disability pay, the amount that is eligible for division during the divorce is the amount that is the difference between what the servicemember would normally receive in retirement pay and the amount calculated by multiplying the base pay amount by the disability percentage. (For more information on how disability percentages are determined, see page 58.) This makes more sense if we look at an example:

A First Sergeant's retired pay, based on twenty years of service and a base pay of $4,700, is $2,350. Let's say the First Sergeant has a disability rating of 40 percent. The rating percentage, 40 percent, is then multiplied by the base pay, $4,700, for a total of $1,880. Because retired servicemembers receive the higher of the two possible benefit payments, the First Sergeant here will receive $2,350 as military disability retired pay.

The difference between these two amounts is $470 (2350 − 1880 = 470). So in this situation, only $470 would be divisible between the servicemember and the former spouse as the disposable retired pay, and no more than half this amount ($235) would be available as the spouse's share. Compare this with the $2,350 that would be divisible for the spouse's share if the servicemember were not receiving military disability pay. In this situation, the spouse's share could be up to $1,175 instead of $235.

Military and VA disability compensation are not divisible with a former spouse. A court cannot use these disability compensation payments in determining the marital share amount owed to a former spouse. However, an indemnification clause can be inserted into the marital termination agreement or the final court order at the time of settlement or trial. To indemnify means to agree to compensate someone if certain events occur, kind of like an insurance clause. In this circumstance, the indemnification clause basically states that the servicemember or retiree will pay back the former spouse any money lost from the marital share if the servicemember receives disability pay or does anything else to reduce the former spouse's share of the military pension.

In some states, VA disability benefits are considered income for purposes of determining alimony or child support. This may be the case even if the disability payments are the member's only source of income. States may still consider VA disability benefits as income even though these payments are not taxed. While not subject to levy, seizure, or attachment, disability payments may be garnished to the extent that the disability payment amount replaces military retired pay. This means if the retiree has waived a portion of military retired pay for disability pay, then this amount may be subject to garnishment for alimony or child support.

Survivor Benefit Plan (SBP) and Divorce

The Survivor Benefit Plan, frequently referred to as SBP, is an annuity program (a form of insurance entitling the beneficiary to a series of payments) allowing retired or retirement-eligible servicemembers to provide continued income to their beneficiary in the event of their death. A designated beneficiary receives a lifetime annuity of 55 percent of the base amount selected. SBP coverage is an option for former spouses; however, this benefit is not automatic; whether a former spouse is covered by SBP should be dealt with in the military pension division order. Many former spouses assume they must or should have SBP. The SBP may not be needed or may not be an advantageous option in all situations. The expense and other limits of the SBP program should be considered before participating or agreeing to former spouse SBP coverage. Here is a list of advantages and disadvantages of this program to consider with your situation.

SBP ADVANTAGES

- Provides financial security for former spouse and/or children in the event of the servicemember's death.

- Does not require either party to qualify for the benefit with a physical examination.

- Coverage cannot be refused or lapse while premiums are being paid.

- The servicemember cannot terminate coverage without spouse's consent once designated.

- Former spouse will receive payments for the rest of his or her life upon servicemember's death (unless former spouse remarries before age 55).

- Premiums are deducted from servicemember's retirement pay, which reduces income for tax purposes.

SBP DISADVANTAGES

- The premiums may be more expensive than term life insurance.

- Once SBP is chosen, it cannot be canceled.

- The benefit cannot be split between a former spouse and a new spouse. If former spouse coverage is elected, a current spouse and additional children will be left without protection of the SBP benefit.

- Entitlement ends if former spouse remarries before age 55.

- If the servicemember has a disability or service-connected condition, an offset of dependency and indemnity compensation (DIC) may reduce SBP.

▶ DEPENDENCY AND INDEMNITY COMPENSATION BENEFITS AND OFFSETS

If the servicemember dies of a service-connected injury or disease, the Department of Veterans Affairs (VA) pays a benefit called dependency and indemnity compensation (DIC) to the surviving spouse and dependent children of the servicemember. DIC is explained in more detail in Chapter 6. However, there is an important connection between SBP coverage and DIC benefits; if SBP coverage is provided by the death of the same servicemember as DIC coverage, the SBP payments will be reduced by the amount of DIC paid to the surviving spouse. DIC payments to or for children do not affect SBP payments. If DIC payments offset the entire SBP amount, no SBP annuity is paid and premiums for spouse coverage may be refunded to the surviving spouse. If an SBP annuity is still paid, minus DIC amounts, a refund of premium may still be given in an amount equal to the difference between the two coverage levels. Special Survivor Indemnity Allowance (SSIA), which went into effect in 2008 and 2009, allows surviving spouses whose SBP annuity has been totally or partially offset by DIC to qualify for monthly SSIA payments, which are taxable. SSIA benefits currently terminate in 2017.

Servicemembers on active duty are automatically covered by the SBP. At retirement, an election must be made. In addition to selection of SBP coverage for the spouse, the servicemember can select no SBP coverage at all, SBP for children only, or SBP at a reduced amount. These elections require the spouse to agree, and all selections must be made in writing. Reserve component members have an opportunity at the twenty-year mark to make an election for SBP coverage. At the time of application for retired pay (normally about a year before the military member turns sixty), there is another opportunity to elect coverage. The same rules apply for spousal concurrence on any coverage less than full coverage. The death of, or divorce from, current spouse or remarriage (if former spouse coverage is not already elected) are other life events that may allow an opportunity to elect coverage.

SBP cannot be elected by divorce decree. Even if the divorce decree awards SBP to the former spouse, the former spouse election must be done within a year of the divorce decree (if submitted by the retiree to DFAS on DD Form 2656–1), and one year from the SBP order (may be different from the date of divorce in some cases) if submitted by the former spouse, in what is known as a "deemed election" letter sent to DFAS. The court order awarding former spouse coverage must be included. If these deadlines are not followed, the parties may have to apply to the appropriate board for correction of military records for relief.

Dividing Other Military Benefits

In addition to military retirement, other federal benefits may be available for former spouses and/or dependent children.

20/20/20 and 20/20/15

These numbers don't refer to vision; they refer to continued military benefits that may be provided for former spouses under certain circumstances if a former spouse was married to a ser-vicemember for at least twenty years. Depending on how both parties view military benefits continuing for the soon-to-be for-mer spouse, it may make sense to seek a legal separation or delay divorce proceedings if the length of the marriage is close to fall-ing into the category of required years. You should talk with your attorney to determine how to proceed. The following benefits may be available under the following conditions:

20/20/20—"Full Coverage"

Under this "full coverage" rule, former spouses are considered dependents and are eligible for all military installation benefits, including TRICARE medical benefits (excluding dental) and other privileges such as Base/Post Exchanges (BX/PX) and commissary access, if:

- The former spouse was married to the same sponsor/servicemember for at least twenty years;
- The servicemember has at least twenty years of creditable service toward retirement pay; and
- All twenty years of marriage overlap the twenty years of creditable (active or reserve) service that counted toward your sponsor's retirement.

20/20/15—"Transitional Coverage"

For divorces occurring on or after September 29, 1988, this "transitional coverage" provides medical coverage for an eligible former spouse one year post divorce if:

- The former spouse was married to the same sponsor/servicemember for at least twenty years;
- The servicemember has at least twenty years of creditable service toward retirement pay; and
- At least fifteen and less than twenty years of marriage overlap the twenty years of creditable (active or reserve) service that counted toward your sponsor's retirement.

Benefits under transitional coverage do not include other military benefits such as access to BX/PX or commissary. For 20/20/15 former spouses, the period for coverage may vary by the date of the divorce as shown below.

A former spouse's eligibility for TRICARE under either type of coverage is determined by DEERS enrollment. Therefore, a former spouse must contact DEERS and enroll as his or her own sponsor under his or her own Social Security number. If the military service determines that the 20/20/20 or 20/20/15

DATE OF DIVORCE OR ANNULMENT	COVERAGE
Before April 1, 1985	You're eligible for care received on or after January 1, 1985, or the date of the divorce/annulment, whichever is later. Your eligibility continues as long as you meet eligibility requirements (also see below)
April 1, 1985 through September 28, 1988	You were eligible for care received from the date of the divorce/annulment until December 31, 1988, or two years from the date of the decree, whichever was later.
On or after September 29, 1988	You're TRICARE eligible for one year from the date of the divorce/annulment.

source: www.tricare.mil

rule is met, the military service will issue a new ID card. A former spouse covered by TRICARE is eligible for the same TRICARE program as the retired servicemember. As a result, the cost of TRICARE benefits and type of coverage for qualifying former spouses may be dependent on whether the servicemember's retirement is under the reserve or the active-duty retirement system.

It is important to note that 20/20/20 or 20/20/15 benefits can be suspended for a number of reasons. These include remarriage, even if the remarriage ends in death or divorce (unless you gain eligibility under your new spouse). In addition, getting health coverage from another entity, for example, purchase of a private health-insurance plan or being covered by an employer-sponsored health plan, may suspend 20/20/20 or 20/20/15 benefits.

> ### ▶ PROVING 20/20/20 OR 20/20/15 ELIGIBILITY
>
> If you are a former military spouse who has not remarried, the following documents should establish your eligibility for coverage:
>
> * Marriage certificate,
>
> * Divorce decree, and
>
> * DD Form 214 or statement of service from the applicable service personnel component.

Continued Health Care Benefit Program

TRICARE will provide transitional health benefits under the Continued Health Care Benefit Program (CHCBP) to former spouses who are not remarried. CHCBP is not a part of TRICARE, but provides benefits similar to those under TRICARE Standard. These benefits are also similar to COBRA benefits for private health insurance programs. Coverage for eighteen to thirty-six months is available after TRICARE eligibility ends, but is not cheap. The current cost of individual coverage is $1,065 per quarter and the cost for family coverage is $2,390 per quarter. Former spouses who qualify for coverage must apply within sixty days of loss of eligibility for either regular TRICARE or Transitional Assistance Management Program (TAMP) coverage.

The following categories of individuals may be eligible to purchase CHCBP coverage:

* **Former active-duty servicemembers released from active duty (under other than adverse conditions) and their eligible family members.** *Coverage is limited to eighteen months.*

* **Unmarried former spouses who were eligible for TRICARE on the day before the date of the final decree of divorce, dissolution, or annulment.** *Coverage is usually limited to thirty-six months; however, some unmarried former spouses may continue coverage beyond thirty-six months if they meet certain criteria. Contact Humana Military for details.*

- Children who cease to meet the requirements to be an eligible family member and were eligible for TRICARE on the day before ceasing to meet those requirements. *Coverage is limited to thirty-six months.*

- Certain unmarried children by adoption or legal custody. *Coverage is limited to thirty-six months.*

Servicemembers Group Life Insurance

The Servicemembers Group Life Insurance (SGLI) program is an optional insurance program for military members to provide life insurance to designated beneficiaries upon the member's death. Servicemembers can designate anyone as a beneficiary under this program. However, this life insurance is also considered a federal benefit, and payment to a beneficiary is generally not considered divisible in divorce. Further, a state court does not have authority to require servicemembers to designate a particular beneficiary in a divorce judgment and decree. (In some divorce proceedings for nonmilitary families, the court may order one spouse to appoint the other spouse as a designee on a life insurance policy during a division process.) Such court-directed SGLI beneficiary designations are invalid and unenforceable.

Servicemembers can voluntarily continue to list their children from a prior marriage or a former spouse as a SGLI beneficiary. Servicemembers who want to provide for their minor children under SGLI should consider establishing trusts to hold the SGLI and other assets of the servicemember rather than identifying a former spouse, current spouse, family member, or guardian as a beneficiary. Establishing a trust to manage the assets passed to any minor children will ensure the money is used for the benefit of the children as required by law. Servicemembers should see their legal assistance attorney at their local military installation Legal Assistance Office or an attorney who specializes in estate planning to set up a will with trust provisions.

Thrift Savings Plan

The Thrift Savings Plan (TSP) is a retirement savings plan available to active-duty servicemembers. The TSP allows servicemembers to save money in the program for use during retirement. Amounts saved as part of this program are in addition to pension benefits provided by the military service. Division of TSP is not required, but TSP is a divisible marital asset, similar to retirement plans available through private employers. The TSP account itself cannot be transferred to a former spouse, but a lump-sum cash payment or a transfer to another retirement account (such as a 401k or IRA) can be made to a former spouse to divide the asset. Another option is to offset the value of this account with another marital asset. Similar to other types of retirement investments, the TSP may be invested in several types of funds that carry varying amounts of financial risk. Therefore, like other investments, a TSP account's value may fluctuate. The TSP provides quarterly statements that may be obtained by logging into the TSP account at www.tsp.gov.

RESOURCES

- **MilitaryOneSource** (www.militaryonesource.mil): Provides marital and individual counseling sessions for no cost.

- **Stateside Legal** (www.statesidelegal.org/interactive-form -waiver-scra): Provides a waiver form that complies with the SCRA.

- **Office of the Secretary of Defense Retirement Calculator** (http://militarypay.defense.gov/retirement/calc/index.html): This resource is useful for ballpark calculations of retirement pay or choosing between the High-3 and REDUX systems.

- **Defense Finance Accounting Service** (www.dfas.mil): This resource provides a variety of information on many types of military pay and benefits.

CUSTODY, VISITATION, AND CHILD SUPPORT

Like most parents, servicemembers and their spouses (or the nonmilitary parent) have concerns and questions about how military service impacts child custody, child visitation, and child support. Frequent moves, temporary-duty assignments, deployments, overseas assignments, and drill and annual training for reservists can all complicate the issues of determining child custody and visitation arrangements.

Before jumping into the nitty-gritty of how military service might impact child custody, visitation, and child support, it is important first to understand *what* court will be making these determinations. Nearly all fifty states follow a pair of uniform laws, the Uniform Child Custody Jurisdiction and Enforcement Act (UCCJEA) and the Uniform Interstate Family Support Act; these laws help determine which court has jurisdiction for custody, visitation, and family support orders.

Jurisdiction is a legal term that indicates whether a court can legally take control over a legal action and issue a decree, or a legal decision. The basis for jurisdiction for initial family support orders, that is, child support and spousal support, may vary by state and are based on the court's jurisdiction over the divorce or over child custody and visitation matters. Jurisdiction for an initial court determination of child custody is determined by the "home state of the child." Under the language of the UCCJEA, and therefore in all the states that have adopted it (forty-nine total), the definition of "home state of the child" is generally the last state the child lived consecutively for six months. Periods of temporary absence do not interrupt the six-month period, and foreign countries are treated as states under the statute. At this point, you're probably beginning to see how these issues can quickly become complicated for military families that move frequently. That is why these matters almost always require the assistance of an attorney who understands child custody, visitation, and family support matters. In some cases, complicated

▶ **UNDERSTANDING VISITATION**

Visitation is the term normally used for the time the noncustodial parent has with the child. Visitation time and duration vary depending on the circumstances between the parents, the age of the children, and the location of each parent. A parent's visitation with his or her children is normally unsupervised by the other parent or third parties. Sometimes circumstances may warrant a parent having temporary or permanent supervised visitation ordered by the court. Courts are usually reluctant to order supervised visitation absent evidence of abuse, neglect, or physical or mental unfitness of a parent.

jurisdictional questions regarding which state has jurisdiction to make an initial determination or a modification may require hiring attorneys in more than one state to ensure that the laws of each jurisdiction are properly understood. Hiring an experienced attorney to draft a thorough child custody and visitation order will save the parties time and expense in the long run.

Options for Child Custody

It's common to hear parents who share custody of children say things like, "We have joint custody of the kids," or "We share the kids 50/50," or "She's the primary parent; I get visitation on the weekends." But, what do these things really mean? In reality, they may mean different things legally depending on the situation. Divorcing parents often feel they have their mind made up at an early stage about custody. Dad may say, "I'm going to fight for joint custody; I don't want to lose my kids." Mom may say, "I don't care what I have to give up; I'm getting sole custody. I don't want him to have anything to do with the kids." On the other hand, the parents may say things like, "We've already agreed on joint custody," when really, the idea of joint custody means different things to each parent. First, let's take a look at the different options for custody and what the terms mean.

Sole Custody

Sole custody generally refers to one parent having primary care and control of the child. Sole custody may be physical, where one parent is the primary physical caretaker of the child, whom the child lives with the majority of the time (sometimes called the custodial parent). Sole custody may also be legal and involve the right to make any decisions affecting the child (generally these include medical decisions and decisions about education, religion, and travel). Depending on the laws of the state, sole custody can be both physical and legal, leaving all care, control, and decisions in the hands of one primary parent, while the other has visitation. Sole custody may also be physical, and with legal custody being shared jointly.

Joint Custody

Joint custody refers to joint parenting between parents and, like sole custody it can be physical and/or legal. Joint legal custody is joint decision-making by the parents regarding the child's health, welfare, and education of the child. Joint physical custody or shared physical custody refers to an arrangement where the child alternates living with both parents on a regular basis. This type of situation works only when both parents agree on major life decisions for the child and live near to each other and plan to stay in the same area, so that a child alternating between each parent's household can still attend the same school and activities throughout the arrangement. However, what if the parents cannot agree? Court orders establishing the joint legal custody arrangement may provide for a neutral "tie breaker" on major life decisions that the parents cannot agree on. Or, one of the parents may be designated the parent with primary physical custody and as the decision maker in a situation where the parents cannot agree. Custody agreements that contain only broad language such as "the parties agree to reasonable visitation" rarely work in the long term. Parents can always agree on arrangements that are different from what the custody decree provides, but in a situation where what is reasonable cannot be agreed upon, it is better to have specific provisions for how communication, transportation, and time with the child will be handled. In addition to a definition of "major decisions" for the child's health, welfare, and education, joint custody agreements frequently provide that:

- the parties will consult with each other and make every effort to agree on "major decisions";

- a specified "tie breaker" method will be used to solve issues when the parents cannot agree on major decisions;

- each parent will make every effort to maintain free access and contact between the child and the other parent;

- the child will be raised within a specified religion;

- schools, health care providers, day care, counselors, and activities will be selected jointly by the parents;

- each parent is authorized to obtain emergency health care for the child without the consent of the other parent;

- each parent will keep the other informed of athletic and social activities, grades, and other events of the child;

- each parent will keep the other informed about issues regarding the well-being of the child;

- each parent will keep the other informed of the current address and whereabouts of the child;

- each parent will keep the other informed of travel that takes the child away from home for longer than an agreed-upon period (often five or seven days);

- each parent ensures regular telephonic and/or electronic communication with the child and will not interfere with the child's communication with the other parent;

- holidays, birthdays, and other family occasions will be handled in a set manner.

Determining Custody

Family law specialist and author James T. Friedman writes, "A fair settlement is better than a good contested victory." In most situations, agreement between the parents is the best (and cheapest!) option. During divorce, tensions and emotions run high, and sometimes the idea of "fighting it out" seems tempting, but the reality rarely matches the fantasy of the judge in black robes giving the other party his or her just desserts. Sometimes trials or hearings are necessary to protect rights or safety, but arguments can be particularly long and financially and emotionally painful. Often in these contests for custody, it is the children who lose the most. But what do you do if you cannot agree? Then it will likely be the job of the judge or court-ordered mediator to make the final decisions. Your attorney is your advocate, and your attorney will also know the laws of your state and how a court would likely view your set of circumstances.

Factors that May Affect Custody

Courts rarely, if ever, grant custody based on the needs of the parent, or how much money a parent makes. Courts most often decide custody based on the arrangement that is in the "best interests of the child." All states have laws that require the interests of the child to be taken into account by the court. There is no standard definition in all states for what "best interests of the child" include; however, frequently the factors include consideration of the following:

- **The importance of family. Keeping the child in their home and/or near other family members with whom the child has a relationship.**
- **Emotional ties between the child and parents, child and siblings, and other family and household members.**
- **Which parent has been the primary caretaker?**

- The capacity of each parent to provide for the health, safety, and protection of the child.

- Whether domestic violence is present in the home.

- The mental and physical health of each parent.

- The ability of each parent to provide a timely, permanent home for the child.

In six states, the court must consider all factors listed in the "best interest of the child" statute. Three states list factors that should not be considered when determining best interests of the child. These include no discrimination based on a parent's disability, no presumption that one sex is a better parent than the other, and no consideration of the socioeconomic status of the parent. The remaining forty-one states provide general guidance in the law and allow courts the discretion to make a determination regarding "best interests of the child."

Marital Fault/Parental Misconduct

Just because one parent is assigned marital fault or may be engaging in activities the other parent does not agree with does not mean that the parent will not receive custody or visitation, or that is he or she will be deemed an unfit parent by the court. Most states now have "no fault divorce," where parties can divorce based on "irreconcilable differences" or "irretrievable breakdown of the marriage," instead of assigning some type of fault to one of the parties as a means to divorce. A number of states also still have fault divorce and may require one of several grounds (such as adultery, desertion, criminal conviction, insanity, or cruelty) to avoid a waiting period for divorce. However, most courts will look at the impact a parent's marital fault or misconduct has on the children before viewing it as a factor for custody determination or parental fitness.

Military Duty

Military duty is not incompatible with parenthood. Military service is not a disqualifying factor for having or winning custody. Still, frequent moves, frequent travel, deployments, and irregular work schedules involved in military duty place a burden on the military parent to show that military duty will not interfere with custody of the children. On the other hand, aspects of the military lifestyle may offer several advantages to children, including:

- **life experience and cultural enrichment of traveling and living in other states and countries;**
- **the quality and availability of day care facilities;**
- **the quality of schools on base; and**
- **availability of youth activities, youth community, and recreational facilities.**

Despite advantages, there is an increasing concern over the last decade about how military deployments and moves impact legal custody arrangements. The recent rise in these types of cases is likely due to the large mobilization of the reserve components and the resulting deployments of thousands of reservists who, other than occasional military deployments, may be very capable of providing a stable living environment for their children. Several cases where the military parent has lost custody during a deployment to the previously noncustodial parent have gained media attention. These custody decisions are seldom, if ever, based solely on the custodial parent's military duties, although the courts have used military membership and duties as a factor. If you think a court is using military service against you during a custody determination, talk to your attorney about how best to handle the situation.

Laws Affecting Custody and Family Support Cases Involving Military Members

In response to cases where custody has been changed due to the deployment of a military parent, state and federal laws have been passed that give some measure of protection to military members in custody situations.

Servicemembers Civil Relief Act (SCRA)

The SCRA, a comprehensive law that offers many types of protection for servicemembers, is most commonly used in custody cases for its stay provisions (the particulars of requesting a stay are discussed in more detail in the previous section on the SCRA). If a non-custodial parent files for a determination or a modification of child custody while the custodial parent is on military orders and cannot appear to defend the case, the servicemember may file a stay of the court proceedings under the SCRA. If the servicemember requests the stay and meets the stay requirements, the court *must* grant a stay of the case for ninety days. Often, though, courts will enter temporary orders for a change in custody despite a servicemember's request for a stay. The courts have repeatedly shown that the primary concern in these cases is the welfare or the "best interests" of the child. In several cases, these temporary custody orders have been upheld on appeal. Temporary custody orders can trump the SCRA's stay provisions, despite new language added to the SCRA stating that the stay provisions apply particularly in custody cases.

The concern normally is not so much for the arrangement the temporary custody order provides for, but the precedent it sets and the effect it has on the return to the previous custody agreement when the custodial military parent returns. If you think this is happening in your case, it is vital that you talk to your attorney immediately and bring this issue to his or her attention.

State Military Custody Laws

Currently, forty states have passed laws that provide some measure of custody and visitation protection for military parents. While these statutes can vary dramatically from state to state, several similar provisions are present in most statutes. Common provisions include:

- No permanent changes in custody during or in defined periods immediately before or after deployment, mobilization, or active duty.
- Temporary orders regarding custody made during or in defined periods immediately before or after deployment, mobilization, or active duty may revert back to original order.
- Deployment may not be considered as a factor in custody determination.
- Deployment does not justify modification or changing a custody order.
- Guardianship or visitation can be delegated or temporarily given to a third party, like a grandparent.
- Expedited/electronic hearings made available for deployed parent.

These differences in state laws and the importance in protecting your rights is part of the reason it is vital to make sure you have the advice of an attorney experienced in dealing with family law cases in your state.

Military Considerations for Custody and Visitation Orders

For situations where one or both parents are in the military, custody and visitation orders should detail what will happen in the event of military PCS, deployment, or temporary military training, or in the case of reservists, drill and annual training. A complete custody and visitation agreement that fully discusses how military duty and child visitation and contact will be handled is the single greatest opportunity to avoid arguments, confusion, unintended consequences, and litigation down the road. The checklist below provides topic that should be discussed between you and the other parent and between you and your attorney when agreeing on custody and visitation.

- ☐ What will the custody arrangement be? Who will have primary physical and legal custody, or will parents share joint custody?

- ☐ If the parents currently live in the same community and custody will be joint, what will the arrangement be in the event the military member must move for military duty?

- ☐ What accommodations will be made in the visitation schedule when military duty interferes with regular visitation? How will visitation time be made up?

- ☐ If the servicemember has primary custody, what will the temporary custody arrangement be during an extended TDY (temporary duty) and/or deployment?

- ☐ What are the terms of the temporary change in custody during a deployment?

- ☐ How and when will the child be returned to the military parent after deployment or TDY?

- ☐ What arrangements will be made for the child to communicate with the military member on a regular basis during military duty (phone time, email, Skype or FaceTime, or similar video access)?

- ☐ What, if any, time will be made available for the child to spend time with grandparents, siblings, or other family members during a military member's deployment or TDY?

- ☐ What arrangements will be made to ensure visitation for the child and the military member during the military parent's leave during a deployment or extended TDY?

- ☐ How will relocation for military duty be handled if the military member is the primary parent? Does the noncustodial parent consent in the agreement to PCS relocation of the child worldwide?

☐ What arrangements will be made for visitation and communication with the noncustodial parent in the event the child moves with the military parent on a PCS move or TDY?

Frequently Asked Questions About Custody and Military Deployment

Why does my mobilization/deployment potentially allow the noncustodial parent to change custody?

The mobilization or deployment of a military parent may allow a noncustodial parent to seek a change in custody; this can occur if the temporary relocation of the child with the noncustodial parent is considered a "change in circumstances" allowing the court to reopen a current custody agreement for modification. Unless the state law that governs the custody agreement (the child's home state under the UCCJEA) provides for automatic return of a child to the military parent after deployment, or the custody agreement provides for this, the noncustodial parent may be able to claim a change in circumstances based on the military parent's absence for military duty. Although the law or an agreement to return the child to the military parent's primary care may prevent a change in custody in most circumstances, there may still be circumstances where a change in custody may occur surrounding a military deployment, where the basis for the custody modification is not the absence of the military parent for duty. Other circumstances affecting the best interests of the child can still arise, such as a parent's mental health, domestic abuse situations, the child's attachment to siblings and family members in the household, and the child's performance in school and recreational activities.

What can I do to keep my custody decree from being modified before, during, or after my deployment?

Not all modifications can be avoided in all circumstances. There is no iron-clad solution. However, the best way to avoid modifications of custody surrounding military deployment is to include agreed-upon terms for temporary change in custody for the duration of deployment in the original custody decree. If this is not possible, another solution is to draft an agreement with the other parent for temporary custody and have it filed with the court. Any informal agreement between parents that is not filed with the court will not adequately protect your custody rights.

Can't I just choose whom I want my child to live with during my deployment? After all, I am the custodial parent and the other parent rarely sees my child. Isn't it my decision?

Sometimes a military member with primary custody wants his or her child to live with a current spouse, parent, or other family member during deployment or military duty, rather than with the child's other parent. Realistically, this situation may work just fine in situations where the other parent is not in communication with the child at all or has no legal parental rights. Legally, though, without court agreement of the other parent, leaving your child with another family member and not the other parent of the child may also have unintended legal consequences. This situation may be considered a change in circumstances that allows the other parent the opportunity to change the current custody agreement. Also, hiding the child from the other parent or failing to notify the other legal parent of military deployment and the relocation of the child is not a good idea. You may face some court sanction for these actions if you have attempted to keep the child from the noncustodial parent in violation of the current custody agreement, and in certain circumstances, you may lose primary custody for these types of actions.

How can I prevent my child from having to live with the noncustodial parent during my deployment? I am worried about my child's well-being.

Merely disliking the other parent is not a basis to keep the other parent from having temporary care and custody of the child during military duty. If there are legitimate concerns regarding the ability of the other parent to care for the child, these should be addressed through legal means. If you suspect abuse or neglect, law enforcement and social services should be contacted. A no-contact order, or order of protection, from a court may be needed to legally prevent an abusive or dangerous parent from contact with the child. In some states, you may be able to file paperwork with the court to designate a third-party temporary or stand-by custodian for the duration of your deployment if certain circumstances exist such as danger to the child, neglect or abandonment of the child, or if you are the only legal parent.

I am deployed and received word that my child is in physical or emotional danger with the other parent or caregiver. What can I do?

In this circumstance, you should contact local law enforcement and social services immediately and ensure that your child is removed from the dangerous environment as soon as possible. If this has already happened, you must normally wait for official notification of a family emergency situation through the Red Cross in order to request emergency military leave from a deployed location where leave may not otherwise be authorized. Emergency leave may be authorized by the chain of command for situations involving the endangerment or abuse of children. In most situations, the military parent will be authorized time to ensure the child is placed in a safe alternative environment and has an alternate family care plan in place for the child before returning to a deployed location. In severe situations, a release from active duty, compassionate reassignment, or hardship discharge may be authorized.

How can I ensure my child is able to spend time with family members on my side of the family while I am on deployment?

Writing up an agreement with the other parent for visitation time with other family members is the best way to facilitate this. You can include these family visitations in custody and visitation decrees or other court-filed agreement as part of the "assignment" of your visitation rights to certain relatives. If this type of provision is not included in a custody agreement, you can petition the court to grant this "assignment" of visitation right to relatives for the duration of a deployment. You will have to show the court that assigning visitation to your relatives is in your child's best interest.

Normally, assignment of visitation rights should be to relatives that the child sees on a regular basis and has a close familial relationship with. Showing that spending time with these relatives is part of the child's routine will help to establish that such an assignment is in the child's best interests. Grandparents may also be able to file for legal visitation rights under a state's grandparent rights statute, but other family members generally have no legal right to visitation with a child, except under extraordinary circumstances where the legal parents are unfit or unable to care for a child.

How can I ensure that I am able to spend my military leave with my child and have frequent telephonic and electronic contact with my child during my deployment?

Custody and visitation orders should include language giving a deployed parent frequent contact with children, as well as visitation with children during leave from the deployment or unaccompanied military tour. These orders should generally state that both parents will ensure communication and contact between the other parent and the child. Most family courts do not look kindly on any attempts to obstruct parent and child contact. In some situations, failure to allow contact between the other parent and the child may be used by the court as a basis to change custody.

What are my options if the other parent relocates to another state with the children?

Relocation of a child, whether in-state or to another state or country, in most circumstances, is considered a "change in circumstances" triggering an opportunity to modify a custody agreement. However, relocation does not necessarily require the court to review or change an existing custody agreement. When courts are involved in determining relocation in a custody situation, the court weighs one parent's right to move, the other parent's right to access to the child, and the best interests of the child. Depending on the state, a court may use one of three standards when considering relocation:

1. A presumption in favor of the move (the parent not moving has the burden to show the court that moving is not in the interests of the child),
2. A presumption against the move (the moving parent must show the court that moving is in the best interest of the child), or
3. The court may review based on "the state's best interests of the child" factors to make the determination. The "best interest of the child factors" or other relocation factors as defined in state law will be looked at by most courts in making this determination.

Many states also have notice requirements to the other parent before relocating. If the noncustodial parent does not agree to the move, or requests a change in custody, the noncustodial parent may have a good chance at preventing the move or gaining custody in this situation.

For military families, moves are frequent. If an active-duty military parent is the custodial parent, the custody and visitation order can include language indicating that the parents agree that relocation of the child for military moves is in the best interest of the child and/or not considered a change in circumstances. A child custody order from one state can be registered in a new state so that the new state can enforce the provisions of the order. Registering the order does not give the new state the power to modify the order, only to enforce the order. Enforcing the provisions of a custody order in another state does not necessarily require pre-registration. If a parent relocates without the permission of the other parent or the court, or refuses to return a child after visitation, the law allows for an emergency hearing to enforce the custody order.

Relocation by one parent or failure to return a child from visitation without the consent of the other parent or the court is normally a very bad idea. Generally, courts look negatively upon such actions, which may be a basis for awarding custody to the other parent; in some situations, it can also result in criminal charges for parental kidnapping.

Child and Family Support

Like other areas of family law, state law governs child and family support issues. While each state has child support provisions specific by state, all states have adopted the Uniform Interstate Family Support Act (UIFSA), which determines how states will resolve issues of jurisdiction, modification, and enforcement of orders that involve more than one state. Military legal assistance attorneys may assist servicemembers and family members with issues of child support, family support, custody and visitation, and paternity. However, military legal assistance is not authorized for a person seeking an initial paternity claim against a servicemember. Once paternity is established, the child will be entitled to military legal assistance as a military dependent.

Initial Determinations

An initial determination of child support may be made as a stand-alone order or in combination with a divorce decree. If a child is born to parents that are not married, paternity of the child must be legally established before the court will enter a child support order. Either parent or the state government may seek child support, normally from the noncustodial parent. Depending on the laws of the state, and the type of custody the parties have, the court may enter a child support order that obligates one or both parents for child support payments. Court orders for child support can be made in the state where:

- the parents and child live,
- the parent responding to the child support order lives,
- the parents consent to jurisdiction, or
- the parents have contacts within the state (this normally can include visiting the state in person or contacting people who live in the state on a reoccurring basis).

Modification

Normally, the state that entered the initial support order will maintain the right to modify the order until the parents and the child leave the state or both parents sign a written consent of jurisdiction in another state.

A child support order may be modified for a number of reasons, including a change in custody or a change in job or income (an increase or decrease). The amount of child support may also change after a periodic (or automatic) review allowed by state statute for increase due to cost of living. Major life events may also justify a change in child support amounts, including the incarceration of one parent, illness or hospitalization, extended visitation, or the remarriage or cohabitation of the custodial parent.

Enforcement

An order requiring a servicemember to pay child support can be enforced through the military or through the state court system. A commander can legally order a servicemember to pay a child support obligation. The servicemember may also set up a voluntary allotment out of his or her military paycheck to pay child support obligations. Another option for enforcement through the military is to file a garnishment order with Defense Finance

Accounting Service (DFAS), the agency that administers military pay, and have the child support amounts taken directly out of the servicemember's paycheck involuntarily. As discussed on page 31, in the absence of a child support order, the military services can order servicemembers to support their families under regulation.

More commonly, child support is enforced through state courts and government agencies. Any state can enforce another state's child support order. Enforcement of support can include collection of ongoing support, arrearages (unpaid obligations), reimbursement of birthing costs, or health care expenses, interest, and fees and costs including attorney fees. Child support enforcement services are offered through county or state agencies. These agencies are often referred to as "IV-D" agencies based on the federal law subsidizing child support enforcement. "IV-D cases" are those for which the county or state is a party to the child support enforcement action because a parent entitled to child support applies for public assistance or requests the state's assistance with enforcement of the child support obligation. To request assistance in the enforcement of a child support obligation, visit your local county court or government building; that is where the child support enforcement agency or a child and family services center is usually housed, and they can offer you information and assistance.

Establishing Paternity

Establishing paternity creates a legal relationship between the father and child. For the child of a male servicemember, establishing paternity is the first step for establishing child support and other legal benefits for the child such as medical and dental benefits, veterans, disability, and Social Security benefits. Paternity is also the first step for establishing a father's visitation rights for parents who are not married. Most states have a "presumption of paternity" law that holds that if a woman is married at the time of either birth or conception, the husband is legally presumed the father. A few states go even further and will not allow legal recognition of a father other than the husband, even through DNA testing.

When the parents are not married, paternity can be established by court order or by the parents, or father, consensually acknowledging paternity by signing legal documents known as a "recognition of parentage" or an "acknowledgement of parentage." If these forms are signed at the hospital, there may be immediate establishment of a legal father and the father's name will appear on the birth certificate. If these documents are not signed at the hospital, normally the parents will have to obtain these documents from the local courts, social services, or child support offices and, once they are signed, file them with the court or local government agency. The obligation to pay support and the right to visitation are often separate processes. Don't assume that because an acknowledgement of parentage has been signed, a right exists for visitation or contact with the child. In some states, these forms may give fathers legal rights for visitation, but in other states, a custody and visitation order may still be required in addition to an acknowledgement of parentage.

Paternity that is contested may be established through genetic testing (normally cheek swabs or blood tests). In the military, commanders cannot order servicemembers to support children born out of wedlock without a court order, and they cannot order a servicemember to take a DNA test; however, the military cannot shield a servicemember from a civilian requirement to submit to a DNA test. DoD policy is to honor court orders for support and paternity. Once paternity is established by court order, an inquiry can be made to the military for family support under military regulations until a support order is established. Once a court order for support is established, the military will honor and enforce this order.

CUSTODY/VISITATION ORDERS	FAMILY/CHILD SUPPORT ORDERS
INITIAL ORDER	

• Establish paternity
• Court with jurisdiction to enter the order is the "child's home state"
  – State where child has physically lived with parent for at least six months
	• Establish paternity
	• Court has jurisdiction to enter an order if:
	  – a parent lives with the child in the state,
	  – a responding parent consents to the court's jurisdiction, service of a summons in person on a responding parent within the state, or
	  – petition filed in the home state of the responding parent.
	  – There may also be other bases for jurisdiction based on contact with the state.

MODIFICATION	

• The child's home state has "continuing exclusive jurisdiction," so the original home state will modify unless:
  – court determines neither the child nor parents have significant connection to the state, or
  – when court determines that child and parents no longer reside in the state.
	• The state that entered the original child support order has "continuing exclusive jurisdiction" to modify until:
	  – Both parents agree to jurisdiction of another state, or
	  – Both parents and the child no longer reside in the state that issued the original order.

CUSTODY/VISITATION ORDERS	FAMILY/CHILD SUPPORT ORDERS
ENFORCEMENT	
• Registration of a custody order with the court of another state allows that state to enforce the provisions of the order, or • File an expedited petition to enforce a custody order from another state. • Contact law enforcement to assist. Criminal penalties may apply for parental kidnapping.	• Register support order with the state. Enforcement is usually by income withholding. • If you have moved, register the child support order and your new state will enforce your current order from another state, but not modify. • Direct allotment from an active-duty servicemember's paycheck. • Through an order for garnishment of military pay sent to DFAS. • File a non-support complaint with the servicemember's chain of command.

Frequently Asked Questions About Child and Family Support and the Military

My child support amount can be based only on my military basic pay, not my entitlements like BAH or hazardous duty pay, right?

Income criteria for calculation of child support obligations vary from state to state. Whether your military entitlements will be considered income for purposes of calculating child support will depend on the laws of the state that issued your child support. Some states consider all sources of income, including military pay and entitlements, military retirement pay, and even VA and military disability pay. Other states will exempt certain categories of military entitlements.

What do I do if I am paying my child support directly to the other parent and now a state is garnishing my military pay and double charging me?

Sometimes, due to frequent military moves or miscommunication between parents, servicemembers are double charged for child support on the same child. Normally this happens when the state where the custodial parent and child are living becomes involved in child support enforcement and sets up automatic garnishment without knowing about garnishment or payment from another source. In these situations, the servicemember should seek assistance from his or her base legal assistance office and provide proof of payment of the child support obligation through canceled checks, bank statements, or an LES military pay statement showing an allotment or garnishment. In most cases, this situation can be cleared up by a legal assistance attorney through phone calls and correspondence with DFAS and state child support agencies. Once overpayment is established, the servicemember can receive reimbursement through the assistance of the state where the overpayment occurred or through agreement between the parents. DFAS will not assist in the recovery of overpayments from a garnishment order.

Can I get an SCRA stay to put a hold on my child support case?

Technically, yes, but in most circumstances a stay is probably not the best solution. Unless there is a question regarding paternity or back child support owed, staying the case is only putting off the inevitable requirement to pay child support and the result is a mounting debt in back child support owed. Some courts will even find that the servicemember's ability to defend in the case is not in question since in many states calculation of a child support obligation depends merely on a formula where income numbers are plugged in. If your child support case is ongoing and your military duty is keeping you from appearing in the case, the most sensible solution is to hire a local attorney to assist you in continuing to resolve the case while you are away on military duty.

Do I have to pay child support while I am deployed to a combat zone if all my income is tax free?

Yes. There is no combat-zone exemption for payment of child support—or other obligations, for that matter. In fact, if you make more income while deployed, the extra military entitlements you receive while in a combat zone, such as tax-free status, hazardous duty pay, and family separation pay, may be a basis to modify your child support obligation. On the other hand, if you are a reservist and are taking a pay cut (which in some cases can be substantial), you may request a modification that is a temporary decrease of your child support obligation for the duration of your deployment.

RESOURCES

- **Defense Finance Accounting Service** (www.dfas.mil/garnishment.html): This website has information on how to begin payment on a garnishment order for child support

DOMESTIC VIOLENCE

Sheila has been married to Marine Corps Gunnery Sergeant Mike Anthony for five years. When Sheila first met Mike, she thought he was sweet, thoughtful, and best of all, he always wanted to be just with her. When he began telling her not to spend time with her friends and family, she thought it was just because he loved her so much and did not want to share her. Soon, they were married, and shortly after, they PCS'ed to Hawaii. Sheila was excited to meet other military wives and make new friends, but once they arrived, Mike started to change. After a "welcome" party, he told her she was not to become friends with the other wives of his fellow Marines because he "didn't like the look of those girls." He became more and more suspicious of Sheila's activities, calling her and texting her every five to ten minutes throughout the day to ask where she was, who she was with, and what she was doing. Mike forbade her to have a job, saying he did not want her gone from the house without him. Sheila became depressed and isolated but was afraid to reach out to anyone because she feared repercussions from Mike. Even though she is unhappy, Sheila tells herself she's lucky because Mike doesn't hit her; he really loves her. Mary Jones, the wife of Gunnery Sergeant Jones, lives next door to the Anthonys. She has heard loud arguing from the Anthonys' home on several occasions and one night shattering glass and a scream. She has grown concerned about Sheila. What options and resources are out there to help Sheila?

Domestic violence may come in many forms, including physical, emotional, and mental abuse. It is not always easy to spot. Both men and women can be abusers or victims. Victims frequently do not report abuse and in many cases protect their abusers. Often it takes a crisis event for a victim to receive help.

The military community is certainly not immune to issues of domestic violence. Domestic violence prevention is a priority for the Department of Defense (DoD) and the military services. Since 2001, the DoD has been working with national victim advocacy groups to improve responses to domestic violence cases involving military personnel. A task force has been formed to study domestic violence in the military, improve resources, and enhance protections for victims. The DoD's policy is to prevent and eliminate domestic abuse (which includes all the military services), and provides for the safety of victims; hold abusers appropriately accountable for their behavior; and coordinate the response to domestic abuse with the local community. There are many military and community resources available for both victims and offenders. This section outlines some of those military resources and then turns to the possible consequences that may stem from a servicemember's conduct.

Military Family Advocacy Programs

Each military service has established a family advocacy program (FAP). These programs serve military members and their families and are available at most military installations worldwide. FAPs provide support for victims of domestic violence, early identification and prevention programs, and intervention and treatment programs for offenders. FAPs ensure victim safety and access to military and community shelters, resources and programs, as well as assisting offenders with treatment and intervention services. Additionally, FAPs provide notification to appropriate law enforcement and child protective service agencies of suspected abuse cases involving military members. Each FAP has programs in the following areas:

Prevention: Initiatives to prevent family violence are coordinated with chaplains, medical clinics, and local civilian resources. These initiatives include couples counseling and classes on topics such as parenting, stress management, and couples' communication.

Identification: Resources are available to educate military leaders and family members to recognize signs of possible domestic and child abuse including education materials, public awareness initiatives, and various training programs.

Assessment: FAPs provide clinical assessment services in cases of suspected child and domestic abuse, including treatment plans and recommendations for the family.

Support for Victims: A victim's immediate safety is paramount. Support services include crisis intervention, victim advocacy services, assistance with access to counseling and medical services, referrals to shelters, and support groups. Two types of domestic abuse reporting are available for adult victims reporting to FAPs: restricted and unrestricted. These types of reporting vary in whether command and local law enforcement are notified about the incident. Talk to your FAP personnel to determine which system makes the most sense for your situation.

Treatment for Abusers: Treatment recommendations for abusers are individually tailored based on the clinical assessment of the abuser and the family. Treatment may include parenting or anger management education classes, individual counseling, group counseling, family counseling, and couples counseling. The primary goals for treatment of abusers are to help the individual recognize abusive behavior, understand that the behavior is unacceptable, and develop skills for appropriate nonviolent conflict and anger management.

FAP professionals also participate on military installation case review committees that bring together a team of experts from different professions to evaluate cases of suspected abuse, make recommendations to military commanders, and come to a determination as to whether each case is "suspected," "substantiated," or "non-substantiated."

National Guard Family Assistance Centers

FAPs are also open to members of the reserve components and their dependents; however, if you are in an area that is not near a military installation and want assistance from a source that understands the unique stresses and issues of military families, National Guard family assistance centers (FACs) are an option for basic support and assistance. National Guard FACs are normally co-located with National Guard armories in communities throughout every state. FACs do not have family violence or counseling programs, but the staff can provide confidential support for military family members in crisis and in need of community resource assistance.

Military Chain of Command

It is important for family members to understand that reports to the chain of command are unrestricted reports. If the military chain of command receives a report of domestic abuse, commanders are required to report suspected abuse to local and military law enforcement and to have the report thoroughly investigated. Commanders are also responsible for ensuring that military members under their command who engage in domestic abuse are held accountable through UCMJ or administrative action.

The military chain of command can provide the following assistance:

- ensure victim, abuser, and other family members are aware of and referred to appropriate resources for medical treatment, referral services, FAP, and legal services;

- ensure victim advocacy is provided within a coordinated community response;

- in coordination with FAP, ensure a safety plan is in place to ensure and monitor victim safety;

- ensure safe housing has been secured for the victim(s);

- direct the military member abuser to secure alternative housing in order to ensure the safety of victims, if necessary;

- issue a military protective order or compliance with a civilian protective order (discussed below);

- if the abuser is a civilian, consider requesting that the installation/garrison commander bar the individual from the installation;

- direct the military member to provide continued family support for victim family members in accordance with applicable military regulation or court order;

- consult with servicing legal office regarding appropriate disposition of alleged abuse; and

- document as needed for an appropriate administrative separation or court-martial that a military member was involved in perpetrating an incident of domestic abuse so that family member victims may apply for transitional compensation benefits.

Military and Civilian Protective Orders

Military commanders may issue military protective orders (MPOs) that apply to military members under their command; MPOs are issued in order to ensure the safety of military family members who are victims of domestic violence, maintain good order and discipline within the command, or control a disturbance. The MPOs' purpose is to keep a military member

▶ HOW TO OBTAIN A CIVILIAN PROTECTIVE ORDER

A protective order, sometimes called a restraining order, can be obtained from courts on an emergency, temporary, or permanent basis. Local city and county courts normally have self-help centers where this paperwork can be obtained online or in person. Family advocacy program personnel, law enforcement, victim advocates, and attorneys can also assist in obtaining and filing this paperwork. The standard of proof for obtaining a temporary protective order is normally minimal. The victim needs to state he or she has been threatened by someone and requires protection. This temporary or emergency order is normally only for the short period between the incident and the hearing for a permanent order, which normally will last for one or two years if obtained. The person against whom the protective order is filed has the right to appear at a hearing for a permanent order and present a defense. Requirements for permanent orders may vary by state, but generally, the victim must prove by clear and convincing evidence that a permanent order is needed. Evidence can include, but is not limited to, in-person witnesses to threats or abuse, video evidence, telephone messages, text messages, emails, letters or notes, photos, police reports, and medical examinations showing evidence of physical abuse. A person obtaining a protective order against a military member should bring this order to the military member's chain of command or the post/base provost martial for assistance with enforcement of this order by the military.

from contacting victims or members of the victim's family. A commander can issue an MPO in addition to, or instead of, a civilian protective order, though an MPO will not contradict terms of a civilian protective order. The applicability of an MPO can go beyond the jurisdiction of a civilian order, for instance, an MPO can apply overseas. An MPO is normally issued on a DD Form 2873, and copies are provided to the subject servicemember and the victim and are placed in the servicemember's personnel file. Violations of an MPO are prosecuted under the UCMJ.

Military commanders must also enforce civilian protective orders issued by civilian courts or magistrates. The Armed Forces Domestic Security Act requires military commanders to ensure that civilian protective orders are given full force and effect on military installations. Military family members with civilian protective orders should provide a copy to their victim liaison or to the chain of command. On some military installations, there may also be a system to register civilian protective orders. To see if a registration system exists on your installation, check with the provost marshall's office, military police, FAP, legal assistance office, or personnel office. All individuals subject to a civilian protective order must abide by the order on DoD installations and are subject to legal action by the court issuing the order. Additionally, if the subject of the order is a military member or DoD civilian employee, failure to comply with the order may result in UCMJ or administrative action as appropriate. Civilians on a DoD installation who fail to comply with a civilian protective order may be barred from the installation.

Benefits for Victims

The military services provide a variety of assistance programs and support for victims of servicemember domestic violence. Some of the more frequently used programs are outlined below. Should you need specific assistance or support, consult your FAP.

Transitional Compensation Benefits

Transitional Compensation Benefits is a congressionally authorized program that allows the DoD to provide financial assistance and limited benefits for military family-member victims when the servicemember is separated from the military for committing acts of domestic violence. Benefits include monetary payments and access to TRICARE and other military installation benefits for a minimum of twelve months and maximum of thirty-six months. Benefits are reported as income, but are not taxable. These benefits are designed to help the family establish a life apart from the abuser; therefore, family member victims living with the abuser will not qualify for benefits. To apply for Transitional Compensation Benefits, a family member should contact the family advocacy program (FAP), installation legal office, or victim/witness coordinator.

Travel and Transportation Allowance for Dependents and Household Effects

Travel and transportation allowances are designed to assist family members who are required to move away from an abuser for safety reasons. To qualify for this benefit, the family member must be the victim of domestic abuse perpetrated by a servicemember. It must be determined that the spouse or child(ren)'s safety is at continued risk and that the safety plan advises relocation. To determine eligibility for these benefits, a family-member victim should contact the FAP, installation legal office, or victim/witness coordinator.

Office of the Inspector General and Installation Legal Office Assistance

The military chain of command can provide assistance with access to most military resources. Most commands have "open-door policies" and encourage interaction with military members and family members. However, military members and family members also have independent access at any time to the Office of the Inspector General and a military installation's legal office.

The Office of the Inspector General (IG) may be able to assist you in contacting or receiving assistance from the chain of command or the FAP and in some circumstances may initiate an investigation into allegations of inaction of the command or failure to comply with regulation, policy or law.

A military installation's legal office may also provide assistance in contacting the chain of command or referral to military and community resources. In addition, the installation legal office provides victims with a victim/witness liaison in situations where UCMJ action is taken against a military member for abuse. The legal office can also assist family members with family law legal services (divorce, legal separation, child support, or family support) or referrals to free or low-cost local legal resources. For more information on locating and contacting your local legal office, see page 6.

Criminal Conviction by Civilian Authorities or Military Court-Martial

There are a variety of possible civilian and military legal consequences for servicemembers who engage in acts of domestic violence.

Abuse of family members may result in criminal conviction by civilian authorities, military authorities, or, in some cases, both. Generally, prosecution in a state court for a crime does not bar federal prosecution for the same crime; therefore, servicemembers may be subject to criminal prosecution by state authorities for domestic abuse and still may be prosecuted criminally by the military under the UCMJ. Domestic violence criminal convictions have additional legal consequences for servicemembers under the Lautenberg Amendment and the Violence Against Women Act.

The Lautenberg Amendment

The Lautenberg Amendment is a federal law that added provisions to the Gun Control Act of 1968. This addition prevents those convicted of domestic violence misdemeanors (state or federal) from shipping, receiving, or possessing firearms. There is no military exception to this law; servicemembers with domestic violence convictions may not possess firearms. Such a prohibition will likely result in a servicemember's separation from military service if the servicemember is not already punitively discharged by court-martial or otherwise administratively separated for the conviction or the misconduct. Additionally, the DoD has made felony domestic violence convictions subject to the same requirements. Servicemembers with domestic violence convictions are required by DoD policy to report their convictions to their chain of command. A determination of whether a conviction falls under the definition of a domestic violence conviction for purposes of the Lautenberg Amendment will be made by a military lawyer, called a Judge Advocate. If the Judge Advocate determines that a conviction is a qualifying conviction for purposes of the Lautenberg Amendment, the command is required to ensure that the servicemember does not have access to firearms until the servicemember can be processed out of military service.

The military command can decide to allow a servicemember up to a year to seek an expungement of a domestic violence conviction. An expungement means that a court clears the conviction as if it never occurred. Expungements, especially of domestic violence convictions, are extremely rare and should not be relied upon as a means of continued military service.

The Violence Against Women Act of 1994

The Violence Against Women Act of 1994 prohibits individuals (including servicemembers) who are subject to a domestic violence restraining order from possessing firearms or ammunition.

Consequently, even a domestic violence restraining order may impact military service.

Administrative Separation from Military Service

As previously discussed, a servicemember may be convicted by a civilian or military court for crimes of domestic violence. In addition, a servicemember may be subject to adverse administrative action up to and including administrative separation from the military service for criminal conviction or act(s) of misconduct. The military may administratively separate servicemembers from the military in addition to any criminal action taken. If administratively discharged for acts or convictions of domestic violence, an active-duty servicemember may lose his or her eligibility for military retirement. Reserve members will still be eligible for retirement under the reserve retirement system if administratively discharged. However, all servicemembers who are administratively discharged with characterizations of service of either general under honorable conditions or other than honorable conditions will lose educational benefits and may lose a variety of Veterans Administration benefits depending on the circumstances. Further, these servicemembers may not be considered for other employment based on an unfavorable military discharge. For more information on these discharges and their impact, see Chapter 9.

Termination of Parental Rights

In cases where a state child welfare agency (sometimes called child protection services) or law enforcement authorities find that children are unsafe in their home with their parent(s) due to suspected abuse or neglect, the child(ren) may be removed from the family home temporarily or permanently for their safety. If children are required by authorities to remain out of the home for ongoing safety concerns, they may be placed with a foster home or in a state-run facility while the child welfare agency and the courts attempt to reunify the family.

If efforts to reunify the family (normally through a rehabilitation case plan for parents required by the state family court) are unsuccessful, termination of parental rights may result. Termination of parental rights normally requires a court trial unless the parent(s) voluntarily terminate their parental rights without trial. If, as a result of trial, parental rights are terminated, the legal effect is that the parents lose all legal rights to the child(ren). The child(ren) then become "wards of the state," that is, the responsibility of the state, until the child(ren) are legally adopted.

Parents facing termination of parental rights for abuse or neglect in family court may or may not also be facing criminal action for abuse and neglect in state criminal or military courts. In some instances of severe abuse or neglect, parents may not be eligible under state law to reunite with their children, and state authorities may move immediately for termination of parental rights.

RESOURCES

- **National Domestic Violence Hotline:** 1-800-799-SAFE (7233) www.ndvh.org. This service provides immediate resources and support for domestic violence victims twenty-four hours a day, seven days a week, 365 days a year.

- **MilitaryHOMEFRONT:** This initiative provides support to servicemembers and their families in a variety of areas including domestic violence and family advocacy. MilitaryHOMEFRONT's webpage on family advocacy includes a link to contact information for all military family advocacy programs and services.

- **Military OneSource:** 1-800-342-9647, or visit www .militaryonesource.mil. This 24/7 resource offers information in a variety of areas including domestic violence. Several options for no-cost marital, individual, and financial counseling are available for servicemembers and their families through Military OneSource.

- **Americans Overseas Domestic Violence Crisis Center:**
  The center serves abused Americans, both military and
  civilian, who are overseas. The center can be reached toll-
  free from over 175 countries using an AT&T USADirect
  Access number, then at the prompt, dial the center's number,
  866-USWOMEN (879-6636); www.866uswomen.org.

- **National Suicide Prevention Lifeline:** This resource has a
  crisis line for military members and their families. Call 1-800-
  273-8255 and press 1, chat online, or send a text message to
  838255 to receive confidential support twenty-four hours a
  day, seven days a week, 365 days a year.

ADOPTION

The number of military families interested in adoption has been
growing in recent years. Adoption can be time consuming and
expensive, and the frequent moves many military families experience can add complications to the adoption process. However,
in turn, the resources and benefits available for military families
looking to adopt a child (or children) have grown as well. If you
are a military member or military family considering adoption as
an option, this section provides basic information on the process
and resources.

How to Get Started

There are many resources available for military members and
families wishing to adopt. The DoD has established family service
centers at most military installations worldwide with resources
including information and referral resources on the adoption
process. Seeking out the resources on your local military installation will also help you identify adoption agencies and programs
specifically targeted to military families looking to adopt. Local
adoption agencies and resources always have recruitment pro-

grams to seek out eligible, potential adoptive parents. These efforts may include those targeted to military families interested in adoption.

Agencies that collaborate with local military installations often have someone in the agency who is a military liaison or frequently works with military families.

Adoption Laws

Generally, state laws govern adoptions. The Interstate Compact on the Placement of Children (ICPC), a law that applies in all states, controls those adoptions of a child from another state; because of the ICPC, all interstate adoptions are handled under the same administrative and legal provisions. The primary objective of the ICPC is to ensure that the best interests of the child are the priority in the adoption process. Both the state where the child is from and the home state of the adoptive family evaluate proposed adoptive placement. More specifically, the ICPC ensures the home state of the adoptive family and the adoptive child's state work together to assess whether the placement is in the best interests of the child and ensures compliance with all state laws regarding the adoption and placement before approving the placement of the child with the adoptive family.

If you are considering the adoption of a child born outside of the United States, the laws of the child's country of origin as well as U.S. immigration laws will apply to the adoption process. For military families stationed overseas, the military legal assistance office on the base where you are stationed may be able to assist you in obtaining country-specific information on the requirements to adopt while stationed overseas. You should ask how the country's Status of Forces Agreement (SOFA) may affect an adoption done while stationed overseas. You can also look up country-specific adoption requirements and find an accredited adoption agency on the U.S. State Department website for international adoption at http://adoption.state.gov/hague_convention/hague_vs_nonhague.php.

In order to standardize the process that applies to international adoptions, seventy-five countries have signed an international agreement called the Hague Convention on Intercountry Adoption. If you are adopting a child from a country that has signed onto the convention, the process is different from adoptions with non-convention countries. The Department of Health and Human Services has a resource on its website (www.childwelfare.gov/pubs/f_inter/index.cfm) explaining the differences to parents wanting to adopt.

Choosing an Agency

Whether you choose a local, interstate, or international adoption, one of the most important decisions you will make is choosing a reputable and properly accredited adoption agency to assist you through the adoption process. Many agencies hold informational meetings where adoptive parents can ask questions and gather information in a low-stress group environment. Adoptive parent support groups, or RESOLVE groups, run by the National Infertility Association, are another resource for gathering information on the adoption process from couples who have adopted and obtaining peer support through the process. The best way to begin researching agencies is to start with a basic, non-biased resource, such as the U.S. Department of Health and Human Services website or the U.S. Department of State website, that have information on accredited agencies and links to other reputable resources.

The Home Study

The home study, also called the family assessment, is a central part of any adoption process, and is required by all states and international adoptions. However, the actual requirements for the study can vary widely from state to state and may change. A home study educates and prepares the adoptive family for the adoption, evaluates the fitness of the adoptive family, and helps the social worker match the family with the appropriate assistance through the process. The process may seem daunting, but your agency or attorney should fully explain the process and requirements. With the right information, the home study process can be an exciting and positive step toward becoming an adoptive family.

The requirements of a home study are the same for military families as they are for other families. Military families may require more background checks than other families simply because military families are highly mobile. A background check is required from every state where the family members have lived. Beginning the adoption process while living abroad with the military will likely require additional steps.

The home study normally takes at least three months to complete. However, it can take up to two years or more for a child to be identified for placement depending on the family situation. Specific state terms for the placement of the child will vary by state. Some adoptions may require several visits between the adoptive child and family before final placement. It is important to discuss the timeframe of the placement period with your agency or attorney. Understanding the timeframe and aligning your expectations with the process will help relieve stress and frustration during the waiting period before final placement.

In the event of a military move, or permanent change of station (PCS), during the home study, your home study documents can be transferred to an agency near your new duty station. If you are required to PCS during the home study, this may add some steps to the process since each agency has its own home study requirements. In certain cases, a military family may be required to delay a move until the adoption process is complete due to the approval requirements of the ICPC.

If a military member is deployed during the home study process, you must ensure the appropriate powers of attorney are drafted to ensure the process can continue to move forward while the service member is deployed. It is also critical to keep your chain of command informed about the adoption process so the servicemember can continue to participate in the adoption process to the extent possible during deployment.

Military Leave for Adoption

Military members may take up to twenty-one days of noncharge-able leave for an adoption. The leave must be taken within twelve months of the adoption. If both parents are servicemembers, only one parent will be authorized the nonchargeable leave. Military members are not entitled to leave under the Family Medical Leave Act. (The Family Medical Leave Act is the federal law requiring certain employers to give employees time off to care for a new baby or sick family member.) Leave in addition to the twenty-one days of nonchargeable leave will be ordinary leave chargeable to the servicemember's leave balance.

Costs

The National Adoption Information Clearinghouse of the U.S. Department of Health and Human Services lists the following cost ranges for the different types of available adoptions:

- Foster care adoption, adoption of a child from the state foster care systems: $0 to $2,500,
- Domestic, licensed, private agency adoption, adoption arranged and facilitated through a licensed adoption agency: $5,000 to $40,000,
- Domestic independent adoption, adoption arranged between a birth mother and a prospective adoptive parent often with the assistance of an attorney: $8,000 to $40,000 (average is $10,000 to $15,000),
- Domestic facilitated/unlicensed agency adoption, a facilitator links a birth mother and a prospective adoptive parent for a fee: $5,000 to $40,000,
- International (or intercountry) adoption, adoption of a child in another country: $7,000 to $30,000,
- Additional Costs: Home study (required for all types of adoption), legal fees, foreign travel, foreign attorney fees, and passport and visa fees.

Paying for Adoption and Payment Assistance

Loans and Grants

Several resources exist for loans and grants to assist families with the costs of adoption. Some will also require a home study and may or may not be based on the financial need of the adoptive parents. One such resource is the Affording Adoption Foundation at www.affordingadoption.com, which has resources for grants for all legal adoptions. A Child Waits Foundation provides loans of up to $10,000 at a low interest rate to assist families with international adoption. The Adoption Council website at www.adoptioncouncil.org provides a list of several resources for loans and grants. Another resource is the National Adoption Foundation at www.fundyouradoption.org, which also provides grants, fundraising options, and other financial resources.

Employer Benefits

Department of Defense Instruction 1341.9 authorizes the military to provide adoption reimbursement to military members of up to $2,000 per child, but no more than $5,000 a year for qualifying adoption expenses. These benefits are paid after the adoption is complete, and members must be on active duty at the time of the completion of the adoption to qualify. If a dual military couple adopts, only one member may apply and qualify for benefits. To file a claim, fill out DD Form 2675 and attach all supporting documentation regarding your expenses. Supporting documentation includes a copy of the court order showing the adoption is final and copies of receipts to substantiate related expenses. Foreign adoptions must include all of this, as well as information showing the qualification of the adoption agency. Foreign adoption documents must be translated to English, and foreign currency receipts must be converted to U.S. dollars. In addition, foreign adoption claims must prove the citizenship status of the child; this can be accomplished by providing one of the following:

- a copy of the front and back of the Permanent Resident Alien Card (green card) showing the IR-3 code;

- a letter from U.S. Citizenship and Immigration Services that states the status of the child's adoption;

- a copy of the child's U.S. passport (page with personal information only); or

- a copy of the child's certificate of citizenship.

This information should be submitted to the installation personnel office. The personnel office will review your claim for completeness and forward your documents to DFAS for payment.

Many other civilian employers also offer adoption benefits to employees, including financial support options and resources and leave programs. Military spouses and military reserve members should check with the human resources department of their employer for specific information. If your employer does not offer adoption benefits, you can encourage your employer to start a program for adoption benefits. The Adoption Friendly Workplace program of the Dave Thomas Foundation for Adoption offers a free guide, which includes information on how a company can roll out adoption benefits, as well as other valuable tools and information for employers. The information about the foundation and its program can be found at www.davethomasfoundation.org.

Federal Tax Credit

In addition to other types of financial assistance, adoptive families may qualify for a federal tax credit of up to $13,170 for qualifying expenses paid to adopt an eligible child, including a child with special needs. This is a refundable credit, meaning you may receive a cash refund for qualifying expenses if your refund amount is more than the amount of the taxes you owe. Families currently earning less than $182,520 as modified adjusted gross income may qualify for the full credit. Partial credits may be available on a sliding scale for families earning up to $222,520. The amount of credit available and the qualifying income amount may be adjusted every tax year, so be sure to check with your tax preparer for current limits. The tax credit can be used to pay for expenses, including:

- **reasonable and necessary adoption fees,**
- **court costs,**
- **attorney fees,**
- **traveling expenses (including amounts spent for meals and lodging), and**
- **other expenses directly related to, and whose principal purpose is for, the legal adoption of an eligible child.**

Questions to Ask an Adoption Agency

Agencies should be anticipating questions and be happy to answer them and provide information. Beware an agency that will not provide information on accreditations or is evasive or defensive when answering questions on its services, experience, or fees. At a minimum, when interviewing an adoption agency, you should ask these questions to ensure proper accreditation and experience with the type of adoption you are seeking.

- **How long has the agency operated?**
- **How many children has the agency placed in recent years?**
- **What is the professional licensure of the social workers working for the agency?**
- **Is the agency registered with the Department of Social Services?**
- **Are there any formal complaints on record against the agency with the Department of Social Services? (You can also check with the Better Business Bureau in your state to check for complaints filed.)**

- What are the agency's professional affiliations? (*Child Welfare League of America, Joint Council on International Children's Services, and/or the Council on Accreditation*)

- What are the agency's fees and when are payments required? (Beware of an agency requiring all fees be paid up front. This is not a generally accepted ethical practice.)

- Can you provide a list of costs and fees associated with every step of the process?

- What are the additional associated costs not covered by agency fees?

- Is there a free orientation?

- What trainings and services does the agency provide for adoptive parents?

- What pre-adoptive and post-adoption services does the agency provide?

- What types of support are offered for adoptive parents through the adoption process?

- What are the agency's adoption matching policies?

- What is the average timeframe for a referral?

- If we are not approved, is there an appeal process?

- Do you have annual reports available for review?

Working with an Adoption Attorney

Even if you choose to work with an agency, an adoption attorney is a highly valuable resource to adoptive families. These advocates can provide an unbiased explanation of adoption resources and options. Attorneys also understand the laws that apply to adoptions and how the laws may impact your adoption situation and options. Attorneys are also best suited to resolve any issue in the adoption process that may become contested. You can work with an attorney in addition to working with an agency, or you may choose to work directly through an adoption attorney without an agency, a type of adoption commonly referred to as an independent adoption, direct placement, or private adoption. In this process, the attorney is the adoptive family's legal advocate through the process.

Working directly through an attorney may provide more flexibility to military families on the terms of the adoption. Often the adopted child is released directly from the hospital to the adoptive parents, instead of being released to an adoption agency as an intermediary. Military legal assistance offices may be able to assist with the legal aspects of the adoption process, but military attorneys cannot provide representation to servicemembers in court for adoption. No matter what, it is a good idea to have an experienced adoption attorney review all adoption paperwork and agency contracts before you sign with a particular agency.

Currently, you may not file your tax return online if you are applying for this credit. In order to claim this credit, you must fill out an IRS Form 8839 and include documentation to support all your claimed qualifying expenses. Therefore, you should keep every receipt for adoption-related expenses in order to prove the amount you are claiming in qualifying expenses. You will also need to include a final decree of adoption or certificate of adoption with your claim to prove the adoption is finalized. If you are adopting a special needs child, you may be eligible to receive the full amount of the credit, even if your expenses do not equal the full amount of the credit authorized. You will need to provide additional information to substantiate a finding by the state that the child meets the definition of special needs. An experienced adoption attorney may also be able to suggest additional state tax incentives or credits available in your state.

Post-Adoption Services

Services and support for adoptive families do not have to end when the adoption is complete. Once an adoption is final, an adopted child is considered a military dependent and qualifies for medical care at a military medical treatment facility and TRI-CARE medical benefits as well as all other military dependent benefits. Military family service centers can provide information for financial reimbursement options and military benefits. Post-adoption support groups are also available in many areas. If you are stationed in the United States, your adoption case worker or agency can direct you to available local post-adoption resources. If you are overseas, you may want to contact the state where you will PCS next to see what resources are available locally.

RESOURCES

- **The US Department of Health and Human Services website** (www.childwelfare.gov/adoption/): A great resource for basic adoption information and links to other reputable resources.

- **The National Foster Care & Adoption Directory** (www.childwelfare.gov/nfcad/index.cfm): This search engine, also on the U.S. Department of Health and Human Services website, offers adoption resources listed by state.

- **U.S. Department of State:** This webpage has search engines for agencies approved for international adoption, and country-specific information relating to adoption, as well as contact numbers and email for answers on international adoption questions from the U.S. State Department: http://adoption.state.gov/hague_convention/overview.php.

- **RESOLVE The National Infertility Association** (www.resolve.org/): This nonprofit website offers a variety of information and resources for adoption and infertility.

- **The Adoptive Families Magazine and Adoption Guide .com:** Adoptive Families Magazine is a national monthly publication that assists families in all aspects of the adoptive process. The Adoption Guide.com website is the website of Adoptive Family Magazine, and it offers information on the adoption process, options, cost, and advice, including a downloadable comprehensive list of questions to ask adoption agencies: http://theadoptionguide.com/process/articles/agency-questions.

CHAPTER 3

Debt and Finance for Military Families

Will, a twenty-three-year-old soldier, never expected to get behind on his bills. He opened up a credit card when he was in community college because the airline points seemed like too good of a deal to pass up. He hasn't spent extravagantly with the card—just buying some gifts here and there, and of course that flatscreen TV that was on sale before the big football game. But between a couple of TDYs and an unexpected trip to the mechanic for his car, Will is now a couple of payments behind on his credit cards. He has heard there are special rules for servicemembers, but he isn't really sure what options he has. Can he get the debt removed? Should he contact the credit card companies directly or the credit bureaus? Will he get in trouble with the Army if he continues to fall behind on his payments?

Credit can be valuable for many consumers, including servicemembers and their families, but it has many potential downsides. However, there are laws and legal requirements in place during the credit lending process to protect consumers; given the many moves and deployments military families face, there are additional legal protections in place to ensure fairness and equality in the lending process when it involves servicemembers. This chapter explains the basics of debt and credit, taking into account the specific protections in place for military families, and then turns to the collections and garnishment processes.

DEBT AND CREDIT

What is "debt"? What is "credit"?

Simply put, debt is money owed by one entity (such as a person or business) to another, and credit is confidence in the purchaser's ability and intention to pay back a debt, displayed by entrusting the buyer with goods and services without immediate payment. The person owing money is known as a debtor, while the person to whom the money is owed is known as a creditor. The debtor has an obligation to pay off the debt, and the creditor has a legal right to receive and enforce payment. For example, a bank or a finance company may lend money to a borrower, who will then have to repay that money, plus any interest agreed upon after a certain period of time. Sometimes businesses will permit a purchaser to buy goods or services directly on credit. The purchaser receives the goods or services immediately, but then has to pay on a debt over a certain period of time to the seller who is now also a creditor.

Establishing Good Credit

If creditors generally have confidence that a person will repay debts, that person is said to have "good credit." On the other hand, if a person show signs of unreliability, that person may have "bad credit." Of course, having good credit is generally desirable because it means that a creditor is more likely to extend credit to you as a purchaser or borrower. Initially, establishing good credit can be difficult. For example, trying to obtain a credit card when you lack any credit history can result in a Catch-22. A consumer often cannot gain credit without having a credit card, but lenders are often reluctant to provide potential customers with a credit card without examining a substantial credit history. However, there are a few steps you can take in order to make the process a little easier.

Start off by opening up a checking or savings account at your local bank. Maintaining a checking or savings account in good standing is a positive sign to lenders that you are not a credit risk. Place utility bills in your name and make sure they are paid on time without fail. If you are having trouble establishing credit, you may also consider obtaining a department store credit card, which is sometimes easier to get than other types of credit cards. Upon obtaining such a card, it is imperative that you make timely payments.

If the checking account, savings account, and department store card options do not work out, you may still try to obtain secured credit. Secured credit is backed by a deposit or asset (for example, your bank account) that may be applied as collateral to the debt if you do not make the required payments. Failure to make payments allows the lender to take the collateral. However, maintaining the account in good standing may allow you to successfully apply for a standard credit card in the near future.

Now that you are aware of the steps you can take in order to improve your chances of establishing quality credit, it is important for you to understand what lenders are looking for in a potential customer. When making their decision on whether or not to extend a line of credit to a potential customer, lenders look to the so-called three Cs: character, capital, and capacity. The three Cs measure gives a lender a fairly accurate idea of a customer's ability to repay debts.

The first "C" lenders look for in a customer is **character**. A customer's character is measured by the willingness to repay the debt. Lenders explore the customers' past credit experiences to determine if they have had trouble with late or delinquent payments. Much of this information can be found on your credit report. (Credit reports are explained on page 128.) Lenders also will examine employment history to see whether or not the customer has been able to maintain a job and a steady income. Frequently jumping from job to job is not seen as a positive quality in the credit calculation. Similarly, periods of unemployment do not receive high marks. Residency history is another basis for

> ## USE THE SAME NAME
>
> Since your credit record is critical to obtaining credit, it is very impor-
> tant that you check to make sure that each item in your credit record
> accurately reflects your own credit history and not that of another
> person. Whenever you apply for credit, you should always use the
> same name. Thus, if you are James R. Jones Jr., always include
> the "Jr." and do not use "J. Russell Jones" sometimes and "J.R.
> Jones" other times.

measuring a customer's character. Creditors are looking for sta-
bility, so a transient lifestyle in terms of residency can decrease
the credit rating. When it comes to assessing an individual's
credit worthiness, owning a home is generally preferable to renting. The necessities of renting and moving often pose a challenge for the military family in establishing good credit, but it
is important to remember that timely and reliable payments on
debts will go a long way even where a person's situation is not
ideal with respect to other factors.

The second "C" lenders look for is **capital**. A customer's
capital is measured by the number of assets he or she owns.
These assets might include personal property, real estate property, or savings accounts. The more assets a person has, the

> ## IMPROVE YOUR CREDIT
>
> If you have bad credit, don't despair. Time will likely help improve
> your credit, but there are a number of steps you can take, including
>
> * Not using all of your credit limit—keep a low balance
> * Paying down your loans
> * Carrying as little debt as possible

larger that person's capacity to repay. Sometimes the existence of assets can provide the creditor with a target for attachment in the event that a debtor does not pay.

The third "C" lenders look for is **capacity**. A customer's capacity is measured by the actual ability to repay the debt. In determining a customer's capacity, lenders here too scrutinize the customer's employment and income. If the customer is employed and earning sufficient income to handle the debt, then the lender will be more likely to extend a line of credit. Alternatively, if the customer is unemployed or has high living expenses or multiple outstanding debts, the lender will be far more reluctant to extend a line of credit.

Establishing good credit is no easy feat. It may take time and become frustrating. However, as a customer, following these steps and keeping the three Cs in mind will increase your chances of establishing quality credit.

LAWS REGULATING THE LENDING AND CREDIT PROCESS

The lending process can be a complicated and expensive process; for many consumers, it can be an overwhelming experience filled with terms and vocabulary unfamiliar to most Americans. Consequently, the federal government and many state legislatures have stepped in and enacted a number of laws to protect consumers. These protections come in many forms, from making information easy to understand to providing recourse for consumers who have been defrauded. Below, we detail some of the most common legal protections.

The Fair Credit Reporting Act

The Fair Credit Reporting Act (FCRA), passed in 1970, was established to protect the consumer's privacy and promote the accuracy of his or her credit file. The FCRA lays out how a lender

▶ UNDERSTANDING YOUR CREDIT REPORT

Credit bureaus record your financial-payment histories, public-record information, and personal-identifying data. There are three major competing credit-reporting agencies: Experian, Equifax, and Trans-Union. Contrary to popular belief, a credit bureau neither tracks all aspects of your personal life nor explicitly evaluates credit applications. Credit bureaus simply collect and transmit information.

Credit reports vary slightly, depending on which of the bureaus compiles them. Generally, the same type of information will be listed, including:

- Your identification information (name, birth date, Social Security number, address)

- Employment history

- Public information such as bankruptcy filings, foreclosures, and tax liens

- Payment history: showing how much credit has been extended to you and how you have repaid it

- Inquiries: all creditors who have checked your credit within the past six months

- Credit score: your score and a list of factors most affecting that score

If you find an error on your credit report, you may challenge the accuracy or completeness by notifying the bureau (see Resources section for contact information). The website of each bureau explains what you must do to challenge an error. If a complaint is justified, the bureau will automatically notify the other bureaus of the change and, if you request it, notify you of any creditor that has checked your file in the past six months. The bureau will also notify you of anyone who has made an employment-related check of your credit within the last two years.

can collect, distribute, and use a consumer's credit information. It also explains the rights and responsibilities of the consumer under this act.

Credit reporting agencies are responsible for compiling and maintaining consumer's credit information. The three major credit reporting agencies are Equifax, Experian, and Trans-Union. These agencies operate by maintaining consumer credit information and then selling it to potential lenders or businesses. However, access to a consumer's credit file is limited to those with a legitimate business purpose. Current and potential creditors, employers, insurers, and government agencies can gain access to a consumer's credit report.

With this in mind, it is only fair that consumers have a right to know what is in their credit file. You can prevent credit-reporting agencies from sharing their credit information for prescreening and marketing purposes. You can request that the reporting agencies exclude these types of organizations from distribution lists sold to creditors and insurers for solicitation purposes.

The FCRA also ensures that the credit agencies maintain accurate information within your credit file. You have the right to dispute inaccurate information with each credit reporting agency. This is why it is important to regularly check your credit report to make sure it is accurate. If the reported information is found to be inaccurate, the reporting agency must remove it from your report within thirty days.

▶ CONTACTING A CREDIT BUREAU

The three main credit bureaus can be contacted at:

- Equifax: 1-800-685-1111, or www.equifax.com

- Experian: 1-888-397-3742, or www.experian.com

- TransUnion: 1-800-916-8800, or www.transunion.com

These companies also have information on their websites explaining how to correct a mistake on your report.

Amendments to the Fair Credit Reporting Act (FCRA) have refined reporting agency guidelines and increased the protections provided for consumers. The Fair and Accurate Credit Transaction Act (FACTA), passed in 2003, amended the FCRA. The updated FCRA provides consumers with greater access to and control over their credit reports, prescreening opt-outs through the reporting agencies, and improved identity theft protection.

Truth in Lending

The Truth in Lending Act (TILA) was enacted in 1968 to protect consumers from misleading lenders who purposefully fail to provide important details regarding credit transactions. Previously, it was normal for creditors to advertise misleading or varying credit terms, confusing the average consumer. The Truth in Lending Act reflected a shift in emphasis from "let the buyer beware" to "let the seller disclose." TILA's main purpose is to require uniform disclosures on credit documents, making it easier for the consumer to compare loan costs and interest rates from competing lenders. The act requires lenders to accurately disclose the cost of credit, annual percentage rate (APR), total cost of the loan, the sum of all loan payments, and the schedule of payments to prospective customers. With this information, consumers are better equipped to make responsible decisions.

TILA also provides consumers with the right to cancel certain credit transactions that involve a lien on their principal dwelling, regulates certain credit card practices, and provides methods for resolution of credit billing disputes. For example,

▶ UNDERSTANDING THE APR

The annual percentage rate, or APR, refers to the amount of interest and certain other fees that you must pay in order to obtain credit. The APR relates your total finance charge to the amount of credit you receive and the amount of time you have in which to repay it.

it is considered a violation of TILA if every borrower or person with an ownership interest in a property subject to a loan did not receive two copies of the required notice addressing cancellation rights. In that event, it is possible to cancel a loan even after up to three years. To rescind a loan under the appropriate circumstances, the borrower has to notify the creditor by mail, telegram, or other means of written communication. The law states that TILA is supposed to be liberally construed in favor of the consumer.

Any credit extended to individuals, families, or farms is subject to TILA, while businesses and commercial interests that apply for credit are not covered by the act. TILA applies to both open-end and closed-end credit. Open-end credit has open usage without a definitive term, meaning the extension of credit stays open indefinitely. A credit card typically entails an open-end credit arrangement. Closed-end credit has a fixed term. These arrangements are typically found in automobile loans or home mortgages.

If a lender violates your rights under TILA, the lender may be subject to a fine or prosecution. Additionally, the lender may be responsible for any damages you incur, including attorney fees and costs. If TILA and a local state law are different, TILA will trump, so it is important for consumers and lenders to understand its requirements and remedies. In order to enforce your TILA or other consumer protection acts, consider bringing your issue to the attorney general's office for the state of your residence or to the local Better Business Bureau office. To pursue monetary remedies you may need the help of a lawyer; you likely want to work with a lawyer who practices "consumer law." You can find more information in Chapter 1 on finding and working with a lawyer.

The Truth in Lending Act was designed to protect the consumer. However, as a consumer, it is your responsibility to make sure that you understand the terms and conditions of any credit contract you sign. Take the time to read the disclosure and understand all the important details of your loan agreement before you sign on the dotted line.

Fair Credit Billing Act

When credit cards were first introduced, they were often stolen and subsequently charged without the original cardholder's authorization. When the consumer failed to make a payment on the unauthorized charge, credit card companies treated the failure as an ordinary delinquent payment. In 1974, the Fair Credit Billing Act (FCBA) was passed to help consumers defend themselves against these unauthorized charges and other credit card billing errors. The FCBA provides consumers with the power to report a billing error, request an explanation of a credit card charge, or dispute a charge without damaging their credit rating.

The FCBA dispute settlement procedures apply only to billing error disputes. Such billing errors include unauthorized charges; charges that list the wrong date or purchase amount; charges for goods or services you did not buy or accept; charges for goods or services not delivered as you had agreed; calculation errors; failure to post payments, returns, and other credits; and failure to send bills to your current address as long as you properly provided the creditor with twenty-day notice, in writ-

CHECKLIST: WHAT TO INCLUDE IN YOUR BILLING DISPUTE LETTER

☐ Your name and address

☐ Your account number

☐ A description of the billing error

☐ Copies of any sales slips, receipts, or other documents that support your position

Keep copies of this information when you send it—don't just send your original receipts. You should also consider sending the letter and its enclosures and include a return receipt that allows you to track it; this allows you to prove the letter was received by the business if there is an issue.

ing, of your change of address. Additionally, the FCBA applies strictly to open-end accounts, such as credit card and revolving charge accounts—not for closed-end credit you repay on a fixed schedule.

If you discover a billing error on your credit card statement, you must follow certain steps in order to report and challenge the disputed charge. First, you must write a letter to the creditor at its billing inquiries address. In this letter, you must include your name, address, account number, and a description of the billing error. This letter must be sent in a timely enough fashion that it reaches the creditor within sixty days after the bill containing the error was mailed to you. It is a good idea to send copies of sales slips, receipts, or other documents that support your position along with your letter.

After receiving your dispute letter, the creditor has thirty days to acknowledge your complaint in writing. The creditor must complete an investigation and decide on the correctness of the disputed charge within ninety days of its filing. During the investigation, you are not obligated to pay the disputed portion of the bill. You are, however, required to pay every other part of the bill that is not being disputed. Many consumers make the mistake of assuming that since they are disputing part of their statement, they are not obligated to pay the remaining charges on that statement. Do not make this mistake! Failure to pay the minimum due, even when certain portions of your bill are in dispute, may result in late charges and may negatively affect your credit.

While the investigation is ongoing, the creditor is forbidden from taking any legal or other action against you to collect the disputed amount and related charges. Although the creditor may report that you are challenging your bill, they may not threaten your credit rating or report you as delinquent while your billing dispute is in progress. Further, creditors may not deny you credit in the future simply because you have disputed a billing error.

Upon completion of the investigation, you and the creditor have different responsibilities depending on whether or not the billing was determined to be correct. If the billing was determined to be incorrect, the creditor must explain to you in writing the corrections or adjustments that will be made to your account. The creditor is also required to clear all finance charges, late fees, or other charges related to the error. If the billing was correct, the creditor must inform you in writing how much you owe and why and provide you with copies of relevant documents. You are required to pay the disputed amount along with any finance charges that accumulated during the dispute, as well as any minimum amount you missed paying as a result of the dispute.

If you disagree with the outcome of the investigation, let the creditor know, in writing, within ten days of receiving the investigation results that you do not plan on paying the disputed amount. If the creditor then reports you as delinquent to the credit bureau, its report must state that you do not think you owe the money and the creditor must inform you of who is receiving the report of delinquency. In the meantime, the creditor can begin collection procedures.

Credit Concerns and Protections
for Military Families

In order to understand how military service might impact someone's credit, it is first important to understand the factors that might negatively impact anyone's credit record. Low credit scores result from harmful information on your credit report. Multiple factors can negatively influence your credit score. Probably the most common credit score problem results from late payments. Because payment history accounts for about 35 percent of your credit score, late payments have the most negative impact on your credit score of all other common credit problems. When a late payment occurs, a negative entry is made on your credit report. Obviously, the more negative entries on your credit score, the more harmful they become. Simply staying organized and making timely payments can prevent you from encountering this common problem.

Another common credit problem results from consumers

carrying too much debt. Thirty percent of your credit score is based on your level of debt. That level of debt is based on the consumer's credit limits and loan amounts. The higher your credit card balance is relative to your credit limit, the lower your credit score will be. Similarly, the closer your loan balances are in relation to your original loan amount, the lower your credit score. Carrying too much debt can be remedied by regularly paying down your credit card and loan balances.

For military members, not only can these common credit problems hurt their credit scores, but they can also affect their military security clearances too. Qualifying for a security clearance can be a requirement for holding a certain military position or even staying in the military altogether. The government believes that military members who have unmanageable debts and bad credit can be subject to the undue influence of hostile nations or organizations, thus posing a security threat.

Recent decisions by the Department of Defense's Office of Hearings and Appeals (DOHA) reflect that excessive and delinquent indebtedness is the number one cause for denying or revoking a security clearance. Between 2006 and 2010, the U.S. Department of Defense denied or revoked 5,059 security clearances for military, civilians, and contractors based solely on financial considerations. Military members suffer from the same financial problems as civilians, including increased credit card debt, spouse layoffs, and overspending. A report from a nonprofit group, Iraq and Afghanistan Veterans of America, found the unemployment rate among military spouses is about 26 percent.

A 2010 military survey found that 27 percent of servicemembers said they had more than $10,000 in credit card debt. Although one of these problems alone may not be cause for concern, multiple debt delinquencies can indicate "lack of self-control, lack of judgment and unwillingness to abide by rules and regulations, all of which can raise questions about an individual's reliability, trustworthiness and ability to protect classified information," according to the Defense Department's Guidelines for Determining Eligibility For Access to Classified Information.

Although debtors' prisons are no longer common in the United States or Western nations more generally, there remains the potential for the military member to be criminally prosecuted for the failure to pay debts. Article 134 of the Uniform Code of Military Justice (UCMJ) contains a provision calling for up to six months in confinement and a bad conduct discharge among the sentencing options if a military member is convicted of such an offense.

Even if a servicemember is not prosecuted criminally in a court-martial, the failure to pay debts can lead to a serious level of nonjudicial punishment authorized by UCMJ Article 15. Among other things, this can result in the forfeiture of pay or a reduction in rank for enlisted personnel. Letters of reprimand, admonishment, and counseling are other measures that the military uses to address a servicemember's debt issues. Such actions are rather unlikely as creditors are likely to get their money from servicemembers through DFAS garnishments (discussed more on pages 147–150).

As you can see, a debt problem can have implications beyond just the repayment of the debt itself. Yet, most military installations have a local agency, such as the Family Support Center, which provides counseling to those who seek it. (Contact information for the Family Support Center can be found in the base directory.) Before financial problems become a disciplinary issue, a trusted supervisor such as a first sergeant or a section commander can provide some assistance as well. Base agencies can be a good source for getting a proper orientation on reputable credit counseling services. There are some credit counseling businesses that end up worsening the situation for the consumer by charging high costs and failing to provide information on how its proposed plan may impact a person's credit rating. Once a military member becomes the subject of disciplinary action, whether criminal or administrative, the member should consider seeking the advice of a military defense services lawyer, often known as an area defense counsel or trial defense service (TDS) attorney. Chapter 1 provides information on finding and assessing an attorney.

Payday Loans and the Military Lending Act

A payday loan is a small, short-term loan secured against a customer's next paycheck. Payday lenders thrive on trapping their customers into long-term debt. They are often called predatory because they charge excessive interest rates and penalties while trying to hide them from the public. With a payday loan, the borrower takes out a loan with an enormous interest rate and agrees to pay back the debt when receiving the next paycheck. However, payday lenders issue an overwhelming majority of their loans to borrowers who cannot pay off their loans in full by their next payday.

The guaranteed pay, assigned duty stations, and financial responsibility obligation required by military law make military members targets of predatory lenders. For years, lenders preyed on military families and trapped them in debt behind usurious interest rates. Usury refers to overly excessive interest rates. Usury is such an old term that it is discussed in the Christian Bible and other documents containing moral codes. While the modern United States has several laws protecting against usury, there will always be those who try to press the boundaries for profit at the expense of others. The Department of Defense estimates that 17 percent of military personnel used payday loans and reported to Congress in August 2006 that predatory lending practices weaken the military and that debt issues threaten the security clearances of military personnel. It said, "Predatory lending undermines military readiness, harms the morale of troops and their families, and adds to the cost of fielding an all-volunteer fighting force." Subsequently, the Military Lending Act (MLA) was implemented on October 1, 2007, in an effort to protect members of the military and their families from predatory lending practices.

The MLA and subsequent amendments to the Fair Credit Reporting Act have gone a long way in protecting military families from the threat of predatory lenders. Although these provisions have not completely dried up the practice of predatory lending in the United States, they have improved the landscape.

A spokesman for the Navy-Marine Corps Relief Society told the *Army Times* in April 2010 that his organization is providing assistance related to payday loans at one quarter of the level it was in 2006.

The MLA specifically targets lending without regard to the borrower's ability to repay the debt, charging excessive fees and interest rates, establishing unrealistic payment schedules, and repeating loan rollovers, refinancing, renewals, or consolidations. Additionally, the MLA requires that lenders inform covered individuals of their entitled protections as well as the loan's terms and conditions. Perhaps the most important provision of the MLA is that it caps annual interest rates for consumer credit to military borrowers at 36 percent, including all fees and charges.

The MLA applies to active-duty military personnel, active National Guard or Reserve personnel, and their dependents with a valid military identification card. It does not cover retired service members, servicemembers not on active duty, or civilian employees of the Department of Defense, unless they are dependents of a covered borrower. Furthermore, the MLA applies only to predatory lending actions initiated through traditional payday loans, car title loans, and refund anticipation loans. It does not provide coverage for credit cards, overdraft loans, mortgage

▶ **GETTING AROUND THE MLA**

Some predatory lenders have designed loans to get around the MLA and other restrictions imposed by various states. For example, payday lenders in Illinois restructured 350 percent interest loans as 121-day installment loans to get around the 120-day minimum loan term established in that state. Military members would not be protected from this product under the MLA, which applies only to loans of ninety-one days or less. As a result, lenders could issue loans with a term over ninety-two days to military members and not be saddled with the thirty-six percent interest cap of the MLA.

loans, traditional auto purchasing and leasing loans, military installment loans, or any form of open-end credit.

For military members needing immediate financial help, there are military aid/relief societies that offer emergency assistance for every service. There are also several nonprofit entities for military members that may offer loans or grants for emergency relief. Military OneSource offers information on these programs and consolidation of debt.

Off-Shore and Internet Lenders

With the implementation of the Military Lending Act and the amendments to the Fair Credit Reporting Act, storefront payday loan shops are becoming less prevalent. More than 20 percent of payday stores in the United States have shut down since 2006, and storefront loan volume has decreased by more than one third since 2007. However, an increase in online payday lenders also has played a role in the shift of payday lending practices. The Internet has made it possible for predatory lenders to reach military families without having to locate their businesses on military base perimeters. In fact, Internet payday loan volume nearly doubled from $5.7 billion in 2006 to $10.8 billion in 2010.

Online lenders are not just targeting active military members. Particularly vulnerable to online predatory lenders are military veterans, who are not covered by the protections offered to active-duty personnel, said Brenda Linnington, director of the Better Business Bureau's Military Line, a service that caters to military families needing financial counseling and advice. According to Linnington, the most recent scams targeting veterans include companies offering to buy their veterans' future benefits in exchange for up-front lump sums. "Those deals are potentially problematic," Linnington asserted. "In the end, you don't get the full extent of your benefit."

Other than targeting veterans not covered by the Military Lending Act, lenders have figured out ways around the act's interest rate cap. Some lenders observe the cap on the surface but circumvent it by imposing fees on their products as high as 50 percent of the initial loan amount. Other lenders bypass the federal law's restrictions by using offshore companies. By offering their loans through offshore businesses, Internet lenders can charge as much as 500 percent in interest. Unfortunately, online predatory lending continues to grow and struggling military families remain only one click of the mouse away from burying themselves in dangerous amounts of debt.

Identity Theft

With the continued growth of the Internet, through online banking, shopping, and social networking, consumers are sharing their personal information much more frequently than they ever have. Unfortunately, the positives associated with these services, particularly with regard to making shopping and banking much easier and faster, can leave your personal information vulnerable to identity theft. Identity theft occurs when someone uses your personal information, such as your name, Social Security number, date of birth, or credit card number, without authority to commit fraud. Identity theft is a serious problem. The Federal Trade Commission estimated that as many as nine million Americans have fallen victim to some form of identity theft. Once your identity is stolen, it can take months of your time and hundreds of dollars trying to repair the damage to your reputation and credit record.

In order to protect yourself against identity theft, it is important to understand how identity thieves can get a hold of your personal information. Experienced identity thieves have multiple methods of gaining access to your information. Older, less sophisticated methods exist, such as stealing and dumpster diving. Identity thieves may simply steal items such as your wallet or purse that contains your driver's license and credit cards, or your mail. They may rummage through your trash looking for bills, statements, or other documents containing useful information. If a thief is able to divert your billing statements to an address other than your own, you may not become aware of what is happening until the thief has already inflicted substantial damage on your assets, credit, and reputation.

Some more sophisticated methods also exist, such as phishing and skimming. Identity thieves engaged in phishing may pretend to be financial companies and send you unsolicited emails offering a great deal, vacation, or other enticing offer. These communications may request your personal information. Identity thieves who are skimming will steal your credit and debit card numbers along with a personal identification number with each swipe of the card through a special card-reading storage device. This practice is used most often at gas station pumps and ATMs.

According to the U.S. Department of Justice, you can help protect yourself from identity theft by using the word "SCAM" as a memory device. First, you should be **stingy** about whom you release your personal information to. Adopting a "need to know" approach to your personal data will make it much easier to be stingy when untrustworthy parties contact you asking for your personal data. Second, you should **check** your financial information regularly. Always make sure you are receiving your statements and that those statements are accurate. If you catch an inaccurate or suspicious charge, contact your bank or credit card company immediately. Third, you should **ask** for a copy of your credit report periodically and review it for any inaccuracies. Finally, you should **maintain** careful records of your banking and other financial accounts. It is a good idea to retain your statements and checks in case you ever need to dispute a particular check or transaction. Although following these SCAM steps will not eliminate the possibility of identity theft completely, it will greatly reduce your chances of being a victim.

If you believe you have become a victim of identity theft, you must act immediately to minimize the damage to your personal funds, financial accounts, and reputation. The Federal Trade Commission suggests taking four steps as soon as possible.

First, place a fraud alert on your credit reports, and review those credit reports. Fraud alerts, which can be placed by contacting one of the three major credit reporting agencies, can help prevent identity thieves from opening additional accounts in your name. After placing the fraud alert, check your credit report for any fraudulent or inaccurate information, and get it removed.

Second, close the accounts that you know or believe have been affected. Once the identity theft dispute is resolved, ask the agency for a letter stating the disputed account is closed and the fraudulent debts are discharged. Keep a copy of this letter and other related correspondence and disclosures.

Third, file a complaint with the Federal Trade Commission (FTC). This can be done online, by phone, or by mail (www.ftc .gov has links to access the online complaint form, the phone number to call, and the mailing address). Fill out the FTC ID Theft Complaint and provide a copy to the police to incorporate in their police report. The ID Theft Complaint and police report together can constitute an Identity Theft Report and entitle you to certain protections. The Identity Theft Report can be used to permanently block fraudulent information from appearing on your credit report, prevent debts from reappearing on your credit report, stop a company from continuing to collect debts that result from identity theft and place an extended fraud alert on your credit report.

Fourth, file a police report where the identity theft took place. Request that the officer incorporate your ID Theft Complaint into the police report and that the officer provide you with a copy of the Identity Theft Report to use in your credit report dispute.

Identity theft is a very real and scary threat to every American. That is why it is important to take the necessary measures to ensure that you are doing everything within your control to protect your personal information from potential identity thieves. If not, you may very well end up as one of those nine million Americans every year scrambling to save their finances and reputation before it is too late. A useful resource called "Credit Repair: How to Help Yourself" can be found at www.ftc.gov/bcp/edu/pubs/consumer/credit/cre13.shtm.

Active-Duty Alerts

The Fair Credit Reporting Act provides an extra measure of protection against identity theft for deployed servicemembers: active-duty alerts. If you are away from your usual duty station for an extended period, you can place an "active-duty alert" in your credit report with the major credit reporting companies. This active-duty alert helps minimize the risk of identity theft while you are deployed. It prevents an identity thief from opening credit accounts in your name and also serves to alert you that your personal information has been compromised if someone attempts to do so.

When a creditor sees the alert on your credit report, the creditor must verify your identity before issuing you any credit. The creditor may try to contact you directly. If you are on deployment, the creditor may not be able to contact you; consequently, the law allows you to appoint a personal representative to place or remove an alert in your absence. Active-duty alerts on your report are effective for one year unless you request that the alert be removed sooner. If your deployment lasts longer than one year, you may place another alert on your report. An active-duty alert also removes your name from the nationwide consumer reporting agencies' marketing lists for prescreened offers of credit for two years. This means you will be leaving a smaller footprint that might attract identity thieves. While it is difficult to eliminate your footprint entirely, this will go a long

> ▶ **WHAT ACTIVE-DUTY ALERT DOES:**
>
> - Provides a notification that you are deployed
> - Requires creditors to take special steps before granting credit in your name
> - Lasts for a standard one-year period, but can be renewed

way toward making you more invisible. If you are about to leave for a long deployment, an active-duty alert can provide some peace of mind that your credit and identity will be protected until your return.

Credit Freeze and Thaw

If you are worried about becoming a victim of fraud or identity theft, you may want to consider a credit freeze. A credit freeze prevents creditors and other third parties from gaining access to a consumer's credit report entirely. This drastically reduces an identity thief's ability to open an account in the consumer's name. Placing a credit freeze does not affect your credit score or your ability to receive a free credit report every year.

Due to the more stringent security features, it is necessary to place a credit freeze separately with each of the three major credit reporting companies. A credit freeze remains on your credit report until you remove it or choose to lift it temporarily. A temporary lift on a credit freeze allows you to apply for a credit card or loan or give someone access to your credit report. The practice of lifting your credit freeze is known as a "credit thaw." You can thaw your credit report by using a special PIN, which is sent to you by each credit reporting agency when you place the initial credit freeze.

It is important to keep in mind that credit freeze and thaw laws vary from state to state. For instance, in some states, only identity theft victims can freeze their credit files. Additionally, the cost of placing, thawing, and removing a credit freeze also varies by state. The cost can range from $0 to $20 per credit reporting agency, depending on multiple factors, including the state of residence, whether or not you are an identity theft victim, and your age.

Servicemembers Civil Relief Act

The Servicemembers Civil Relief Act (SCRA), formerly known as the Soldiers and Sailors Civil Relief Act, affords a variety of protections for military members on active duty. Many of the SCRA protections pertain to consumer issues, contract obligations, and personal finance. These protections apply to members of all service branches on permanent active duty, and under certain circumstances, those in the Guard and Reserve.

One of the most popular provisions when it comes to finances is the ability to reduce the interest rate on a qualifying loan to 6 percent. The loan must have been taken on before the entry of service. Any interest above the 6 percent is forgiven, not deferred, meaning the servicemember is not required to pay the additional interest. This provision applies to numerous obligations, including home mortgage and business loans and those debts the servicemembers hold jointly with their spouses. The SCRA's interest rate provision is a federal law, but some states have bolstered the interest rate protection further with their own laws.

The SCRA also permits a military member to have any type of civil court action stayed while on a period of active duty where the ability to participate in the proceeding is materially affected by the qualifying service. To get a stay, merely being on active duty is not enough. Military members are subject to the same laws as the rest of us and can be compelled to appear at court proceedings. Yet, a military member can make an application to a court where he has a case pending and ask the judge to temporarily delay the proceedings if the legitimate obligations of military service make it difficult to participate. The application includes a letter from the military member's commander and

> ### WHAT IS A DEFAULT JUDGMENT?
>
> A default judgment is a legal order entered against a defendant who does not file the proper response to a court action within the time allowed or who fails to appear in court when directed. A default judgment can have the same effect as if a court hearing or trial was conducted and the judge or jury ruled against the defendant.

from the member or his lawyer explaining the circumstances. The law requires a statement explaining why the military member cannot appear and when he or she will be available. The member should also include a copy of his or her military orders to prove military status. The command letter must state that current military service prevents the member's appearance and that leave is not authorized. Upon proper application, the SCRA requires the court to issue a stay of proceedings for at least ninety days. The court can grant longer periods if it deems a longer stay appropriate. Once the court issues a stay, the member can reapply in the same fashion for a further extension or the court can choose to extend the stay of its own accord without the necessity of further application.

The SCRA affords several other types of protection that can impact a military member's debt and credit situations. If a member has been legitimately unable to respond to a lawsuit and a default judgment has been entered as a result, the SCRA provides the military member with the ability to ask the court to vacate or throw out the default judgment. In fact, the SCRA requires that an individual or business seeking to have a default judgment entered against someone must file an affidavit. If the party seeking the judgment fails to file such an affidavit, a military member has a basis for asking a court to undo the default judgment.

For certain types of contracts, such as automobile leases and apartment leases, the SCRA permits a military member to unilaterally terminate the contract upon giving adequate written notice. To terminate an automobile lease, the military member must have received permanent change of station orders or deployment orders for more than ninety days. To terminate an apartment lease, the military member must have received permanent change of station orders for a location outside of the continental United States or deployment orders for more than 180 days. The legal assistance office on your local installation can help you enforce your SCRA rights and ensure that any contracts or judgments to which you are a party meet SCRA obligations.

Active-duty, Reserve, and National Guard members are entitled to legal assistance regarding most SCRA issues. If you think the SCRA may be able to help your financial situation, contact the local installation office of the Staff Judge Advocate. Chapter 1 has more information on finding local legal assistance and working with a lawyer.

COLLECTIONS AND GARNISHMENT

According to the U.S. Department of Labor, wage garnishment "occurs when an employer is required to withhold [a portion of] the earnings of an individual for the payment of a debt in accordance with a court order or other legal or equitable procedure." Title III of the Consumer Credit Protection Act (CCPA) limits the amount of an employee's earnings that may be garnished. The law protects everyone receiving personal earnings in the form of wages, salaries, commissions, bonuses, or other income. This includes earnings from a pension or retirement program. The CCPA prohibits an employer from firing an employee whose earnings are subject to garnishment for any one debt. The act does not, however, prohibit the firing of an employee whose earnings are separately garnished for two or more debts.

The amount of pay subject to a garnishment is based on an employee's "disposable earnings," which is the amount left over after legally required deductions are made. Examples of these deductions include federal, state, and local taxes, Social Security, and retirement withholdings. Further information on wage garnishments can be found in the Department of Labor's Fact Sheet at www.dol.gov/whd/regs/compliance/whdfs30.pdf.

Wage garnishment laws apply to all members of the military, including active-duty, reserve, retirees, and even civilian employees of the Department of Defense. Military members may have their wages garnished by creditors seeking payment for unpaid debts. These debts include commercial debts, child support payments, orders for spousal support, and back taxes.

Below we look at some of the specific types of garnishments a military member may be the target of and then turn to other debt collection practices.

Active-Duty Garnishments

A creditor can sue an active member of the military and attempt to obtain a wage garnishment judgment in nearly the same fashion as a civilian consumer counterpart. One important difference: The request for garnishment of a military member must include the submission of an income withholding order to the Defense Finance and Accounting Service (DFAS), a branch of the U.S. Department of Defense, or the Pay and Personnel Center for the Coast Guard. There have been instances where parties that have obtained a garnishment order have had some difficulties in the execution with DFAS when the language of the order has been overly complicated or unclear.

A military wage garnishment is limited to 25 percent of that member's disposable weekly earnings. However, if the wage garnishment reduces the military member's weekly earnings to less than thirty times the amount of the federal minimum wage, then the garnishment amount must be reduced. For example, the federal minimum hourly wage in 2011 was $7.25. Therefore, in 2011 a military member must have been left with at least $217.50 of his weekly earnings after a wage garnishment.

Different wage garnishment rules exist when military members are responsible for child and/or spousal support. If a military member is supporting a second spouse or child, then a weekly wage garnishment may not exceed 50 percent of disposable earnings. If, however, the member is not supporting a second child or spouse, then the weekly wage garnishment may not exceed 60 percent of disposable weekly earnings.

Civilian Spouse Garnishments

The Uniformed Services Former Spouses' Protection Act (USF-SPA) recognizes the right of state courts to distribute military retired pay to a spouse or former spouse and provides a method of enforcing these orders through the Department of Defense. A former spouse, under USFSPA, can seek assistance collecting retired pay from a former military spouse through the DFAS.

Under some circumstances, the former spouse can request garnishment from the military member's income in order to pay for alimony. To properly request garnishment, the former civilian spouse must serve DFAS with a court order specifically directing the government to withhold alimony and direct the required payments to the former spouse. Again, if the language of the order is overly complicated or unclear, DFAS may have difficulty in executing its terms; this can result in more legal costs for the party seeking a garnishment because that party may have to seek an amendment or clarification of the order from the issuing court. Family support orders are dealt with in more detail in Chapter 2.

Retiree Garnishments

Retired pay may be garnished for enforcement of a retired military member's legal obligations to provide child support or make alimony payments and payments from retired pay to a former spouse under a divorce decree. (Chapter 2 on Family Law has more information on enforcing these types of orders.) Upon receipt of a valid court order, the DFAS may initiate the wage garnishment process of a retired service member's weekly benefits. The garnishment amount must not exceed 50 percent of disposable pay if the retiree is supporting a second family or 60 percent if the retiree is not supporting a second family. Only the retiree's disposable retired pay is subject to garnishment.

Assets Subject to Garnishment

Along with wages, other assets are subject to garnishment, including bank accounts, cash, investments, personal property, and real estate. However, bank accounts are the most common type of asset, other than wages, garnished by creditors. In order for a bank account to be garnished, the creditor must obtain a money judgment from the court. To obtain this, the creditor must file a lawsuit against you. If you fail to successfully contest the lawsuit by showing that the creditor filed the lawsuit incorrectly or that you have already paid the debt, the court may issue a judgment against you. The judgment allows the creditor to obtain a writ of garnishment to take some of your assets. Typically, the creditor will then contact your bank and use that judgment to freeze the funds in your bank account. The bank can then send nonexempt funds in the account to the court that issued the judgment for payment of the debt. Collectors typically try to notify the bank before notifying you because they want the bank to freeze your account before you can withdraw any funds. The account freeze applies only to the funds in your account at the time your bank was served.

During the garnishment period, your bank cannot honor checks or other orders for payment of money drawn against your account, including outstanding checks, until the garnishment is paid. However, if your account has more on deposit than the total amount of the garnishment, then the bank can honor checks until the funds in your account fall below the amount of garnishment. Once the entire garnishment is paid, the freeze on your account must be lifted by your bank.

Debt Collections and the Law

The Fair Debt Collection Practices Act (FDCPA), which became effective in 1978, was designed to eliminate abusive, deceptive, and unfair debt collection practices. Today, it outlines the primary protections for consumers subject to debt collections. The FDCPA also encourages consistent state action to protect consumers against debt collection abuses and seeks to insure that those debt collectors that refrain from using abusive debt collection practices are not competitively disadvantaged. The FDCPA focuses primarily on establishing guidelines and a code of conduct for debt collectors. However, it also describes the rights of consumers involved with debt collectors and prescribes penalties and remedies for violations of the act.

The FDCPA applies only to the collection of consumer debt incurred primarily for personal, family, or household purposes. Such debts include auto loans, home loans, medical bills, and credit card accounts. It does not apply to the collection of corporate debt or debt owed for business purposes. Under the act, a "debt collector" is any person, other than a creditor or its employees, who regularly collects debts on behalf of creditors. For communications with a consumer or third party in connection with the collection of a debt, the term "consumer" not only includes the consumer, but also the consumer's spouse, parent (if the consumer is a minor), guardian, executor, or administrator.

Limits on Contact

The FDCPA limits the contact that a debt collector may have with a consumer. Without prior consent of the consumer or express permission of the court, a debt collector may not communicate *with a consumer* in connection with the collection of any debt before 8 A.M. or after 9 P.M. or any place known to be inconvenient to the consumer. Also, a debt collector may not contact the consumer at the consumer's place of employment if the debt collector knows the consumer's employer prohibits the consumer from receiving such communication. If the debt collector knows the consumer is represented by an attorney with respect to such debt, and the debt collector can readily discover the attorney's name and address, then all communication must be with the attorney unless he is unresponsive or gives consent.

Without prior consent of the consumer or express permission of the court, a debt collector may not communicate, in connection with the collection of any debt, with any outside third parties. This means that a debt collector cannot contact your boss or a coworker about your debt. The only exceptions to this include the consumer, the consumer's attorney, a consumer reporting agency (if permitted by law), the creditor, the creditor's attorney, or the debt collector's attorney.

If a debt collector is unable to locate a consumer, he may communicate with a third party to acquire location information about the consumer. Location information, under the FDCPA's definition, includes a consumer's home address, telephone number, and place of employment. In these communications, the debt collector must adhere to specific guidelines established by the FDCPA. The debt collector must identify himself and state that he is confirming or correcting information regarding the consumer's location. He must not identify his employer unless expressly asked by the third party, and he must refrain from stating that the consumer owes any debt. The debt collector is prohibited from communicating with the person more than once, unless requested to do so by the person, or the debt collector believes the third party answered erroneously or not completely the first time and has since acquired correct or complete location information. Finally, the debt collector must not communicate by postcard or use any letter or telegram if the envelope or content of the communication indicates he is a debt collector.

You can stop a debt collector from contacting you about your debt. If you notify the debt collector in writing that you refuse to pay the debt or wish the debt collector to cease further communication with you, the debt collector must stop communication with respect to such debt. The only exceptions are if the debt collector tells you that the collection effort has ceased or to notify you that he may invoke, or intends to invoke, a specified remedy such as bringing a lawsuit.

Prohibited Conduct

The FDCPA prohibits certain conduct of debt collectors. A debt collector may not intentionally harass, oppress, or abuse any person in connection with the collection of a debt. Examples of this include the use of threats, violence, or obscene language or repeatedly calling someone with the intent to annoy or harass that person. Additionally, a debt collector may not use any false, deceptive, or misleading representations when trying to collect debt. For example, the debt collector may not falsely represent that he or she is an attorney, falsely represent the amount or legal status of the debt, threaten to take any action that is not intended or legal, or falsely represent that nonpayment of the debt will result in the seizure, garnishment, attachment, or sale of any property or wages, unless such action is legal and intended by the debt collector. Furthermore, a debt collector may not use unfair or unconscionable means in an attempt to collect a debt. Examples of these unfair practices include collecting any interest, fee, charge or expense not authorized by the agreement or permitted by law or threatening to take possession of property if the debt collector has no intention or legal right to take possession of the property. If a debt collector violates the law while attempting collection of your debt, is possible that you may be able to bring a lawsuit to collect damages such as lost wages and medical bills that are directly connected to the violation. Whether or not you experienced actual damages, it is possible for the court to make the debt collector pay the debtor $1,000. It is important to understand that this does not extinguish the debt. You would still owe the debt even if the court found against the debt collector. When multiple people have been aggrieved by the same debt collector in the same way, they can sometimes bring a lawsuit together, known as a class action.

Within five days after the initial communication with a consumer about a debt, the debt collector must send the consumer a written notice unless the consumer has paid the debt. The written notice must contain the amount of the debt, the name of the creditor, a statement that the consumer has thirty days after receipt of the notice to dispute the validity of the debt or it will be assumed to be valid, a statement that if the consumer notifies the debt collector in writing within the thirty-day period that the debt is disputed, the debt collector will obtain verification of the debt or a copy of a judgment against the consumer, and a statement that the debt collector will provide the consumer with the name and address of the original creditor, if different from the current creditor. If the consumer notifies the debt collector in writing within the thirty-day period that the debt is disputed, or that the consumer requests the name and address of the original creditor, the debt collector must cease collection of the debt until the debt collector obtains verification of the debt or a copy of the judgment, or the name and address of the original creditor.

Remedies for Violations

Any debt collector who fails to comply with any provision of the FDCPA is subject to liability for actual damages, punitive damages up to $1,000, and costs and attorney fees. However, a debt collector is not liable under the FDCPA if he shows by a preponderance of evidence (i.e. that it is more likely than not) that the violation was unintentional and resulted from a bona fide error notwithstanding reasonable efforts to avoid any such error. A debt collector also is not liable for any act done or omitted in good faith in conformity with an advisory opinion of the Federal Trade Commission, even if the opinion is amended, rescinded, or determined to be invalid for any reason. Such challenges under the FDCPA must be brought within one year of the date of the violation.

Although compliance with the FDCPA is enforced by the Fair Trade Commission, you may still want to file a complaint with a state governmental agency. If the applicable state law is inconsistent with the FDCPA, then the FDCPA preempts that state law only to the extent of the inconsistency. However, a state law is not considered inconsistent if it simply provides greater consumer protection than the FDCPA. The FTC may exempt certain classes of debt collection practices within a state if it determines that the state law requirements are substantially similar to the FDCPA requirements and that there is adequate provision for enforcement.

CONTRACTS

A contract is an agreement that the law will enforce. Contracts are express, which means the agreement is put into words, or implied, which means the agreement is assumed based on the parties' conduct. At its basic level, a contract consists of an offer, an acceptance, and some form of consideration. In general, state law controls contracts.

An offer is the manifestation of willingness to enter into a bargain. In other words, it is a proposal to make a deal that gives the other party the ability to accept. The offer remains open until it is accepted, rejected, withdrawn, or has expired by its own terms. The acceptance of an offer is a manifestation of assent to the terms of an offer in a manner invited or required by the offer. This means that the offer indicates the party's willingness to agree to the terms of the offer and that acceptance is indicated in the manner the offer required (for example, in writing or via fax). Consideration is the bargained-for exchange. Often, money is a part of the consideration in an exchange, but it does not have to be. Consideration can be anything of value. Usually, even a small amount of consideration can be enough to form a contract. If any part of the offer, acceptance, or consideration is not valid or complete, then the contract is not properly formed.

Some contracts are valid despite the lack of a written agreement. In any situation where there is a verbal contract, proving its existence can be problematic. That is why it is a good idea to put contracts in writing. Yet, it is important to understand that the mere lack of a document does not necessarily mean a contractual arrangement is invalid in all situations.

Automobile Leases and Cellular Telephone Contracts

The Servicemembers Civil Relief Act (SCRA) has terms specifically dealing with the termination of automobile leases before the contract period expires. The act allows a military member to change the terms of the original contract under certain circumstances. The military member must give notice to the person or company who leased the member the vehicle (the lessor). The automobile lease can be terminated upon a qualifying period of active-duty lasting at least 180 days. A vehicle lease may also be terminated upon receiving permanent change of station orders. Although the lessor may not impose an early termination charge,

▶ **SOME MUST BE WRITTEN**

Some types of contracts are not valid unless they are in writing. These contracts fall within what is called the Statute of Frauds (which has nothing to do with fraud in the common sense). There are several categories of contracts in most state that fall within the Statute of Frauds. These are marriage contracts, contracts for the sale of an interest in land, contracts that cannot be performed within one year of their making, contracts between merchants, contracts for the sale of goods for a price of $500 or more, and contracts to answer for the debt or duty of another (surety).

any taxes, title fees, and registration fees are due at the time of termination and must be paid by the lessee.

The SCRA provides military members similar rights to cancel cell phone contracts upon activation or deployment. To determine whether you qualify for these cancellations or to get the most up-to-date information on these rights, your best bet is to contact your local Legal Assistance office. Chapter 1 of this book has more information on finding such help.

Installment Contracts

An installment contract is an agreement by which payments of money, delivery of goods, or performance of services are to be made in a series, usually on specific dates or upon certain events. Installment contracts are common in the sale and shipment of goods. Buyers in installment sales do not have the same rights of rejection as buyers in other sales. In an installment contract, even if one installment is substantially nonconforming, the buyer may not cancel the entire contract unless the problem with the one installment substantially impairs the value of the entire contract. Instead, the buyer must give the seller the opportunity to cure the defective installment. Additionally, failure to pay an installment when due is a breach in which damages can be assessed based on the portion that has not been paid and is an excuse for the other party not to perform further. In many installment contracts, failure to make a payment gives the seller of an article the right to repossess.

If a servicemember has an installment contract, the SCRA may be able to help if the member's service interferes with his or her obligations under the contract; it prevents the rescission, or termination, of contracts entered into with a servicemember for the purchase of real or personal property. However, this provision applies only if the servicemember paid an installment or deposit before the servicemember entered a period of qualifying military service.

RESOURCES

- **Military OneSource** (www.militaryonesource.mil): Includes information and resources on financial counseling and debt management.

- **Defense Finance and Account Service** (www.dfas.mil): The site for the DoD agency charged with providing payment services; it has information on garnishment and allotments.

- **Stateside Legal—Consumer Law Section** (http:// statesidelegal.org): site for military legal issues with a specific page on consumer financial resources and info.

- **Federal Trade Commission** (www.ftc.gov/index.shtml): The government agency charged with preventing business practices that are unfair to consumers or deceptive. Provides information on filing a complaint for identity theft and consumer fraud.

- **Better Business Bureau** (www.bbb.org): Nonprofit organization that seeks to increase marketplace trust; includes an online database allowing you to search a business's records and learn of any complaints filed by other consumers. You can also file complaints for misleading advertising, improper selling practices, and nondelivery of goods or services, complaints about nonprofit/charitable organizations, or the misuse of personal information.

- **Bankrate.com** (www.bankrate.com): Offers one-stop shopping for tools and information to help consumers make the best financial decisions, including information on credit cards and mortgages, as well as investments, banking, and taxes.

- **Consumer Financial Protection Bureau** (www.consumer finance.gov): Government agency charged with ensuring fairness for consumers during financial transactions including applying for a mortgage and choosing among credit cards. Search "servicemembers civil relief act" for information about the SCRA and how to access available protections.

- **National Consumer Law Center** (www.consumerlaw .org): Works to protect consumers and promote marketplace justice; consumer publications include those on foreclosure presentation and surviving debt.

CHAPTER 4

Housing, Real Estate, and Landlord-Tenant Issues

William and Jane were recently married and have been excited to set up their new home together. William is a PFC, and the newlyweds have just signed a lease for an apartment located between the base and Jane's current job as a teacher at a local elementary school. Unfortunately, William just learned that he will be expected to move before the lease is up. Will William and Jane be able to get out of their lease? Will they have to continue to pay rent on the apartment, assuming they can even afford that? Should they buy a home in the next location rather than rent?

Real estate law is full of tradition. In an agricultural economy, land was the most important resource; and many of the general principles of real estate law date back to English common law. Until relatively recently, for example, a tenant still had to pay rent under a residential lease even if the house was destroyed! In the last half-century, the law came to recognize that the country's economy was less land-centric; and many states enacted landlord-tenant codes that finally recognized the rights of tenants.

As far back as the Civil War, Congress created special rules for those whose military service took them away from their homes, businesses, and farms in the service of their country. Servicemembers, especially those in the National Guard and Reserve, must be able to transition smoothly between civilian and military status, often on very short notice. Because servicemembers, in the words of the Supreme Court many years ago, have "dropped their affairs" in order to answer their country's call, they enjoy rights not possessed by any other class of individuals to modify or rescind contracts that would otherwise be

▶ THE SERVICEMEMBERS CIVIL RELIEF ACT AND HOUSING

The Servicemembers Civil Relief Act of 2003 (SCRA) is the successor to the Soldiers and Sailors Civil Relief Act of 1940. That statute in turn was the successor to similar laws enacted during the Civil War and World War I. The SCRA has eight titles. They are:

Title I: General Provisions
Title II: General Relief
Title III: Rent, Installment Contracts, Mortgages, Liens,
    Assignments, Leases
Title IV: Life Insurance
Title V: Taxes and Public Lands
Title VI: Administrative Remedies
Title VII: Further Relief
Title VIII: Civil Liability

The attorney general of the United States has authority to enforce the SCRA by filing a civil suit. It is completely up to the attorney general whether or not to file such a suit. Such a lawsuit doesn't prevent the servicemember or others with rights under the SCRA from joining in or from pursuing other private rights of action. The SCRA provides you the right to sue and a number of possible remedies, including the recovery of monetary damages, your legal costs, and your attorney fees. You should first talk with your military attorney about whether you might have an SCRA case. Your military attorney can advise you, but cannot represent you in suing the other party. Chapter 1 has more information on finding and working with a civilian attorney.

Some SCRA sections can be prosecuted by the Department of Justice as misdemeanor offenses, including:

Section 521, Protection against default judgments
Section 527, Maximum rate of interest on pre-service debts
Section 531, Evictions and distress

Section 532, Protections under lease or installment purchase agreements

Section 533, Mortgages and deeds of trust

Section 535, Termination of residential and vehicle leases

Section 536, Protection under life insurance policies

Section 537, Enforcement of storage liens

Section 566, Perfection or defense of rights.

enforceable against them. When it comes to housing and real estate, these additional rights apply to leases and the landlord-tenant relationship and the lending-debt process.

RENTING BASICS

Before turning to rights specific to servicemember-tenants, it is important first to lay out the groundwork of the landlord-tenant relationship. The landlord-tenant relationship is created when a landlord and tenant choose each other. The tenant has to want to rent from the landlord, and the landlord must accept the tenant's application to rent. Usually, the parties sign a lease that sets forth each party's rights and obligations using standard provisions that are common to most leases. In some situations, a lease can be oral; however, the rights and options of both the landlord and tenant are better protected if everything is in writing.

Most options are negotiable and will depend on what each party wants; for example, the length of the lease, the amount of rent, whether the tenant can own pets, and whether fees will be charged for late rent. If you are considering renting a home, make sure you read the entire lease and understand it. There is no such thing as a "standard" lease. You should ask for changes before you sign. Negotiating does not mean accepting whatever is offered. Simply because a lease includes a particular provision, it doesn't mean that the provision is legally enforceable.

If it sounds ridiculous, it just may be. Nonetheless, tenants are usually not in a favorable bargaining position, particularly in today's real estate market where demand for rental housing has increased significantly in the past several years, and the reality is that tenants are often presented with a landlord's form of lease as a "take it or leave it" proposition. A tenant may be able to afford only a certain amount of rent, may need to live in a particular location, and may face stiff competition to secure a decent rental property, while a landlord may feel none of these same types of pressures and in fact may elect not to even work with a prospective tenant who tries to renegotiate terms if there are other parties lining up to lease the property.

Servicemembers and Landlords

Career servicemembers move regularly. Rather than continue to burden a servicemember with the responsibility to negotiate into their lease a "military orders clause," Congress has effectively included such a clause into servicemembers' leases by way of amendments to the Servicemembers Civil Relief Act of 2003 (SCRA). Under its predecessor, the Soldiers and Sailors Civil Relief Act of 1940, a servicemember had to protect himself or herself against the landlord by insisting that the landlord terminate the lease if the servicemember's military duties required him or her to move to another duty station. Under the SCRA, however, if the servicemember gets permanent change of station (PCS) orders, a servicemember is entitled to terminate his or her lease. This is true whether the lease is of a home, a farm, or an office. For members of the National Guard and Reserve, orders to active duty trigger the same right. The right to terminate the lease also includes not being subject to "self help" remedies sometimes available to landlords under state law, such as seizure and sale at auction of the tenant's belongings.

Under the SCRA, the servicemember must give notice, including a copy of the military orders, to the landlord. The servicemember then owes rent for the rest of the month in which the notice is given as well as the next month. Thus, it is beneficial to the servicemember if his or her orders come in close to the end of a month, assuming that rent is due and payable on the first of the month. There is a statutory ceiling on the monthly rental of a residence subject to the SCRA. The SCRA currently has a ceiling that has been raised annually through a cost-of-living adjustment; the ceiling is $2,975.54 as of August 2011.

The landlord is also not allowed to simply keep the servicemember's security deposit in lieu of "lost rent." Anything beyond the above-described one to two months' rent is forgiven and not a debt against which the security deposit may be offset. If the state landlord-tenant code imposes requirements on the landlord in dealing with the security deposit, those requirements must also be followed. The state landlord-tenant code may, for example, require that deductions from the security deposit be accounted for and paid within a certain time; such regulations must be followed by the landlord of a servicemember terminating a lease due to a PCS. Violations may trigger rights to greater damages or even attorney fees. Landlords who violate the SCRA's provisions without a court order may be criminally prosecuted, as recently occurred when a Michigan landlord seized and sold a servicemember's belongings without a court order after getting the servicemember's notice under the SCRA. The landlord's sentence was suspended pending repayment in full to the tenant, but the court left no doubt that the landlord would pay the full amount before the end of the period of suspension or be jailed for the full sentence imposed.

Landlords who for some reason doubt that the servicemember's orders are genuine or who believe that they as landlords are entitled to it may seek reformation of the lease or other equitable relief from the court. For example, suppose that the servicemember who terminates the lease is one of a number of tenants in a common apartment. The lease is terminated, but perhaps the other tenants wish to remain. The landlord can certainly seek either a new lease with the remaining tenants or reformation of the old lease if the other tenants want to remain and the landlord wants them to hold over. Under the SCRA, however, there is no partial termination of the lease. The servicemember has an unqualified right to terminate the lease, not just his obligations under it. Some states have enacted into their landlord-tenant codes provisions similar to or perhaps more generous than those in the SCRA. Certainly a landlord would be wise to comply with the most-stringent applicable standard.

Under the SCRA, a landlord can ask the court to rewrite provisions of the lease to be fair to the landlord. So, using the previous example of the servicemember terminating the lease, if the servicemember happened to be responsible for significant damage to the leased premises, the landlord might want to ask the court to impose those damages on the servicemember under a revised lease rather than await the outcome of protracted litigation with the other tenants while the servicemember seeks a stay of the proceedings.

Tenants in Possession—Or, What to Do If Your Landlord Sells?

In most states, someone who buys a residence is on notice of the rights of any tenants in possession of the house. Even if the seller does not specifically tell the buyer the terms of the lease, the buyer is expected to observe that there are tenants in possession of the house and to inquire about the extent of their lease interest in the process. Of course if the seller misrepresents the tenants' interest, such as by saying they are month-to-month tenants when they are actually tenants for a fixed term, the seller incurs additional liability for the misrepresentation. The buyer must either buy the tenant out or allow the tenants to remain in possession for the balance of their lease terms. If the tenant in possession is a servicemember, the new owner must follow SCRA obligations. Thus, if someone buys a home inhabited by a tenant expecting to rent to that tenant for some time to come, the buyer should find out whether the tenant is in the military and has the right to terminate the lease.

Landlords also have a duty to maintain their interest in the property. A landlord who doesn't pay the mortgage on the property may lose it to foreclosure. Any court considering a foreclo-

▶ **A LANDLORD'S OTHER DUTIES FOR MILITARY TENANTS**

Landlords have legal responsibilities beyond the SCRA. Under state or local law, landlords must maintain their properties at least to the point that building codes and other safety and health regulations are met. This is frequently a legally required term of a residential lease (regardless of who the tenant is). Military tenants not only have the rights afforded them under state law, they also can, if the landlord refuses to comply with the law, ask the installation commander to place the landlord's establishment "off limits," so other assigned military personnel are prohibited by the installation commander from renting from that landlord. If such a request is made, the landlord will be provided notice and be given an opportunity to be heard before the commander's final decision; but if the "off limits" order were imposed, it would almost certainly dent the landlord's wallet if the landlord is dependent upon military tenants for a large percentage of its rental income.

sure action on a property housing a military tenant might be asked to consider granting relief to the tenant if the new owner wants to evict the military tenant or to treat the proceedings as if the tenant were the owner of the property, so as not to further disrupt the military servicemember's existence. If you, as a servicemember, live in a rental unit and your landlord is facing foreclosure, you should consider reaching out to your local tenant association or legal assistance office to find out your options.

SERVICEMEMBER HOUSING BENEFITS: HOUSING IN KIND AND BASIC ALLOWANCE FOR HOUSING

At some large installations, government housing is available for all military personnel who want it (referred to as housing in kind). This is very seldom the case with reserve component personnel on Active Guard/Reserve (AGR). Many, if not most, military personnel get their housing not in kind, but through the basic allowance for housing (BAH). Reserve component members can draw BAH only when on active duty (including AGR duty).

BAH is computed on the basis of zip codes of duty station or home of record and is paid monthly to the servicemember at the "with dependents" or "without dependents" rate. Although the BAH is not taxed as income, it is ordinarily included in computations of the servicemember's gross pay for the purposes of calculating child or spousal support obligations.

Servicemembers with dependents draw the allowance at the higher "with dependents" rate than do those without dependents. Male servicemembers with out-of-wedlock children can draw BAH at the with dependents rate (this can be true even if paternity hasn't been established). Any single mother of such a child aware that the father is drawing BAH at the higher rate should ask the family court to treat this fact as an admission warranting the entry of an order of paternity and an order for child support. This may or may not succeed; the Joint Federal Travel Regulation still permits a single parent to tell the Defense Finance and Accounting Service he's a parent without telling the state, the family court, or the other parent.

Payment of BAH at the "with dependents" rate is based on the completion by the servicemember of Department of Army Form 5960 or some similar form prescribed by regulation. The information is provided by the servicemember subject to the False Claims Act (which imposes liability on individuals who defraud the government); and is certified by a commander or other officer who incurs potential liability to the government if the information certified isn't true. Additionally, acceptance of the BAH without providing the required amount of support to one's dependents is a crime under the Uniform Code of Military Justice, so the potential penalties for the servicemember are substantial.

All the armed forces require their servicemembers to support their families. If the parties are separated, the servicemember should have a written agreement for support or a court order for support (these orders are detailed in Chapter 2). Failing that, the BAH is the basis for the amount of support that military regulations require be paid.

SCRA AND SERVICEMEMBER-HOMEOWNERS

The SCRA doesn't just protect tenant-servicemembers, it also provides protections for servicemembers who own their homes, particularly with regard to real estate taxes and mortgage obligations. SCRA tax relief applies to real estate taxes initiated by the taxing authority (the city, county, or state) during a period of military service. If, for example, your state taxing agency imposes a new real estate tax that offers a right of appeal for the person who is taxed, the SCRA can "toll" or, in other words, stop the running of the appellate period, if you are on active duty during the portion of the period during which the appeal must otherwise be filed and thereafter. This provision applies to any kind of appeal or reassessment petition imposed by the taxing authority. Thus, the "end date" by which any kind of appeal of a tax assessment must otherwise be filed is extended by the period of military service.

Congress has also passed laws in favor of property-owning servicemembers who get behind on their mortgage obligations. For example, a servicemember "materially affected" by entry into active duty may get his or her mortgage rate reduced to no more than 6 percent per year, although this is largely a non-issue in the current market for any new mortgages (due to the historically low interest rates). Any interest in excess of 6 percent is forgiven, not postponed. This means that the interest in excess of 6 percent is no longer owed to the lender by the servicemember. The servicemember should insist on a new loan amortization schedule, which is the schedule showing how much of each payment goes to principal and interest. As a loan matures, more of each payment goes to principal rather than interest; the same is true if the interest rate is decreased under the SCRA. Obviously, the loan payment must go down or the amount paid on principal must be increased if the payment stays the same and the interest rate is reduced.

Some servicemembers default on their mortgage obligations, whether or not the lender has complied with the SCRA. If a lender brings mortgage default proceedings against a servicemember, the member may ask a court to stay (meaning postpone) the hearing for ninety days automatically if military service materially affects the servicemember's ability to defend himself or herself during the proceedings. Deployment to a remote location and inability to return on leave are factors in deciding if the servicemember is materially affected. In addition to this stay of proceedings mandated by the SCRA for servicemembers, the servicemember may argue that the case should be stayed beyond ninety days. Any such request must be supported by a copy of the servicemember's orders and by correspondence from the commander of the servicemember indicating when the member can be available for the proceedings, or as is often the case, that the servicemember can't participate until the deployment ends. The court must ensure that the servicemember's rights are protected before any foreclosure order is granted.

The protection of the servicemember's rights may include appointing local counsel to contact the servicemember to determine the attitude of the servicemember toward the claim and to ensure the servicemember's SCRA rights are observed. If the servicemember doesn't dispute the claim and his or her SCRA rights have been observed, the servicemember still has a right to delay any foreclosure order (as discussed later). If the servicemember disputes the claim and has a valid defense but is unable to afford a lawyer, the servicemember's defense should be presented to the court by appointed counsel, whose fees and expenses will likely be taxed as court costs by the court. If the servicemember has no defense, then the court-appointed counsel's role is simply to assure that the member's SCRA rights are observed by the lender, advising the court if they aren't. Congress has imposed a period of delay on the entry of foreclosure orders against servicemembers; that period is currently nine months from the date of release from active duty, commonly abbreviated as REFRAD. So any order for the foreclosure and sale entered before that date is premature and subject to being appealed or vacated (voided) under statutes and court rules.

SCRA Protections During the Real Estate Lending Processes and Debt Collection

Servicemembers also have unique rights in the lending process. These rights start as early as the credit report: If a servicemember has previously asserted his or her SCRA rights, no negative entry reflecting this fact may appear in the credit reports. A lender might give a credit reporting agency some suggestion that the servicemember didn't fulfill his or her obligations under a loan agreement; the lender may even have issued an IRS Form 1099 reflecting income to the servicemember derived from cancellation of the part of the interest above 6 percent per year. However, if the servicemember was entitled to relief under the SCRA, the servicemember's credit report should not reflect any noncompliance with the loan agreement since as a matter of law, that noncompliance is forgiven. Obviously, if such a negative entry exists, the servicemember should attack it using the Fair Credit Reporting Act, requesting first reinvestigation of the entry by the credit reporting agency; if that's unsuccessful, the servicemember should insert an explanation of the right under the SCRA into the credit report if the credit reporting agency insists on the accuracy of the entry in the report.

If a servicemember has a debt, that debt may be collected from the servicemember. If a debt collector is employed, the servicemember may exercise his or her rights under the Fair Debt Collection Practices Act (FDCPA); these include the right to be called only at reasonable times (and not later than 8 P.M.) or not to be called at all, to demand proof of the debt, or not to be contacted further by the collector. Complaints about debt collectors should be directed to the Federal Trade Commission (www.ftc.gov), the federal agency with authority to enforce the

▶ REAL ESTATE LENDING—THE BASICS

Unless you can pay cash for a home, you will likely need to borrow money to finance the purchase, which is why it is so important to understand the lending and debt rights for servicemembers. However, it is important not to forget the basics that apply to all prospective homeowners. Today, a wide variety of financing mechanisms exist to finance a home purchase. The most common form is provided by a financial institution, such as a bank. The buyer agrees to pay interest on the money borrowed, and the lender retains a lien (that is, a mortgage) on the property. Obtaining a loan requires a lot of paperwork and fortitude. When applying for a loan, it's a good bet that you will be asked about all aspects of your financial history. Loan applications vary, but most require: employment history, salary history, credit history, assets, and the source of your down payment. The term down payment refers to the approximate difference between the purchase price of a home and the amount of money borrowed to finance the home—that is, the cash that the buyer contributes when making a purchase.

Federal law requires that the lender reveal all costs of the loan, including items such as appraisal fees, escrow fees, fees for the lender's lawyers, service charges, and, of course, the interest rate on the loan. The interest rate must be expressed in terms of an annual percentage rate (APR). This is calculated by including the interest to be paid along with other fees, such as any points paid to originate the loan. Points are interest charges paid up front when a borrower closes a loan or fees imposed by a lender to cover certain expenses associated with making the loan. Points are usually expressed as a percentage of the amount loaned—for example, one point is typically equal to 1 percent of the loan amount.

Borrowing money is an expensive, and sometimes complicated, process; oftentimes, your home loan will be the largest debt you owe. Consequently, it is important to understand what you are getting yourself into and what will be expected of you before you sign on that dotted line.

FDCPA. If the debt has not been entered as a judgment, the servicemember's commander has little to do when contacted by the lender other than to tell the servicemember to address the situation with the lender.

If the lender's claim is now a judgment, then the claim is a "just debt" that the servicemember is ethically (under the Department of Defense Joint Ethics Regulation) and legally bound to pay. The lender may contact the servicemember's commander to persuade the commander to order the member to satisfy the debt or may simply seek an "involuntary allotment" from the servicemember's pay. An involuntary allotment is the military equivalent of a garnishment order. The process for seeking one consists of first obtaining a judgment, then giving the Defense Finance and Accounting Service (DFAS) Cleveland Center notice of the judgment and of compliance with the servicemember's SCRA rights. The DFAS then provides the servicemember with due process before implementing the involuntary allotment consistent with the Fair Debt Collection Practices Act. Details of the involuntary allotment process can be found on the DFAS website (www.dfas.mil). Finally, though many states use the term "garnishment" to apply to a court order withholding a portion of the debt from the debtor's pay, "garnishment" in military parlance is exclusive to withholdings for child and spousal support. These linguistic distinctions can be a source of confusion.

Congress has limited "payday loans" to servicemembers. The rates lenders can now charge servicemembers for these loans has been limited to well below what is usually permitted under state law. Since these changes, it appears that there is less interest in making these loans to servicemembers, since there seem to be fewer such establishments near posts and bases. States have been encouraged to adopt parallel laws, which are often enforceable by state agencies or by state attorneys general.

Although it is no longer required that a debt be adjudicated to be "just" under the Department of Defense Joint Ethics Regulation, a judgment against a servicemember is certainly evidence that the creditor isn't just blowing smoke. Needless to say, if judgment was taken by default against the servicemember on active duty, the servicemember's SCRA rights need to have been observed. To determine if the servicemember is on active duty, the creditor should use the SCRA portal found on the Defense Manpower Data Center (DMDC) website; the DMDC can be found via a link from the DFAS website, www.dfas.mil, and clicking on "Military Members," then "Military Employment Verification." With this electronic means of determining military status available, a creditor employing an affidavit stating that the debtor isn't in military service rather than a certificate from the DMDC website should be closely questioned if there is any doubt about the military status of the debtor.

Servicemembers, especially those who go back and forth from active duty to civilian life with some frequency, may experience economic dislocations not experienced by civilians to the same extent. They may benefit from consumer credit counseling or even bankruptcy relief if their debts warrant such steps. Commanders and creditors alike should consider the totality of the servicemember's situation when considering nonpayment of debts. Since both unpaid debts and bankruptcy can affect a

▶ **SCRA AND SPOUSES**

It is important to note that many of the SCRA rights outlined in this chapter also apply to military spouses. Some creditors will seek to expedite the proceeding by dismissing the servicemember as a defendant and proceeding only against the spouse or dependents, not realizing that the spouse may also have rights under the SCRA independent of those of the servicemember. Any such dismissal may not address all the rights of all the parties, nor include all whose interests are affected by the outcome of the lawsuit in the case, and so, such a dismissal shouldn't be permitted. The primary goal of the legal system in adjudicating the rights of servicemembers ought to be fairness, not expediency, and cases construing the SCRA certainly support this concept.

servicemember's security clearance, that should be considered also. Obviously, loss of security clearance can mean loss of the ability to serve. Consequently, servicemembers should be aware of this possibility when taking on debt and should be careful not to get into debt; if you do find yourself in financial difficulties, diligently pursue every possible avenue of assistance and resolution to prevent detrimental effects on your career.

Homeowners Assistance Program Helps
Servicemembers During Housing Crisis

The American Recovery and Reinvestment Act of 2009 provides a considerable benefit for certain servicemembers who purchased a home prior to July 2006, moved to a new duty station, and were left financially devastated because of the housing collapse. The U.S. Army Corps of Engineers' Expanded Housing Assistance Program (HAP) is designed to help certain government-connected individuals navigate an often hopeless housing situation. HAP allows qualifying soldiers, spouses, or Department of Defense employees to receive support on an underwater house in one of four ways: reimbursement for some of the loss in selling the home, assistance in paying off the mortgage, government purchase of the home or help in a default situation.

Congress passed the Demonstration Cities and Metropolitan Development Act of 1966 as a mechanism to assist military personnel and civilian employees who suffered a loss in home value as a result of military installation closures, or "base realignments." The 2009 expansion applies to servicemembers who suffered a loss in home value during a change in duty station. While the Recovery Act still assists personnel affected by base closures, the expanded program is designed to support the following categories of individuals:

1. **Servicemembers assigned to a new duty location between February 1, 2006, and September 30, 2010. To qualify, the servicemember must have orders to move fifty miles beyond**

the current base. The house must have been the primary residence of the servicemember and the value of the home must have decreased by at least 10 percent.

2. Wounded or ill personnel—those members who were injured in a deployment after September 11, 2001, owned a home at the time of the injury, were permanently moved for medical treatment of the injury, and can establish a nexus between the injury and the reason to relocate from the primary residence.

3. Surviving spouses of soldiers killed in action during a deployment who moved within a two-year period after the death.

4. Certain Coast Guard or DoD civilian employees injured during a deployment after September 11, 2001, who owned a home at the time of the deployment and can establish a nexus between the injury and the reason to relocate from the primary residence.

Given that the maximum loan amount used in calculating reimbursement costs is $729,750, HAP benefits for PCS members are profound. According to the Army Corps of Engineers, qualifying members can be paid up to 90 percent of the original purchase in a private sale that resulted in a loss. The fair market value at the time of the sale of the house is subtracted from the 90 percent value to form a "basic" reimbursement amount. For military personnel, closing costs (up to 7 percent of the sale price) can be reimbursed and are then added to the base amount. Alternatively, if the home has been on the market for at least 120 days and has not sold, the individual could receive 75 percent of the purchase price or a mortgage payoff, whichever is greater.

This program can help servicemembers who are continuing to hold property that is valued at less than the original purchase price. HAP is another tool to assist those affected by the housing crisis. For more detailed guidance, contact the U.S. Army Corps of Engineers at http://hap.usace.army.mil or 1-800-861-8144.

RESOURCES

- **U.S. Department of Housing and Urban Development** (www.hud.gov): Provides regulations information on government federal public housing, fair housing and housing discrimination. Also includes additional information about the SCRA.

- **National Housing Institute** (www.nhi.org): Provides information and referrals for local tenant organizations.

- **National Fair Housing Alliance** (www.nationalfairhousing .org): National organization dedicated to eliminating housing discrimination.

- **Defense Finance and Account Service** (www.dfas.mil): Provides payment services for the U.S. Department of Defense.

- **Federal Trade Commission** (www.ftc.gov): The federal agency charged with protecting consumers; enforces various federal debt collection and lending laws.

- **Save and Invest** (saveandinvest.org): Free online resources by the FINRA Investor Education Foundation providing free financial information and tools to help servicemembers and their families manage their money.

- **VA Veterans Home Loan Program** (www.benefits.va.gov/ homeloans): FAQs on the program, applying, and eligibility.

CHAPTER 5

Motor Vehicle Sales, Finance, and Repair

Samantha and Mark are young, married, and live near Norfolk, Virginia, where Samantha is stationed with the U.S. Navy. Samantha and Mark currently have only one car, a gift from Mark's parents when they got married; this arrangement has worked out fine as Mark works at a local store blocks from their home. However, Mark was recently asked by his boss to take on additional responsibilities at a new location that will require Mark to drive to a neighboring city. With Samantha's hours, there is simply no way they can share one car. How should they finance the car? Can they afford a new car or should they buy used? Should they purchase a neighbor's old truck or go to a dealership? Several used car dealerships near their home advertise in the base newspaper, does that make them safe? What should they be on the lookout for if they purchase a used vehicle? What protections are there for a used vehicle purchase?

In a job where tardiness and absenteeism is a criminal offense, having a reliable automobile is vital for most servicemembers. In many cities, it is a necessity from the basics of getting to base and to the more complicated details of transporting a family to school, civilian employment, and other obligations. Your vehicle is your connection between your military responsibilities and your civilian life. However, purchasing and maintaining a motor vehicle are fraught with tension and risks, particularly for servicemembers. This chapter outlines the process of purchasing a vehicle, including the financing process, and highlights some of the pitfalls and traps so you can be on the lookout.

THE MISSION—OPERATION
AUTOMOBILE PURCHASE

In the military, engaging in risky activities can be a part of your daily life. Understanding the nature of the risks you face and training for the eventual encounter with the opposing force keeps you mission-ready and safe. In combat, the risks and hazards are understood, appreciated, and reduced by training. In the civilian aspects of your life, there are missions with risks and hazards that are not fully understood or appreciated until it is too late. One such mission is the automobile purchase. The automobile purchase is a major decision that can impact your morale, financial well-being, and military readiness. Since they are less expensive than homes, and even junior servicemembers are often able to easily obtain financing, automobiles are something virtually every servicemember can purchase. However, just because you can purchase a vehicle, it does not mean you have the financial maturity and experience to appreciate the risks and hazards.

Servicemembers need training and protection when purchasing an automobile because they may be uniquely susceptible to deceptive sales tactics. The automobile purchase is one of the few places where military training will work against you. Dealerships that target the military know this and exploit it by employing retired or separated servicemembers. These are the special forces of the sales staff. Their mission is to disarm you, get you to trust them, reduce your willingness to question their direction, and get you to buy the car they want to sell. These salespeople look like you; they talk like you; they will have or create a military history to share with you. They have access to your base, galley, and recreation center. They can pick you up at the Exchange, Commissary, or your Command. They will tell you to trust them because they are your brothers or sister in arms. If you do it, if you lower your guard, if you are not armed with tactical consumer knowledge about the automobile purchase engagement, they will defeat you and you will fall prey to the risks and hazards of the automobile purchase.

Getting the right automobile at the right price has many benefits; not only will you have reliable transportation at an affordable price, but such a purchase builds credit, making future purchases more affordable. However, making bad decisions when purchasing an automobile can result in: overpayment and reduced resources for basic needs, unreliable transportation, missed work, expensive repair bills, damaged credit, low credit scores, low personal and family morale, disciplinary problems, security clearance challenges, denial of mission opportunity, separation from the military, reduced command mission readiness, and unemployment. This is a tough and expensive lesson that you should not learn while at the dealership.

It is important that you tackle each stage of the automobile purchase as though it was a high-risk military engagement filled with hazards. The four stages of the automobile purchase process are outlined here in depth:

1. **Selecting a Vehicle**
2. **Deciding Where to Purchase It**
3. **Negotiating the Purchase Price**
4. **Paying for the Vehicle**

You can control the risk and reduce the hazards of purchasing an automobile by understanding and exercising informed options at each stage of the automobile purchase process.

SELECTING A VEHICLE

In every military encounter, the key to victory is controlling the field of engagement. When purchasing a vehicle, the battlefield is your mind. The salesperson and dealership want to control both the sales process and you. They do this by disguising the risks so the process does not appear to have hazards. Buying an automobile is a simple process: Just pick the car, sign, and drive. What can go wrong? The dealership helps you identify a vehicle, arranges financing, and provides a service contract for protection. It's a guaranteed success. Not so fast! The dealership is able to direct this process only because they know the game, wrote the rules, and have most, if not all, of the information. Information is power! To regain tactical advantage and control, you must possess or develop equal knowledge, starting with what type of vehicle you want. If you already know what you want, it is much more difficult for the dealership to divert you from your tactical plan and on to theirs.

The vehicle choice should be made prior to arriving at the dealership, where psychological games can be played to pressure you into a purchase. A salesperson might make a statement like, "This car rides like a man's car. It may need some maintenance, but that's what men do and you can afford it, can't you?" If you are responding to this comment, you have to know what it means to be a man in your own mind and differentiate between being a man who can or wants to do maintenance. Additionally, you have to be able to differentiate among what you can afford, what you want to afford, and what is none of the salesperson's business. This game is meant to play on your ego. Who wants to admit to your new best friend and salesperson what he cannot afford?

Needs vs. Wants

The right vehicle is a balance among needs, wants, and budget. The primary purpose for a vehicle is transportation—getting a person and/or cargo safely from one location to another. Beyond basic transportation, there is a graduated scale of needs moving toward wants. You do not need power windows and locks; you want them for convenience. You must know what you need and what you want so that you are not persuaded to buy more than you need or can afford. Start by determining the primary use of the vehicle. Do you plan to transport just yourself or a family? Is your family small, growing, or large? Do you have a short local commute or do you commute out-of-state on the weekends?

Will you carry lots of gear for work or play, or just a backpack? Answering these questions will narrow the field of acceptable vehicles. The next consideration is gas mileage. Consider the fuel costs for different types of vehicles. For example: You are down to two vehicles. Each has a twenty-gallon gas tank. Gas is currently at $4 per gallon. One vehicle gets twenty-two miles per gallon while the other gets thirty miles per gallon. The cost to fill up the gas tank of each vehicle is the same, $80. The first vehicle will travel 440 miles on that twenty-gallon tank. The second vehicle will take you 600 miles on that same twenty gallons. The traveling difference between the two vehicles is 160 miles, bringing an extra $29 of savings per fill-up for the higher-mileage vehicle. Do you need or want the sportier vehicle with lower gas mileage? If you fill up every two weeks, you could save $754 a year with the more economical vehicle.

Consider Total Costs to Own

In choosing the right vehicle, consider the total cost to own. The total cost to own a vehicle includes more than just the purchase price or the monthly payment; it includes all costs associated with the operation of the vehicle. You should review the costs for insurance, annual maintenance, and repairs for the year, make, and model of vehicle you are interested in purchasing. Good sources of information on the cost to own a particular vehicle are websites such as www.Edmunds.com and publications such as *Consumer Reports*. These resources provide valuable information on the total cost of ownership. A search may reveal that the sporty convertible you want has a history of high maintenance costs and frequent repairs with poor reliability. If you find that your first choice will cost more to own than you can or want to afford, it's time to make another selection.

Be wary of luxury models if you have a limited budget. New luxury vehicles can have very good street reputations and high curb appeal; however, you must consider the necessary maintenance and possible repairs on a luxury vehicle. If you can afford to make the purchase, you have to be able to afford the upkeep. Luxury vehicles have luxury costs for maintenance, repairs, and parts. Some repairs or maintenance on luxury vehicles can be performed only at the dealership, which may not be the best value for service. Many manufacturers of everyday vehicles offer a luxury version; Toyota has Lexus, Nissan has Infinity, Ford has Lincoln, and Chevrolet has Cadillac, to name a few. Buying the value-level luxury model could result in more expenses, as the lowest level luxury model may not be as reliable as the nonluxury model from the same manufacturer.

New or Used

After identifying the type of vehicle you want and narrowing the choice down to a few makes and models, the next decision is whether to purchase "new" or "used." There are advantages to each choice. With a new vehicle there was no previous owner and there are no concerns about prior driver abuse or maintenance neglect. Parts on a new vehicle should not need replacement for some time, saving on maintenance costs. New cars come with a manufacturer's warranty that covers major system and part failures. On some models, manufacturers will offer free or no-cost maintenance and bumper to bumper warranty coverage for limited periods of time or mileage. No previous owner, new parts, and a warranty—all of this equals worry-free driving, but it comes with the new car price.

Most manufactures have a large investment in the name brand and want to build brand loyalty so that customers come back to purchase more products made by the manufacturer. The manufacturer of a product provides a warranty as a guarantee that the product will perform to the specifications advertised. Only the manufacturer can provide a warranty. Presumably, the better the product, the longer and better the warranty; for example, three years and 36,000 miles on one vehicle compared to ten years and 100,000 miles on another. A manufacturer's warranty is usually limited by time or number of years, usage/

number of miles, electrical systems, or power train. The new car warranty usually means that if the product or part of the product does not perform as specified, it will be repaired or replaced. An aftermarket guarantee for the quality of a vehicle is called a service contract. Service contracts are frequently sold with a used vehicle by the dealership but can be purchased from an independent provider. Service contracts are essentially insurance policies for the vehicle. If a covered part fails, the administrator of the contract will pay for the repair. Be very careful when purchasing service contracts. Like insurance companies, the companies that offer service contracts make money when they do not have to pay claims. Check for the history of the provider. Read the contract carefully. Some service contracts will have broad coverage of the vehicle and exclusions that would prevent payment of a claim. For instance, any damage in the first ninety days is considered pre-existing and not covered. Other contract language may indicate that the failure of any lubricated part is covered. However, the owner has to maintain the vehicle's lubrication. It is rare for a lubricated part that is maintained to actually fail. Last, when a product is sold "as is," that means that the seller does not warranty or guarantee the product. Be wary of products sold "as is" because the seller knows where he or she acquired the vehicle and inspected it prior to purchase. If he or she is not willing to offer a service contract on the product, it may mean that the vehicle is in poor condition.

Purchasing a used car may allow you to get more car for the money and avoid the initial depreciation in value that new cars experience. Another advantage to a used vehicle is the opportunity to evaluate new models. If you can wait a year or two for the market to test a vehicle and obtain maintenance costs, repair requirements, and reliability ratings, it is possible to determine whether the improvements are worth the price. A used car has a history that allows the buyer to determine where it was owned, whether it was owned by a company (leased) or an individual, how often it was sold, and if there was any major damage or repairs.

History Review

Don't be pennywise and pound-foolish; paying for a vehicle's history is a small pre-purchase expenditure that can help you avoid major expenses that would flow from a bad purchase decision. For example, spending just .4 percent of a $10,000 purchase or $40 for a history report will provide a wealth of information. A history report is always money well spent. There are several companies and organizations that track vehicle ownership records and provide them to the public: www.autocheck.com, www.carfax.com, your state Department of Motor Vehicles, or the National Motor Vehicle Title Information System are just a few. Each of these services provides previous titling and ownership information. Some provide service records, insurance reports, and/or auction inspection reports. Beware: The vehicle history and service reports are not perfect. The reports only contain information that is provided. Since the value of a vehicle is reduced when it sustains significant damage, there is motivation to conceal accidents and major repairs. It is possible to have an accident and get the vehicle repaired without reporting it to the insurance company or have it serviced off the grid so major repairs are not reported by a dealership. Rely on the history reports for the information they contain, understanding that the report may not contain all of the history. Reports of title transfers, prior ownership, and location can be a warning that the vehicle was placed on the market after a major weather incident, like the flood-damaged cars released to the market following Hurricane Katrina.

Inspection Time

After reviewing the vehicle's history, you should perform a physical inspection. If the car you are buying costs $10,000, spending 1 or 2 percent of the amount of purchase or $100 to $200 for a mechanical inspection is a wise investment. Many automobile repair facilities offer pre-purchase inspections. Servicemembers can use the base auto shops for inspections. These shops are manned with trained, certified mechanics, and they do not have a dog in the fight; they are not trying to sell you anything. Discovering presale that the brakes need to be replaced and negotiating an adjustment in the price or a repair can save you $400 for the brake job. A good mechanical inspection will also check the fluids for contaminants. The mechanic should analyze engine performance for variances beyond factory standards relative to the year and mileage of the vehicle. Additionally, the inspection should cover the condition of the wires, belts, and hoses for wear and tear.

The inspection should include a visual, audible, and mechanical review and analysis of the condition of the vehicle. You should inspect the interior, looking for both excessive wear and brand new materials. Excessive wear tells its own story. New materials could indicate that substantial damage occurred that required total replacement of the part (think fire, flood, blood, and accidents). Conduct an external inspection in good bright light. Examine all of the body panels, trunk, door, and hood.

CHECKLIST: WHAT TO LOOK FOR DURING VISUAL INSPECTION

There are a couple of important things to look for when visually inspecting a car, including:

☐ Are the panels even?

☐ Do the panels line up?

☐ Are the seams between the panels of equal distance?

☐ Does the color look the same in tone and reflection on all panel surfaces? After an accident, some cars get new panels; others get cosmetic resurfacing that looks like the original panel but is really bonded material that can crack, shrink, and peel in later years.

☐ Is the "metal" really metal? Use a magnet to test metal surfaces and see if they are in fact all metal.

For the audible test, take the car on the highway. When next to a vertical structure like a jersey wall, roll down the window and listen to the car. You should hear wind and possibly engine or exhaust sounds, but other sounds may indicate trouble.

DECIDING WHERE TO PURCHASE IT

There are three possible sellers of vehicles: the current private owner, a used car dealership, or a franchise dealership. Each comes with certain positives and negatives. We look at each of those options below, but not before a note of caution.

Who Owns the Vehicle?

Regardless of whether you are purchasing from an individual, used car dealership, or new car franchise, only buy from the owner of the vehicle. The problem with purchasing the Brooklyn Bridge, even at a great price, is that the seller probably does not own the bridge. No matter how many contracts are signed with the address and pictures of the bridge, the seller cannot convey title and ownership of the bridge. Similarly, automobiles, like land, are transferred by title. After the contract to purchase, called a "Bill of Sale" or "Buyers Order," is signed, and even after you transfer the funds to the owner or dealership, you do not own the vehicle until the title has your name on it. Use extra caution with long-distance and Internet purchases because it is more difficult to inspect for quality and to confirm ownership. If you are buying a used vehicle, you need to see the title. You want to know if there are unsatisfied liens listed on the title. The best way to verify the status of the title is to see it. It is possible to perform a title search with companies such as Auto Check or Car Fax or through the National Insurance Crime Bureau. If a seller cannot convey clean, clear, unencumbered title with no liens, you should not purchase that vehicle.

Cars, like houses and land, are transferred from owner to owner by deed or, in the case of cars, by title. Titles to vehicles are issued by the state where the vehicle is purchased and registered. This is a secure document that cannot be duplicated. If there is an error on the title, the owner must order a duplicate title from the state. The title lists the owner and any person or institution that has a lien on the vehicle from lending money to purchase the vehicle. When you purchase a vehicle, the current owner endorses the title indicating intent to convey it to you, and your endorsement indicates acceptance of the property. The title must then be sent to the state department of motor vehicles so it can issue a new title with the new owner's name.

Private Owner Purchase

The private owner selling his or her car has no overhead expenses and will usually provide a better price than a dealership. The private owner also should know the history of the vehicle; be sure to get detailed information about a car's history of repairs, accidents, and maintenance. The private owner should have service records for you to review. Ask questions, listen to the response, verify answers, and review the documents. Used vehicles purchased from individuals do not have a guarantee or service contract to back their condition and operation. This is an "as is" purchase. Unless the manufacturer's warranty is still active and transferable, what you see is what you get, period.

Make sure that the private seller is selling a car that he or she purchased, owned, and operated for a period of time. The fact that an individual owns the vehicle does not mean that he or she is the original purchaser or that he or she owned the vehicle for an extended period of time. Some people buy vehicles cheap at a junkyard, auction, or insurance lot and flip them like houses. They make cosmetic repairs that may be unsafe and sell the car quickly for a profit. Do not take the private seller for granted or be disarmed by the appearance of equal experience and understanding; do your research, ask for records, and perform visual, audible, and mechanical inspections before you buy. Always get the title signed when you make the purchase.

Buying from a Dealership

Automobile dealerships, like military commands, have a mission and a number of personnel in place to execute that mission. The dealership's mission is to sell cars. Many dealerships do this by offering good vehicles, at a fair price, with great customer service. However, some dealerships take advantage of the transitory nature of servicemembers, the unending stream of new recruits to bases in their area, and the ease that money is made available to servicemembers to maximize the profit potential. These dealerships will take advantage of the new recruit's youth, military training, and lack of experience to extract every possible dollar. Some of the tactics used include:

1. **Overpricing: prices that are thousands of dollars above fair market value. The fair market value is determined by averaging sales prices for similar vehicles in similar geographical markets. Car pricing services such as the National Association of Automobile Dealerships (NADA), www.nada.com, and Kelly Blue Book (KBB), www.kbb.com, will provide the fair market value. We have a free market economy based upon capitalism. Profit is good; taking advantage of servicemembers to their detriment is not.**
2. Power booking: A dealer may provide the prospective buyer or lender a retail price from NADA or KBB. When a dealer power books a car, they use the make and model of the vehicle but they add accessories like sports or towing packages, sun roofs, custom wheels, or an upgraded technology system to increase the value. Dealerships using this practice may also use a different geographic location where vehicles carry a higher value, like the West Coast.
3. Add-ons: can benefit the dealership in two ways. One, if the vehicle has a high loan value (a lender will loan more money than the fair market value), selling add-ons will allow the dealership to obtain the full loan value and keep the additional profit from the add-on sales. The second is when the dealership values the vehicle above the loan value. In

this case the sale of add-ons financed by a third-party lender, not the bank loaning the funds to purchase the vehicle, will provide the dealership the profit from the sales to add to the profit from the sale of the vehicle so the dealership receives the total cash value from the sale. Add-ons may be in the form of:

a) Service contracts (agreements to repair a used vehicle);

b) GAP insurance or waivers, which cover the difference between the fair market value and the balance due after a total loss of the vehicle due to an accident;

c) Extra options like undercoating, window tinting or etching, radios, navigation systems, wheels, and tires; or

d) Items unrelated to the vehicle such as microwaves, computers, and even cameras.

4. Assigning loans to lenders based upon the point yield spread they provide the dealership: The point yield spread is the difference between the lender's offered interest rate and the rate offered to the servicemember by the dealership. In a point yield spread situation, the dealer keeps the difference as additional profit. (The point yield spread is discussed more on page 200.)

The Used Car Dealership

Used car dealerships, sometimes called independent dealerships because they are not affiliated with an automobile manufacturer, frequently offer the best value in car buying. Unlike the private owner, the used car dealership has an ongoing relationship with the public and a reputation behind its business. It has professionals to inspect vehicles prior to sale. The vehicles on a used car dealership's lot will also have a Buyers Guide. The Buyers Guide is a sheet of paper in the window of the vehicle that informs the buyer whether the vehicle is covered by a warranty or being sold "as is." Absent fraud, deception, or coercion, a vehicle sold "as is" is just that—"as is." The operational condition of the vehicle is not guaranteed and all implied warranties are waived. Implied warranties are guarantees that a product will function in the manner intended by the manufacturer. For example, beyond the basic power train function items, such as that power windows should go up and down and air conditioning should cool the vehicle. An implied warranty covers the whole vehicle.

Time is on Your Side

Used car dealers usually borrow funds to acquire the cars they sell. The cars are purchased at wholesale prices, which means the dealership has the potential to turn a large profit from the sale of used vehicles. However, the longer a car sits on the lot, the more the vehicle costs the dealership as it will have to make payments on the loan. This growing expense eats into that profit. A patient buyer who tracks a vehicle's life on the lot may find a motivated seller and get a deal. On the other hand, knowing the history of the vehicle and conducting a thorough inspection may tell the tale of why the vehicle is taking so long to sell. Similar to a transaction with a private seller, it is important to pay attention to where the car came from and the operating condition(s). As always, buyer beware.

Bad Credit Can Cost More

If you have questionable credit, a used car dealership may be more willing than a new car dealership to help you find financing. Sub-prime financing for those with challenged credit comes at a premium. Because the risk of default is higher, such lenders will charge a higher interest rate; buyers with challenged credit could see interest charges between 10 and 24 percent or more, depending upon state law. If the dealership has a high percentage of sub-prime borrowers, the vehicles on its lot may be marked above fair market value. Sub-prime lenders frequently discount the loans they purchase from dealerships. If the dealer sells a vehicle with a fair market value of $10,000 and finances it through a sub-prime lender, the dealership may receive only $8,000. Federal law prohibits the dealership from having one price for credit sales and another price for cash sales. This means that a dealership that tends to have a lot of customers with bad credit must mark up the prices of all vehicles in order to account for the possible reduction in profit associated with working with a sub-prime lender. If you are providing your own financing or want a better price, you will need to know the fair market value of the vehicle and negotiate for a fair price. Credit is your ability to access someone else's money and how much that institution will charge you to use their money. The way you use money and credit is tracked by credit rating bureaus, like Equifax and Trans Union. If you pay your bills on time and don't have too much credit extended, your credit rating will be high and your interest rate will be low. The interest rates advertised at 0 percent or 2.9 percent are for the consumers with the highest credit rating, 750 to 800. Consumers with a lower rating will have to pay a higher rate of interest on loans. The higher the interest rate, the higher the monthly payment, which increases the total cost of the vehicle.

Source of Inventory

The used car dealership's inventory comes from one of three sources: trade-ins, auctions, and/or transfers.

Trade-Ins. Trade-ins come from previous customers, who, when purchasing their own new vehicles, turn in their old vehicles and frequently receive credits toward the new purchase. When an owner decides to trade in his or her current car, there is a reason. It could be that the prior owner trades his vehicles at three years or 60,000 miles (end of warranty), that the new model is just too much to resist, or that the current car had or is about to have significant problems. These problems include increased maintenance needs and costs, accident damage, or a value diminishing event, such as floods or long-term abandonment. Hurricane Katrina flooded tens of thousands of vehicles, and a large number of these flood vehicles were released to the market by the insurance companies without the title noting the flood event. Vehicles that were in the flood areas during Katrina are suspect and may have been damaged. Flood vehicles are subject to electrical problems, engine and transmission issues, body rust, bacteria, mold, and other problems. When you buy used, you could be getting the problems the last buyer avoided or covered up. This is why the maintenance records, reliability reports, and car history are so important.

Auctions. Many of the vehicles on a used car dealership's lot were purchased at auction. At an auction, the dealer will have a brief opportunity to inspect and assess the condition of the vehicle, and then the bidding begins. The vehicles sold at auction have been sent there from dealerships, insurance companies, and banks. The vehicle could be a cream puff, with low miles in like-new condition that was returned to the bank, or a flood vehicle that avoided the junkyard.

Transfers. The last source for vehicles at the used car dealership is transfers. Vehicles can be transferred fairly easily from dealership to dealership. Each dealership lot has traffic flow passing its business location every day. If a vehicle does not catch someone's eye in a week or two, it may not be appealing to the market in the area. A car that is not selling is a growing bill. The dealership can transfer (sell wholesale) the slow moving vehicle to another dealership.

New Car Dealerships

New car dealerships are also called franchise dealerships because they are associated with an automobile manufacturer. These dealerships can have millions of dollars invested in their inventory and showroom. That investment means that their name and reputation are important; a new car dealership is less likely to "knowingly" engage in activities that could damage its reputation. That sizable investment also means that there is a lot of overhead to cover on each sale. The lush showrooms, enticing advertisements, and beautiful new cars are there to relax you into signing on the bottom line.

The formality of a franchise dealership can include some benefits for you. New cars come with a manufacturer's warranty that provides a degree of security for the buyer. New cars also have a manufacturer's suggested retail price (MSRP) with an itemized list of standard and optional accessories on the vehicle. This listing helps to prevent confusion over what type of equipment is on the vehicle and the value of the equipment.

The price the dealership pays the manufacturer for the vehicle is called the invoice price. If you are about to begin negotiations with a new car dealership, you should research the invoice price. Knowing it allows you to consider the profit the dealer will make on the vehicle. Offering a flat amount like $500 or $1,000 over invoice is one tactic in purchasing a new vehicle. Several banks and credit unions offer buying services that provide additional savings on the purchase of a new vehicle. These buying services leverage the lending power of the bank in favor of the buyer to get the dealership to offer the vehicle at a reduced price.

One disadvantage in a new vehicle purchase is depreciation. Once purchased, what was previously new is now used, and the vehicle can lose as much as 20 percent of its value when you drive it away.

NEGOTIATING THE PURCHASE PRICE

The automobile business is simple supply and demand. The dealership supplies the vehicles that the servicemember demands. The dealership's mission is to maximize the profit on each transaction. This is not a bad thing. Every business wants to make a profit; that's why it exists. If the servicemember is equally prepared with information on the vehicle, its costs, and the cost of borrowing money, this is a fair and equal transaction. The problem arises when the parties are not equally matched. When information like the vehicle history is not known, when the knowledge about the fair market value or loan value of the vehicle is not known, or when information on the cost to borrow funds is not understood, there is a disparity between the seller and buyer, with the advantage going to the seller. Information is power in a negotiation.

Adjusting Your Perspective

Understand who you are in this process. You can be a mechanism for delivering money to the dealership, a kind of ATM where the dealer pushes the right buttons and you hand over money, or an informed, powerful, respected negotiator. You are a person who is about to deliver what the dealership wants and needs most—a sale! The dealership is not doing you a favor; they are selling you a car. If you did not qualify for the loan or have the money to make the purchase they would not talk to you; it would be a waste of their time.

Time is Money

When you buy an automobile, you spend three, four, maybe six hours at the dealership. The salesperson spends, at most, half of that time with you. The salesperson gets a base salary and a commission. On a per-car basis, the salesperson may make from $500 to $1,000 on your sale. During the purchase/sale process, the salesperson is working for you and you are paying more than $100 per hour for their service. When you pay $100-plus per hour for a service, it should be good service and you should be respected, not rushed or misled.

The Economic Power of "No"

Your economic power is your ability to say "no" and walk out of the dealership. If you walk, the salesperson and dealership invested time, money, and effort into a losing enterprise. Every minute spent on a lost sale is lost money to the dealership, which could have invested that time in a buying customer. If you walk because of the dealership's conduct or the terms of the sale, it may have to change its conduct or terms to stay in business. You have the power! As you decide which car to buy and how much to pay, visualize that you are about to take $20,000 out of your savings account and deliver it, dollar by dollar to the salesperson for the vehicle. Your money and credit is your buying power.

The Purchase Process

Once you identify a vehicle you want to purchase, the business side of buying a car kicks in. Looking for a car is a search with an identified goal guided by reality based on research. Buying is a legal engagement establishing your obligation to purchase, which will be solidified in the Bill of Sale or Buyers Order. Your method of payment will be detailed in the Retail Installment Sales Contract or RISC (should be "risk"!). The last legal step is when the seller conveys title to the vehicle to you. If only it were that simple!

The Buyers Order will contain the following:

1. The amount the vehicle costs;
2. The additional fees the dealership is charging for processing, such as taxes, tags, and title;
3. The amount, if any, paid to you for your trade-in, usually in the form of an allowance against the amount you owe for the new purchase;
4. The negative equity (the amount you still owe), if any, on the trade in; and
5. The cost of any add-ons, such as service contracts, insurance, and GAP and any down payment. Buyer beware! This can be a shell game where the dealership hides the real numbers from you and the banks to assure approval and profit.

The RISC will contain the following information:

1. The name of the buyer and creditor/seller;
2. The category of vehicle—new or used, the year, make, and model of vehicle, and the vehicle identification number (VIN);
3. The annual percentage rate, the total finance charge, the amount financed, the total debt including interest and principle, and total cost to purchase on credit including down payment;
4. The total number of payments, the amount of each payment, and when the payments are due;
5. A breakdown of the amounts paid for or received for trade-in and amounts paid to third parties for negative equity, taxes, and other fees; and
6. Provisions for optional insurance and other contractual provisions

The Add-On Shell Game

The dealer, even if it is a buy-here-pay-here dealership, may want to bundle your loan with others and sell them to a lender. When a dealer sells your loan to a lender, the lender steps into the position of the dealer with regard to you; your payments and fees for the line of credit will start going to the lender. Packaging loans like this gives the dealership more liquid capital (cash) for its business. If the loan is held by a bank, the bank may also want to package and sell the loan to the securities market.

In order for the dealer or bank to be able to sell your loan to a lender, it needs to be appealing to the buyer. A buyer of loans wants to see three things:

1. That the purchaser (you!) does not have other obligations that will interfere or compete with his or her ability to pay the loan.
2. That the property being purchased is of reasonable quality and will work. If the property does not function, the

purchaser will have to pay for repairs or replacement and may not want to or be able to pay the loan.

3. That the purchaser has equity in the vehicle. Equity in this setting means that because of your trade-in, down payment, or negotiation skills, the loan to purchase the vehicle is for an amount that is less than the value of the vehicle. Lenders believe that if the buyer has equity in the vehicle, he or she is less likely to walk away from the vehicle and stop payments because he or she will lose the cash value of the equity.

The dealership accomplishes these three tasks through a number of questionable activities. First, the dealership may try to cover any negative equity in your trade-in with an allowance of equal amount. If you owe $7,000 on your car, but it is worth only $4,500, you have $2,500 in negative equity. The dealership should give you an allowance only for the value of your vehicle, or $4,500. You are responsible for the negative equity of $2,500 to the previous lender. The problem with this is that if you keep the negative equity, you will have to pay on two loans and possibly have to choose between the two. Additionally, the dealership cannot get title to sell your trade-in until the loan on that vehicle is paid off. The negative equity must go—but where? The dealership will frequently hide that negative equity in the purchase price. Since the loan value is ten to forty percent over fair market value, there is room to hide that $2,500 in negative equity in the new sales price.

Second, the dealership can sell a service contract to protect the functionality of the product. The service contract provides coverage for failure of a covered part or system on a vehicle. Service contracts may cost the dealership $300 to $500 and are routinely sold for $1,000 to $2,500 and more. Service contracts are usually offered for sale in conjunction with a used vehicle. Service contracts for new vehicles with warranties are called extended service agreements. Service contracts are a major profit source for new and used car dealers.

Be cautious when purchasing a service contract. A service contract that does not expressly require the provider to fix or repair the vehicle upon the occurrence of a reasonable event is of no value. Service contracts are similar to an insurance policy that the vehicle will perform and not need repair. The provider loses money if the vehicle needs repairs covered by the contract. The provider makes money if the repairs are not covered or are subject to exclusion. The provider is betting that it will not have to make repairs so that it will make money, have a profit, and stay in business. Service contract providers are usually regulated by the state. The issuer of the contract should have a bond or reserve to cover possible claims so it has funds on hand to repair your vehicle. Not all companies are equal and may not pay reasonable claims. If the service contract requires that you provide routine maintenance and covers only the failure of any internally lubricated part, there may be no coverage! Rarely does an internally lubricated part fail without some neglect or improper maintenance, making it the owner's fault and not covered.

Third, dealers may create equity in the purchase of a vehicle from the positive value of the trade-in or a down payment. This provides the appearance that you have equity in the purchase because you paid down the purchase price. Beware, some unscrupulous dealerships will write in a down payment of $500 or $1,000, but explain to you that you don't have to pay it. "The money is just to help the lender approve the loan." The Buyers Order is being submitted to a lending institution as part of an application for a loan. Where does this money come from if you are not paying it? Where does it go? This is more of the shell game.

The down payment is hidden in the price for a 0 percent gain and net loss as you have to pay taxes on these fictional amounts. Note: Federal law prohibits false or fraudulent statements in loan applications. When the dealership does this, it is breaking the law. If you knowingly comply, you are breaking the law, too. When the servicemember wants to assert that he was taken advantage of by the dealership, his credibility may be questioned if he knowingly committed a fraudulent act with the dealership.

The Negotiation Process

This is not a battle between good and evil, but a negotiation between the informed and uninformed or misinformed. To negotiate successfully, you must be informed.

The salesperson and dealership has information on the vehicle, its history, cost, market value, and loan value. The salesperson is also an expert at evaluating the customer. This is particularly easy when dealing with the military. Military personnel can be identified by haircuts, mannerisms, and uniforms. Dealerships that deal with the military seek and hire former military as sales personnel. In casual conversation, the salesperson will ask information about your employment, life, and interests. When dealing with a servicemember, this information provides access to the amount of pay and allowances. A good salesperson will know your income based upon your rank and years in service and the allowances made to you based upon your family status. Some unscrupulous dealerships will take your military ID or driver's license when you take a test drive and use that information to run your credit so they even know your debts. It's all right (though not always smart) to trust your salesperson, but it's respectful and professional to confirm the facts in a business transaction.

You know your income, debt structure, and automobile needs. In making the purchase, you need the rest of the story, information regarding the history, quality, vehicle cost, market value, relative value, and loan value of the vehicle being purchased. Use this information to guide your negotiations. Take the time to research, even if it's just on your smart phone. Always know what you are willing to pay monthly, total price, and for upkeep and maintenance. Be willing to say "no" without an explanation. Be willing to walk out if you cannot get what you want. If the dealership wants to sell a vehicle, they will meet you at a reasonable price without games. If they will not negotiate in good faith, you will know to leave and not waste your or their time.

PAYING FOR THE VEHICLE

Unless you have enough cash to cover the entire purchase price of the vehicle, you will be financing your purchase with someone else's money. While there are buy-here, pay-here dealerships that provide financing to purchase vehicles, most automobile dealerships are not banks. There are many other ways to finance your automobile purchase, including coming in to the dealership pre-approved by a bank or credit union; or, you may allow the dealership to act as an automobile loan broker and find financing for you.

Credit and Mission Readiness

Your ability to borrow money is dependent upon your credit score. Your credit score tells creditors how risky it is to lend you funds. Your credit score can impact much more than automobile purchases. Knowing what your credit score is, building and improving your credit score, and protecting your credit score are important for mission readiness. Credit issues can impact your household budget, family morale, sailor morale, individual readiness, security clearance, and in the end, command mission accomplishment. Like your security clearance, your credit score should be protected.

> ▶ **CREDIT ISN'T FREE**
>
> When a lender extends credit to you, this isn't free money lent to you out of the goodness of the lender's heart. The lender is in this business to make money, and credit isn't free. From interest rates to various fees, the lender will charge you a fee for the use of his or her money.

You cannot change your history, but you can make adjustments to change your future. If you have a low credit score, get assistance from a reliable financial counselor such as those at the military family support centers, a bank, or a credit union. These organizations and institutions can help you develop a plan to pay down your debt. With consistent regular payments, over time, you will increase your credit score.

Costs of Financing

If you navigated through the maze of which vehicle to get and where to get the vehicle and negotiated a good price, you are left with the last trap: how to pay for the vehicle. Where do you go to get a quick $10,000, $15,000, or $20,000? How much will it cost to borrow the money, and how long will you have to pay it back? These are the important questions to consider when using someone else's money. There are many options, and adjusting the term (three, four, five years), the interest rate (3.5 percent, 7.5 percent, 15 percent), and the monthly payments will change the costs of borrowing money. For example, a sixty-month loan for $15,000 at 7.5 percent will have a monthly payment of $315 per month and cost $3,935 in interest charges for a total purchase cost $18,935. That same loan at 15 percent will cost $374 per month and $7,481 in interest charges for a total purchase cost $22,481. The interest charge and the $3,546 difference between the two rates is the cost of borrowing money. Shopping for the best credit terms will save you money.

How to Shop for Credit

In 1968, Congress decided that the economy would be more stable and competition between lenders would improve if consumers had more information about their use of credit. Using credit can be risky if you don't understand the costs associated with borrowing money. To address the lack of information in the credit extending process, Congress has created laws to assure the meaningful disclosure of credit terms. Understanding the terms of credit allows you to compare various credit options and make an informed decision. Your government wants you to shop around for the best borrowing opportunity.

This law, the Truth in Lending Act (TILA), in a nutshell, requires that automobile dealerships (or any institution lending money) provide you the terms of your proposed financing in a format that you can take with you prior to signing and becoming obligated, so that you can shop for credit. The mandatory disclosure terms of your credit are: the annual percentage rate, finance charge, amount financed, total of payments, total of sales price including down payment, number of payments, amount of payments, and the due date for payments. You are then able to take these disclosures and compare them with offers from other lenders to get the best deal.

It is illegal for car dealerships to tell you that they cannot give disclosures to you or give you a paper without the information. Dealerships may deny you this disclosure because their business is competitive and if you shop for a better loan deal or better car price, you may just find someone who will offer a better deal, costing the disclosing dealership your business. There are two things you can do if the dealership refuses to provide the documentation. The first is to simply leave the dealership. The potential loss of the sale may motivate the dealership to follow the law. The second is to gather as much information as you can before you go to the dealership. You should know the average price for the vehicle you want to purchase by checking the NADA or KBB values on the Internet. You should check your credit report and score to make sure that it accurately reflects your credit status. You should apply for an auto loan at your local bank or credit union. This information will allow you to determine if you are getting the best deal from the dealership.

Go Ahead, Apply

Applying for a loan is really the only real way to know how much credit will cost you. Go to your credit union or bank and apply for a loan to buy a car. You do not have to take the money right then, but you will know if you qualify and on what terms the loan will be offered. When you begin to shop for your previously identified vehicle, you already know what you can afford and how much it will cost you to borrow the money. The dealership now has to meet or beat the established standard.

If a lender declines to offer you credit, you will be informed in hours or days. Within thirty days of being denied credit, the lender will send you a letter explaining why it declined your credit. This provides you an opportunity to critically evaluate your credit and make changes. If a bank or credit union cannot approve you, you may apply through the dealership for a loan with a subprime lender. However, when applying for credit from or through the dealership, do not sign the papers. Signing is buying. The law requires the dealership to provide you with a copy of the RISC or at least its terms unsigned so you can shop for credit.

Various Types of Lenders

You will have to look for the best deals on financing. On new vehicles, the manufacturers and the financial institutions associated with them that loan money to purchase vehicles may offer incentives like no-down payment and/or low interest for purchases. On new and used vehicles, the bank and credit union market is very competitive and shopping around will pay off in better lending terms.

If a servicemember cannot get approved through a traditional bank or credit union, he or she will usually allow the dealership to act as an automobile loan broker. In this capacity, you are asking it to find the best rate to save you money and offer it to you. Dealers use an Internet-based system to solicit purchasers for your loan. The dealership enters your RISC terms and personal credit information into the system and lenders make offers to buy your loan. If the dealership receives an offer it likes, it can accept that offer and agree to assign your loan and payment obligation to that lender. Be aware that the dealership independently determines if the offer by the lender is acceptable. You will not know what the dealership's criteria for an acceptable and best offer is until you get the paperwork. The accepted offer may allow the dealership to apply a "point yield spread." With a point yield spread, the lender offers to purchase the RISC accepting the terms on the form but offering the dealership a lower interest rate. The dealership could convey that information and savings to you, but some unscrupulous dealers use the point yield spread to their advantage and keep the difference as additional profit. Everybody's happy, you get the contract and vehicle, the dealership gets a sale and additional funds, and the creditor gets a loan. The creditor may lose two points on a loan, but it will build volume with more loans from a select group of debtors (servicemembers) for whom it's a crime not to pay a just debt. There are three problems with this model. First, you are misled into thinking that the dealership is working for you, in your best interest, as a fiduciary, when the dealership is actually working for its own best interest. The second is that it establishes a system where instead of transparency and informed use of credit, the real transaction is concealed and you are deceived into allowing the misuse of your credit. The third is that in an economy where, due to recession, there are massive numbers of new borderline borrowers, there can be an incentive for the dealership to feed the loans to subprime lenders that charge a higher interest and can offer larger point yield spreads.

You can also negotiate the price for a specific vehicle, then look at the financing offer and decide to shop around at other dealerships for the best deal on both. The dealership will not like that plan and want you to be obligated to purchase from them before they allow you to see the credit terms. The best tactic in this case is just to stick to your guns. Even if you are in a situation where you need a car, remember that the dealership needs the sale. This issue is on whose terms the deal will be made.

WHAT TO DO IF THINGS GO WRONG

If you find that even with your best efforts, the salesperson, dealership, mechanic, inspector, warranty, or service contract failed to meet your expectations, seek assistance, but first take time to help yourself. Before you go to see an attorney, you should type up a narrative of the event. Be thorough, listing everything that happened in chronological order including each event, what happened, who said what, and the names of the people and businesses with addresses and phone numbers. Copy all of your documents. The auto sales industry is highly regulated. Dealerships are licensed by the state and operated under statutory requirements. If the dealership violated any of the legal requirements for the conduct of its business, you have several options.

1. Ask a person with the authority to make the decision (general manager or owner) in a professional and polite manner to provide the desired resolution.
2. Send a professionally worded letter to the general manager or owner requesting resolution of your problem. Writing is a tool frequently overlooked by consumers. Phone calls are fast, but they do not document the problem or request for resolution.
3. File complaints with the Better Business Bureau (www.bbb .org), state Consumer Protection Agency, state dealership licensing authority, Federal Trade Commission (www.ftc .gov), Consumer Protection Bureau (www.cfbp.gov), and Armed Forces Disciplinary Control Board (AFDCB). Attach your professional letter and documents to the complaints. The civilian agencies each have an interest in protecting consumers and can address the problem through public reputation, licensing, civil fines, criminal prosecution, and other sanctions. The AFDCB is a regional military board that protects servicemembers from unscrupulous merchants whose business practices impact individual and mission readiness by causing harm to the health, safety, welfare, or

morale of the troops. The AFDCB can ban military personnel from a business by placing that business off limits. For those businesses that target the military and soliciting sales from the military, a ban can directly impact the sales, profit, and bottom line.

4. If the above efforts fail, you can seek resolution through the courts. On occasion, the mere fact that you are represented can motivate an offending party to settle the matter because the costs of litigation can be excessive. Also, many federal and state laws protecting the consumer have a fee-shifting provision that would allow the court to order the offending dealership to pay the attorney fees of the servicemember. If you need an attorney, you have free attorney support from the legal assistance office nearest you. Go to www.legalassistance.law.af.mil to find the closest office. Additionally, the American Bar Association (ABA) maintains a list of legal assistance programs that are free or low-cost for servicemembers and their families. It can be found in the "Program Directory" at www.abahomefront .org. The ABA also has a pro bono program that in some instances can provide an attorney free of charge. The ABA Pro Bono Program can be found at http://apps.americanbar .org/legalservices/probono/directory.html. Many state bar associations and local city bar associations have pro bono assistance for servicemembers. The National Association of Consumer Advocates provides a list of attorneys by state and by area of practice who may be able to assist with a multitude of consumer issues. Go to www.naca.net to find a consumer law attorney.

Repair

If you have problems with the vehicle after purchase, first document the problem. You need to know under what circumstances the event occurs, when it occurs, and if possible what is happening.

Problems with New Cars

If you purchased a new vehicle, the defects should be covered under the warranty. Because the vehicle is new, there is a presumption that any defects were caused in the manufacturing of the vehicle and should be repaired by the manufacturer. Your state lemon law may allow you to return a vehicle for a refund or repair if it is a new vehicle that cannot be repaired or that has recurring problems. Lemon laws vary from state to state. Most will provide protection against defects in the vehicle for the initial warranty period offered by manufacturer. Others extend that coverage beyond the initial warranty period for months to years.

There are usually two tiers of defects under lemon laws. The first tier is a defect that causes or risks substantial damage or serious harm, such as the failure of a major safety system or component. This tier of defects has to occur only once for a lemon law to apply. The second tier consists of defects that affect the use of the vehicle and that cannot be repaired after a set number of attempts or after a specified period of time. The number of attempts and period of time for the dealership to complete the repairs vary from state to state. New vehicles come with a warranty book that contains a card to be used to notify the manufacturer and dealership of the defect. If you are dealing with a defect to a new car, the best bet is to use the address on the card, but send the notice by certified mail to assure the receipt of the complaint and the date of the receipt.

Problems with Old Cars

If you purchased a used vehicle, but it is a newer vehicle, the original warranty may transfer to you and you may have the protections of the lemon law. If the defect is such that it substantially impairs the value or use of the vehicle and it could not be found by reasonable inspection prior to purchase, you may be able to return the vehicle to the dealership for repair under an implied warranty or terminate the purchase. An implied warranty comes with any vehicle that has an express (written warranty) or that has a service contract sold with the purchase or within ninety days. The implied warranty covers the car and warrants that the components perform as specified or as is the usual function for that component. For example: Power windows should raise and lower by power and air conditioning should cool the interior of the vehicle. In order to take advantage of an implied warranty, you have to return the vehicle to the dealership, provide notice of the problem, and allow the

▶ **THINGS TO REMEMBER**

1. In any negotiation, information is power. Before you arrive at the dealership, empower yourself with information about the type of vehicle you want to purchase, the average cost of the vehicle, and what options you need, want, and can live without.

2. Get a copy of your credit report. Get your credit score. Get any errors on your credit report corrected.

3. Before you arrive at the dealership, you should shop around for a loan. This will tell you what your buying power is and how much it will cost you to finance the purchase. The dealership may be able to offer you a better interest rate.

4. When purchasing a vehicle, you are the one with the money. You are the boss. Demand respect. Use your economic power and walk away if the transaction is not right.

5. Remember, this is a business transaction, not a long-term relationship. As a good business person, you are not offending the salesperson if you ask questions about the condition of the vehicle, the purchase price, or the financing. If you choose to trust the salesperson, trust with verification.

6. Take the time to read the financial documents and contracts. Ask questions. Get your answers in writing. You will be strictly held to the terms you agree to in the contract. Make sure you understand what you are about to sign.

dealership the opportunity to cure or fix the problem. If after a reasonable time the dealership has failed to fix the problem, you can request that the purchase be terminated. This process is difficult, and you should seek guidance from an attorney on the specific rule for revocation of acceptance under the Uniform Commercial Code.

Dealing with Repair Facilities

If you are at a repair facility, you should always ask for a written estimate with an itemized list of parts and labor. These steps will protect against unauthorized repairs and surprise charges. If you have any uncertainty about what the repair facility is telling you, get a second opinion. If the vehicle came with a warranty or you purchased a service contract, review the documents to see if the problem the facility is telling you about is covered.

RESOURCES

- **Edmunds** (www.edmunds.com): Provides pricing information and consumer education.

- **Kelly Blue Book** (www.kbb.com): Provides pricing information for used vehicles.

- **National Automobile Dealers Association** (www.nada.com): Provides pricing information for used vehicles.

- **Autopedia** (www.autopedia.com): Provides links to auto purchase resources.

- **National Motor Vehicle Title Information System** (www .vehiclehistory.gov): Provides tips and history and sells educational resources.

- **Carfax** (www.carfax.com): (fee) Provides service, damage, title, and mileage history.

- **AutoCheck** (www.autocheck.com): (fee) Provides service, damage, title, and mileage history for vehicles.

- **Consumer Guide** (www.consumerguide.com/auto): (fee) Provides history, repair, and costs.

- **Consumer Reports** (www.consumerreports.org): (fee) Provides history, reliability, repair, and maintenance costs.

- **Military Legal Assistance Office Locator:** www.legalassistance.law.af.mil.

- **Federal Trade Commission:** www.ftc.gov.

- **Consumer Financial Protection Bureau:** www.cfpb.gov.

- **The National Association of Consumer Advocates** (www.naca.net): Provides a list of attorneys by state and by area of practice who may be able to assist with a multitude of consumer issues.

CHAPTER 6

Wills and Estate Planning

Noelle, a Private First Class in the U.S. Army, is twenty-two years old and just had her first child, a bouncing baby boy. She and her husband don't have a ton of money but are very proud of the home that they have made for their family. Because they are so young, and because they don't own a lot of assets, Noelle and her husband are pretty sure they don't need a fancy will or any complex estate planning. The last time Noelle deployed, she filled out a basic will, and she figures that should be enough. However, that was before she became a mom and her husband doesn't have one in case something happens to him. Does Noelle need to update her will? What would happen to her husband's savings account and car if something happened to him? And now that she is thinking about it, Noelle would really like to make sure that her son is provided for. Can a will help her do that?

Estate planning is meant to plan for emergencies during life and for a smooth transition of your assets after death. Most people are unaware of the broad scope of estate planning because they tend to focus solely on the will. A will is a necessary piece of an estate plan, but it is just one piece. This chapter explains the basics of estate planning, including wills, but also the other parts of an estate plan and their significance.

ESTATE PLANNING BASICS

The process of estate planning and the legal tools that make sense for you and your family will vary depending on your circumstance and what you hope to get out of the process. However, there are some basic tools and considerations that are likely going to be a part of any estate-planning process. This section details the common ones, including wills, trusts, and important tax considerations.

Wills

A will is a formal written document that sets out certain instructions that are to be followed upon your death. These instructions normally will cover: distribution of your personal property, pets, and real estate (such as a house); appointing a guardian for your minor children if both parents are deceased; nominating a person to be the executor of the instructions in your will (and stating whether or not the executor should post a bond with the court); directions with regard to payment of estate taxes and debts; and funeral, memorial, and burial instructions. Wills can go by a number of different names, including "Last Will and Testament." What a will is called, whether or not it may be handwritten or must be typed, if it needs to be notarized to be valid, how many witnesses must sign the will, and how changes to the will may be made all depend on the law of the state where the person making the will is located. There is a federal law that creates an exception for "Military Testamentary Instruments" (Title 10, United States Code 1044d). This law covers wills prepared and executed (signed) by military legal assistance lawyers and states that they shall be accepted in any state where filed for probate.

To get the most accurate, up-to-date information for your state, it is best to make an appointment with your local military legal assistance office; the staff there can walk you through these issues and ensure that you are following the applicable rules in your case.

Care must be taken when writing a will. Estate settlement costs can be expensive if not properly planned for. Estate settlement fees can include attorney fees for the attorney assisting with the probate of the estate and fees to the executor. As detailed on page 217, estates that exceed certain amounts may

▶ **AN EXECUTOR OR PERSONAL REPRESENTATIVE**

Appointing an executor (or a personal representative) is an important part of estate planning. The executor is your personal representative who you appoint to administer your estate; in other words, this is the person who will make sure that your instructions are followed, that your property gets where it is supposed to, and that any necessary taxes and fees are paid. There's no consensus about who makes the best executor; some states may give your surviving spouse preference. It all depends on your circumstances; a good choice is often your spouse or the person who will be the main beneficiary of your will. This person is naturally going to be interested in making the process go as smoothly as possible and with minimal expense. For larger, more complicated estates, you may want to consider naming a professional, such as your bank, accountant, or lawyer.

be subject to both state and federal death taxes. If the estate's assets are not arranged correctly, there may not be enough cash or liquid assets to pay estate settlement costs. There might not be enough assets or income to care for a spouse or child who survives your death. For all these reasons and more, it is incredibly important to make sure you are thoughtful in writing a will and getting all your ducks in line; the best way to do that is to start with a military legal assistance lawyer.

Transferring assets to your beneficiaries can be a complex process after your death. Estate assets may be subject to the delays and expense of probate. (Probate is the process by which the state government makes sure that your will's instructions as to property and asset distribution are followed—after your estate's debts and bills and taxes are paid. For many military members, their Servicemembers Group Life Insurance (SGLI) at $400,000 is their largest asset, and this in almost all cases is not included in the probate process. In addition, most states have a short-form or summary probate proceeding, which is very quick and not burdensome.) Assets transferred to minors may be held in guardianship accounts until the minors reach a certain age, such as eighteen or twenty-one (depending on state law). To structure a guardianship of funds in advance, a trust instrument can be created or included in your will, which would allow the grantor of funds to make the rules about how these funds should be distributed to a minor. If not structured in advance, a court-supervised guardianship may be required. This would mean that the court would approve of the guardian appointed and may require the guardian to report at certain times to the court concerning the status of the guardian's money.

Trusts

Trusts are documents that establish a legal entity that can hold and manage assets according to the instructions contained within the trust document. Some people find it easiest to envision the trust as a box, where you put all of your assets. The box has a lid that is locked. Who owns the box, who can get inside the box, and who is allowed to receive the items in the box are dictated by the terms of the trust. There are three people involved in a trust. The first is the grantor (also called settlor). To refer back to the box analogy, the grantor is often the person who owns the box. If you are creating a trust for your assets, you are the initial grantor. The grantor establishes the trust, funds it, and provides the instructions by which the trust assets are to be managed by the trustee. The trustee is the person who has the key to the box. The trustee manages the trust in accordance with those instructions, for the benefit of the beneficiary. The beneficiary is the person who gets the use, value, and enjoyment of the trust assets that have been placed inside the box. When and how the beneficiary is allowed to receive these assets is set out in the trust document.

There are several types of trusts. The trust most often created by servicemembers is a trust for the benefit of your children that is contained in your will. If your children are your only surviving beneficiaries at the time of your death, your property, including the proceeds of your SGLI life insurance, will go into this trust and can be managed by a trustee until your children reach an age you have predetermined. If your estate is smaller and consists basically of your SGLI, this type of trust can be quickly processed in a small or summary probate with very little delay and cost. This process can usually be done at a military legal assistance office and requires careful coordination between your will and your SGLI beneficiary choice. The SGLI (SGLV 8286) must be reviewed by the attorney who prepares your will.

The following are trusts that are not included in your will and in most cases will not be prepared by the military legal assistance attorney. The intricacies of SGLI, the death gratuity, SBP, or other military benefits (all discussed later in this chapter), can be rather complicated, and it is likely best that you see a military legal assistance attorney first and request that he or she work with your civilian attorney, who can help you set up these additional types of trusts.

A **revocable living trust** is one that the grantor can amend, change, or revoke during his life. While the assets in the trust do not go through the probate process, they are still considered part of the grantor's gross estate for federal estate tax purposes. Upon the grantor's death, the trust continues to operate in accordance with the grantor's instructions. Revocable living trusts can be used to avoid probate, establish college funds for children or grandchildren, or prevent heirs with poor money management skills from being subject to lawsuits from predators or creditors. Often in a revocable living trust, the grantor is also the trustee and the beneficiary. It sounds confusing, but if you think of the box analogy again, the grantor is merely placing his assets in the box to avoid the probate tax but still retains the rights to distribute all of the assets as he wishes and enjoy them as he sees fit. This arrangement also allows grantors/beneficiaries who are preparing for some type of future incapacitation (for example, a chronic illness) to put provisions into the trust allowing a new, independent trustee to be appointed if the grantor/beneficiary is unable to manage his own finances. As Americans live longer, this type of planning for future incapacitation is becoming even more invaluable. At the end of a grantor's live, a revocable living trust is then turned over to another trustee to manage funds as explained above for a new beneficiary.

An **irrevocable trust** is a trust that the grantor establishes but then gives up any right to amend, change, or revoke and also gives up rights to the assets in the trust. The most common reason for this type of trust is to place assets outside the grantor's gross estate for estate tax purposes. A common example is an irrevocable life insurance trust, where the grantor takes out a life insurance policy on himself, makes the trust the beneficiary, and then assigns ownership of the policy to the trust, paying for the policy's premium payments as a gift to the trust. The benefit is that the trust beneficiaries will have money to use according to the terms of the trust, and those proceeds are not included in the grantor's taxable gross estate.

Irrevocable trusts may also be used to divest one's self of assets in certain situations such as estate planning to become eligible for social services. Medicaid planning is a good example of this type of planning. This concept is explained more in the health care section in Chapter 7.

Supplemental Needs Trusts

Certain individuals with disabilities may qualify for means-tested governmental assistance programs such as Medicaid, Social Security Disability Insurance, or Social Security Supplemental Security Income. These individuals receive health benefits, income, and special program access due to their disability and their low or nonexistent income (such as group homes, mental health care, and other non-income assistance). If an individual who is eligible to receive such assistance receives a substantial inheritance, he would be in danger of losing his

COMPARING TYPES OF TRUSTS

TYPE	GENERAL USE	RESTRIC- TIONS	BENEFITS
Testamentary Trust in Will	Catches and manages assets from estate or life insurance, and assets are usually maintained for children.	The assets in the trust are still considered part of the grantor's estate for tax purposes.	Permits management of children's benefits until they reach the age you decide.
Supplemental Needs Trust	Contains assets and cash for the supplemental needs of a disabled person such as entertainment, travel, utilities.	Assets cannot be spent for the health, education, maintenance, or support of the disabled person.	Maintains a disabled person's eligibility for needs-based programs like Medicaid and Social Security.
Revocable Trust	A trust that can be amended, changed, or revoked during the grantor's lifetime. Revocable trusts are generally used to avoid the probate process.	The assets in the trust are still considered part of the grantor's estate for tax purposes.	Grantor can use assets in trust as he or she sees fit. If original grantor becomes incapacitated, a trustee can be appointed to manage the grantor's assets, if no co-trustee is named.
Irrevocable Trust	The grantor cannot change, revoke, or amend the trust during his or her lifetime.	Grantor gives up the right to the assets in the trust.	Assets in the trusts are not considered part of the grantor's estate for tax purposes. Can be used to make the grantor eligible for certain social services.

eligibility. A supplemental needs trust may be appropriate in such a case.

A supplemental needs trust is a special type of trust that contains assets and cash for a disabled person's supplemental needs such as entertainment, travel, utilities, and other expenses that are not directly tied to health, education, maintenance, and/or support. Because the assets and cash are in the trust and do not belong to the disabled individual, and because the trustee cannot spend for the beneficiary's health, education, maintenance, or support, the trust's assets and cash are not considered resources available to the disabled individual and thus do not affect his eligibility for the means-tested programs. This area of law is highly complex, and you should consult with an attorney who is experienced in this area to determine if this type of trust is an appropriate tool for your family.

Estate Taxation Issues

The federal government imposes a tax on estates over a certain dollar value. (Certain states impose an estate tax as well, but that is beyond the scope of this book.) The federal government's estate tax exempts a certain amount of the estate from taxation and will impose a tax on the amount of the estate over that exemption. For example, in 2012, the federal government did not impose a tax on the first $5 million of a person's "gross estate" (defined below) and imposed a 35 percent tax on the gross estate above $5 million. This exemption and tax rate may vary from year to year, so be sure to check with your estate-planning attorney each year to see if your estate plan needs to be updated due to changes in the tax code. Note that under current law, for a married couple, there is no estate tax on the transfer of marital assets from the deceased spouse to the surviving spouse.

So, what is the "gross estate" that is subject to the federal estate tax? It is quite broad, and you may be surprised at what is taxed. Assets that you own in your own name will be included, such as a house, a car, stocks, bonds, cash in the bank, and other tangible and intangible property. However, many people are surprised to learn that other items can also be included in the gross estate, such as the death benefit of life insurance policies that you own and the assets owned by a revocable living trust you have established. For this reason, estate planning can also include creating an irrevocable trust that puts certain assets outside of your gross estate.

Let's take an example to illustrate this. If you are single, own a $500,000 life insurance policy on yourself, own a $250,000 house, and own $300,000 in stocks and bonds, you have a gross estate of $1,050,000. If the federal tax code says the first $5 million of gross estate is tax-exempt, then you would pay no estate tax. But if the tax code has changed so that the exemption is lowered to $1 million, you now have $50,000 of taxable estate. That $50,000 will be subject to the federal estate tax rate, which could be as high as 55 percent (which at the time of writing was scheduled to happen at the start of 2013 unless Congress changes the law). Now your executor is faced with having to come up with cash to pay the IRS the estate tax, either by selling the house, by selling the stocks and bonds, or by asking the life insurance policy beneficiary for the cash.

If you have a large amount of assets and life insurance that you think may subject you to the federal and state estate tax, make an appointment with an estate planning attorney in your state.

When Should You Review Your Estate Plan?

Once an estate plan is completed and signed, it is often placed in a file cabinet, desk drawer, or safe deposit box where it is forgotten about until it is needed. However, it is important to periodically review and update your estate plan, depending on the type of document and which circumstances have changed (you would be shocked to learn how many people never bother to update their will if their designated executor dies first!). Here is a list of events that may require updating of a will or other document in your estate plan:

- Marriage
- Divorce
- Death of a spouse
- Disability of a spouse or child
- Moving to another state
- Death of executor, trustee, guardian, or agent
- Change in business interest
- Retirement
- Change in health
- Change in tax, property, or probate law
- Birth of child or grandchild

Also, remember that if no one knows you have an estate plan or where to find the plan, it is like it doesn't exist! Notifying the people pivotal to implementing your estate plan that they are in the plan is key to the success of this planning. Choosing where to keep your documents and making them easy to locate is also important—for example, if you put your plan in a safe-deposit box at a bank, make sure your executor has access to that box and knows to look there for your will and other documents.

Advance Directives

Everyone eventually faces the reality that one day we may become mentally incapacitated and no longer able to take care of our own affairs or make our own decisions. If that happens, you hope that you have a support system in place that can step in; but legally, where do you stand? Thinking about this and making plans for it are often referred to as "advance planning" or writing advance directives. Several tools and methods are key to advance planning, and the more common ones are outlined below. Of course, these tools can be incredibly complex and you would be well served to talk to an attorney to make sure your interests and desires are best protected.

Powers of Attorney

A power of attorney is a written document in which you (the "principal") delegate to another person (the "agent" or, in some states, the "attorney-in-fact") the power and authority to perform certain acts in your name. Neither party to a power of attorney actually needs to be an attorney. Powers of attorney are another area of the law where Congress has created specialized forms for military members and their families under Title 10, United States Code 1044a, which creates military powers of attorney. These must be prepared by military legal assistance providers. When you meet with your military legal assistance attorney, he or she will help you understand if this option is appropriate for your situation. Chapter 1 outlines how to find a legal assistance attorney in your area.

These powers given through an advanced directive can be limited to one topic in what is called a "special power of attorney." Examples include a special power of attorney for a spouse agent to sign an income tax return for the other spouse, or a special power of attorney for a friend to sell your car if you are moving overseas and will not be able to sell it before your departure. Another common special power of attorney is one that allows an agent to authorize medical care for the principal's child; these are particularly common when children are physically out of the parents' locality. Often, special powers of attorney are given for a specific amount of time and limited duration.

The powers given to an agent can alternately be broad and general in scope, referred to as a "general power of attorney." The general power of attorney grants the agent authority to act for the principal in all areas in which the principal could act, such as buying and selling assets, operating a business, and accessing bank accounts to name a few. As you can imagine, a general power of attorney is a very powerful tool and should be given only to someone you completely trust. These also may be given for a limited duration or specific period of time.

Powers of attorney can take effect immediately or they can

> ### WHEN POWERS OF ATTORNEY ARE MOST COMMONLY USED BY SERVICEMEMBERS

- Special powers of attorney for childcare (often used when the servicemember/parent must deploy or go out for field exercises, etc.).

- Special power of attorney to receive household goods (when a spouse or someone trusted needs the ability to sign for your household goods shipment because you are still en route).

- Special power of attorney to move goods (when you are unable to be present as the packers are coming through to begin a PCS move).

- Power of attorney to handle financial transactions (giving someone the ability to pay bills on behalf of the servicemember while he or she is deployed, etc.).

take effect only upon a certain set of circumstances, such as the principal's incapacitation from dementia, injury, imprisonment, or disappearance.

Depending on the state, a power of attorney may end at the principal's incapacitation. This means that if you lost the capacity to do something like enter into a contract (for example, if you suffered an injury that impaired your cognitive functions), your agent under a power of attorney would not be able to enter into a contract on your behalf either. However, many jurisdictions allow principals to create a durable power of attorney that specifically allows the agent to continue acting on the principal's behalf despite the incapacitation. In most states, if you are incapacitated and cannot handle your personal or financial affairs, someone must petition the court to establish a guardianship of your person (to handle personal matters, such as authority to set your doctor appointments) and establish a conservatorship of your estate (to handle your money and assets, such as authority to pay your bills). This can be expensive and time consuming. Luckily, a general power of attorney or durable power of attorney may make such processes unnecessary, particularly if the power of attorney contains language nominating the agent to be the guardian and conservator. When determining which language is best for your situation, it is best to talk to your military legal assistance attorney, who can help ensure that your power of attorney will fulfill your needs.

Advance Medical Directives

Modern medicine can now keep a person alive in situations that previously would have resulted in death. Frequently, a person in such a situation is unable to communicate his or her wishes with regard to the type of medical care to be provided. Many individuals feel that once death is inevitable, life should not be artificially prolonged through the use of medical technology. Others believe that life should be maintained at any cost. All too often, families are left fighting about what a relative "would have wanted" to happen, leaving strains on these relationships that may never heal. The decision to provide or withdraw such life-sustaining support, and who is permitted to make that decision for the incapacitated person, can be made easier with advance planning.

The term "advance medical directive" refers to two different documents: a health care power of attorney and a living will. The health care power of attorney is a kind of special power of attorney that allows you (the principal) to grant powers to a person (the agent) to make medical treatment decisions for you if you are incapacitated and/or unable to communicate your wishes as a result of dementia, disease, or injury. The health care power of attorney will spell out your agent's authority to hire and fire physicians, to approve medical procedures, to approve whether or not to donate your body or organs after death, and more.

The living will is a written statement of your wishes if you have a terminal illness and are incapacitated and/or unable to communicate. The living will should state under what circumstances you do or do not wish to receive artificial respiration, cardiopulmonary resuscitation, feeding tubes, and hydration. This is a matter of your personal and religious beliefs and val-

> ### ITEMS TO CONSIDER BEFORE MEETING WITH AN ATTORNEY
>
> There are several topics you should think about before meeting with an estate planning attorney. These items include:
>
> - who would best be able to cope with raising your minor children;
>
> - who would be best suited to handle the details of paying your debts and death taxes and distributing the remaining assets to your beneficiaries named in your will;
>
> - who is responsible enough to be your agent under your powers of attorney and whether that person can be actually available to perform those duties; and
>
> - how you want your property distributed to your heirs.

ues. In the absence of your guidance, your physician will be duty-bound to provide life-prolonging treatment even if your family disagrees. Because family members may disagree about the right course of treatment for you in these circumstances, you can save yourself, your physician, and your family a great deal of trouble by having a living will or directive for your physicians to follow.

Another document that has become extremely necessary for agents acting under a health care power of attorney and/or living will is an explicit HIPAA authorization. HIPAA (or the Health Insurance Portability and Accounting Act of 1996) regulates the use and disclosure of a person's private "protected health information." You likely have encountered HIPAA when you go to the doctor's office and have to sign acknowledgments that you have read and understood when your health information may be shared or used. Creating an authorization that allows your agent to have access to your health care records, lab results, and other documents makes the agent's job that much easier when communicating with your doctors and other health care providers. This is another area of the law in which Congress has cre-

COMPARING POWERS OF ATTORNEY AND ADVANCE DIRECTIVES

TYPE	SCOPE	WHAT IT DOES	DOES IT STILL APPLY IF PRINCIPAL IS INCAPACITATED?
General Power of Attorney	Broad and general in scope.	Allows the agent to act in all ways that the principal would be able to act. Some states require that the power of attorney list the activities the agent is authorized to undertake.	Generally no; however, some states may allow the power of attorney to stay in place depending on how it is written—confirm with your attorney either way.
Health Care Power of Attorney	Use is limited to health care decisions.	The principal gives the agent the ability to make medical decisions for the principal should he or she become incapacitated.	Yes
Living Will	Limited in scope.	Gives instructions as to end-of-life desires should principal become incapacitated and/or unable to communicate. May include a statement about the principal's moral views on medical technology prolonging life.	Yes

ated special rules and documents for military members (usually called military advanced medical directives); your military legal assistance provider can help you understand how this works in your situation.

LIFE INSURANCE

Life insurance is a contract (called the policy) between you and an insurance company, stating that the insurance company will pay a set amount of money (called the death benefit) to the person you designate to receive the money (this person is called the beneficiary). Life insurance comes in several different types, which will be discussed below. The price for a life insurance policy will vary based on several different factors, including your age at the time you purchase the policy, your life expectancy, your gender, your health history, your history of tobacco use, and the amount of life insurance you are purchasing.

Types of Life Insurance

Permanent Life Insurance. Permanent life insurance is a life insurance policy that does not expire as long as you continue making the payments (which can be made monthly, quarterly, or annually). Generally speaking, the amount of the payments will not increase over time. There are several types of permanent life insurance, including whole life and universal life. Whole life policies will have a set payment that remains the same throughout your life even as you age, and a set death benefit. Whole life policies also have the benefit of building a "cash value" that you can borrow from if necessary. Universal life policies allow you to vary the amount of premium you pay and death benefit your beneficiaries receive. The benefit of both policies is that as long as you make your payments, the policy will not expire and cannot be cancelled by the insurance company (except under certain circumstances, such as suicide within the first few years or fraud in the application).

Term Life Insurance. Term life insurance is a life insurance policy that has a fixed payment for a stated period of time, and the policy expires at the end of that period of time. It does not build a cash value (meaning that you wouldn't be able to borrow against the value of the policy like you would be able to with a permanent policy). The benefit of term life insurance is that such policies are normally cheaper than permanent life insurance. The downside is that term life insurance can be much more expensive at older ages, and some people may be uninsurable due to advanced age.

Establishing a Beneficiary

The normal way to establish a beneficiary to a life insurance policy is to complete the specific form required by the life insurance company on which you name your beneficiary. You can have multiple beneficiaries who each receive a stated share of the death benefit (for example, you may wish to leave the death benefit in equal parts to each of your children, or you may opt to have your spouse receive 50 percent of the benefit and your two children each receive 25 percent). You can also have contingent beneficiaries, who receive the death benefit if none of the primary beneficiaries is alive at your death. Be very careful to update your beneficiary designation if you marry, divorce, or remarry; most of the time the insurance company will pay the death benefit to the named beneficiary on their form, not the spouse or surviving children! You would not want to leave your life insurance policy death benefit to your ex-spouse and leave nothing to your current spouse and children simply because you forgot to fill out the necessary paperwork to change your beneficiary, would you?

Servicemembers Group Life Insurance

Most traditional insurance policies will not provide coverage for death as a result of combat or military service. Therefore, Servicemembers Group Life Insurance (SGLI) was established to provide coverage for deaths resulting from military service. SGLI is a program of low-cost group life insurance for servicemembers on active duty, ready reservists, members of the National Guard, members of the Commissioned Corps of the National Oceanic and Atmospheric Administration and the Public Health Service, cadets and midshipmen of the four service academies, and members of the Reserve Officer Training Corps. Servicemembers are often signed up for SGLI during introduction to the military. Before deployment, SGLI is almost always one of the documents that is reviewed at a readiness program with the servicemember. SGLI coverage is available in $50,000 increments up to the maximum of $400,000. There have been several instances where tragedy has occurred because the SGLI has not been properly coordinated with the servicemember's estate plan or will. Be extremely careful in this area, especially if you have a trust in your will for minor children. SGLI is "a creature of Federal Statute," meaning that mistakes cannot be easily corrected in state court with the rest of your estate plan.

Servicemembers with SGLI coverage have two options available to them upon release from service. They can convert their full-time SGLI coverage to term insurance under the Veterans' Group Life Insurance program or convert it to a permanent plan of insurance with one of the participating commercial insurance companies. The SGLI Disability Extension allows servicemembers who are totally disabled at the time of their discharge to retain the SGLI coverage they had in service at no cost for up to two years.

How Much Life Insurance Do I Need?

The answer to that question depends on your particular situation. Some common factors to take into consideration in determining the amount of life insurance you may need are the cost to cover the payment of burial and memorial expenses, replacing the loss of your income to your family resulting from your death, paying estate taxes or debts, and providing your children's guardian with funds with which to raise them. Consulting with a financial adviser will allow you to make an informed decision.

DEATH BENEFITS FOR VETERANS AND THEIR FAMILY MEMBERS

The United States takes very seriously its debt to the families of servicemembers who die while in service to their country; consequently, the government provides a number of benefits to these families. The most common death benefits and their details are outlined here.

Death Gratuity

The Department of Defense provides a death gratuity to families of servicemembers who die while on active duty or within 120 days of release from active duty if their death was related to their service. This tax-free payment of $100,000 may be paid to the person the servicemember designated. If the servicemember did not choose someone to receive this payment, then the law provides that the payment will go first to the servicemember's surviving spouse. If there is no spouse, the money will then go to the children of the servicemember, then the servicemember's parents, then the administrator of the estate, then to the next of kin. Families can apply for this benefit using a DD Form 397 (Department of Defense Form) and turning the form in to the local finance office.

Burial Benefits

Families of active-duty servicemembers are entitled to receive an allowance to help cover the costs of burial. This benefit also comes through the Department of Defense. The amount a family will get varies depending on where the servicemember is to be buried and who arranged for the preparation and casket for the member. If the family arranges for the preparation and casket, they will be given an amount that is currently more than $8,000 to help cover those expenses if the member is buried in a civilian cemetery and more than $7,000 if the member is buried in a government cemetery. If the military service arranges for the casket and preparation, these amounts are decreased and vary between $1,000 and $6,000 depending on where the member is to be laid to rest.

Many servicemembers would like to be buried in a national cemetery. Our national cemeteries are run by the Department of Veterans Affairs. Burial in a national cemetery is available to the following groups of servicemembers: all active-duty personnel (including reservists who pass away on active duty); reservists who have twenty years of service; and veterans who served a certain period of time on active duty (normally twenty-four months) and were discharged with an "other than dishonorable" discharge. A word here about the "other than dishonorable" discharge requirement for Department of Veterans Affairs benefits: The Department of Defense does not issue a discharge called "other than dishonorable," so it can get confusing for veterans and their families when they try to figure out if a veteran's service is "other than dishonorable." While it sounds like all discharges other than an actual "dishonorable" discharge would entitle a veteran to benefits from the Department of Veterans Affairs, that is not always true. For most purposes, an "honorable" or a "general" (sometimes referred to as a "general under honorable conditions") discharge will entitle a veteran to all of the benefits discussed here. Veterans with other discharges ("other than honorable" or "bad conduct discharges" or any other type of discharge) should contact their local Department of Veterans Affairs office to determine eligibility. For more information on the various types of discharge, see page 287.

For those families who would like military funeral honors at their servicemember's funeral, these are also available. Veterans who were discharged under conditions other than dishonorable (again, this normally includes honorable and general discharge recipients) are entitled to these honors as well. The Department of Defense has a website with information on these services, including points of contact and phone numbers: www.dmdc .osd.mil/mfh.

Pay and Leave Balances

A servicemember normally designates in advance who is entitled to receive all pay, allowances, and accrued leave benefits upon his death. If the member fails to make this choice himself, the law provides that these benefits be paid in the same order as death gratuities are paid above: to the spouse, then children, then the member's parents, then the member's estate.

Casualty Assistance Officer

Each branch of the military has individuals who make the first notification to the primary next-of-kin (spouses, parents, or children) concerning the casualty's status (i.e.: death, whereabouts unknown (DUSTWUN), missing, ill, or injured). Each branch calls the person who fills this role by a different name. In the Navy, they are referred to as the casualty assistance calls officers (CACO). The Army refers to this person as the casualty assistance officer (CAO). Whatever name he or she goes by, this person is the official representative of the relevant secretary (Navy, Army, or Air Force) who provides information, resources, and assistance to the member's next of kin in the event of a casualty. According to the Navy, the CAO's "full time responsibility and mission is to assist families during a difficult time and ensure they receive the benefits and entitlements due." These individuals ensure that the family has the support it needs during the planning of a memorial. This officer ensures that the next of kin know what benefits they may be entitled to and helps the family apply for these benefits. The support the CAO provides to families during this time of grief is invaluable; these services help relieve the stress on a member's loved ones.

SURVIVOR BENEFITS

Survivor benefits are a constantly changing area of benefits. Below is a general list of benefits, but to confirm eligibility for benefits and the extent of these benefits, seek the help of the legal assistance office at the installation's Judge Advocate General (JAG) office nearest you, the CAO assigned to help you identify and apply for benefits, or in some cases the Department of Veterans Affairs representative in your local area.

Continued Benefits

Dependents who lose a loved one in active-duty service are still entitled to receive a number of benefits from the Department of Defense, including access to the post exchanges and commissaries, certain types of legal assistance at the JAG office on the nearest military installation, some medical care, travel and shipment of their household goods from the member's last place of duty, and the ability to occupy family housing on base for one year following the servicemember's death (or basic allowance for housing if not in military on-base housing).

Survivor Benefit Plan

The Survivor Benefit Plan (SBP) is a type of insurance that is available to active duty, retirees, and certain other categories of reservists. This program allows servicemembers to make certain that their survivors receive a monthly payment for their support. Survivors usually include a member's surviving spouses and/or dependent children, but may extend to a person with a financial interest in the member if there is no spouse or child, for instance, a dependent parent. The SBP plan is implemented and paid by the Department of Defense. When a servicemember is enrolled into the SBP, a premium is withheld from his or her pay. The premium amount depends on the "coverage" the servicemember chooses to provide his survivors. The minimum coverage is a payment of $300 a month to the survivor. The maximum is the entire amount of the member's monthly retired pay. Of course, the member can choose to provide survivors with any amount in between. The SBP payment to a survivor after a member's death is taxable income to the beneficiary. Problems with SBP normally arise in the context of a separation agreement or divorce, and this is an extremely technical area. Please see Chapter 2 on family law, which should provide you with an overview of how SBPs may be divided and the importance of working with an experienced legal adviser during that process.

Dependency and Indemnity Compensation

Dependency and indemnity compensation (DIC) is a monthly tax-free payment available to surviving spouses and dependent children of a servicemember/veteran. DIC is approved and paid for by the Department of Veterans Affairs. To be eligible for DIC payments, the family's member must have: died while on active duty, died due to service-connected disabilities, or have been totally disabled due to service-connected disabilities— even if those disabilities did not cause the veteran's eventual death. Surviving spouses must have been married to the member at the time of his or her death and continually co-habitating with that member. Remarriage of the surviving spouse before the age of fifty-seven will end the DIC payments, but the payments may be reinstated if the subsequent marriage is terminated by death or divorce. Dependent children are defined as unmarried and under the age of eighteen or twenty-three, if they are still in school. Dependent parents of a member may also qualify for DIC.

Death Pension/Housebound/Aid and Attendance Benefits

Surviving spouses or dependent children of veterans who served during a time of war and find themselves in a low-income, low-asset situation may be eligible for payments from the Department of Veterans Affairs that are referred to as "death pension." A veteran's service will qualify survivors for this benefit if: the veteran served at least one day during a time of declared war; the veteran served for at least ninety days on active duty (twenty-four months if the veteran entered service after September 7, 1980);

and the veteran was discharged other than dishonorably (as with almost all benefits administered by the VA, this includes honorable and general discharges). The surviving spouse and/or dependent child will be eligible for the basic death pension if he or she meets certain income and asset requirements and age/disability requirements. If the surviving spouse or child needs additional assistance due to his or her disability, there are two different special payments permitted on top of the pension. These payments are referred to as "housebound" benefits and "aid and attendance" benefits. Current payment rates for surviving spouses range from a little more than $8,000 a year in basic death pension benefits to a little more than $13,000 for a surviving spouse receiving aid and attendance benefits. Surviving spouses who remarry are no longer eligible for these benefits. Children must be under eighteen or twenty-three, if still in school, or must have been incapable of caring for themselves before the age of eighteen. These pension payments are tax-free.

Priority for Death Gratuity Benefits

A servicemember's benefits are distributed to an individual selected by the member before all others; if a person has not been selected then all benefits are distributed to the servicemember's spouse. If there is no lawful surviving spouse, then the benefits are distributed to the servicemember's children and

> **BENEFITS DISTRIBUTION:**
>
> Benefits are distributed in the following order:
>
> 1. Individual selected by member,
> 2. Spouse,
> 3. Children,
> 4. Parents, or
> 5. Member's estate to be distributed to next of kin.

then parents. In cases without these individuals present, all benefits are given to the member's estate to be distributed to next of kin.

RESOURCES

- **AARP's Estate Planning** (www.aarp.org/money/estate
-planning): Includes estate planning to-do lists and information on paying for your long-term care.

- **American Bar Association Wills and Estates Public Information** (www.ambar.org/wills): Links to helpful national, state, and local resources on wills, trusts, and estates.

- **Estate Planning Answers** (www.estateplanninganswers
.org): Website hosted by the National Association of Estate Planners and Councils; includes information on estate and financial planning broken down by life stages.

- **U.S. Department of Veteran Affairs SGLI Information** (www.insurance.va.gov/sgliSite/SGLI/SGLI.htm): SGLI website run by the VA; has information on coverage and application.

- **Veterans Benefits** (www.benefits.va.gov/benefits): The VA's Veterans Benefit site includes a summary of the various benefit programs and application information.

- **Secretary of Defense's Survivor Benefit Plan Site** (http://militarypay.defense.gov/survivor/sbp/01_overview.html) Survivor Benefit Plan overview and information provided by the Secretary of Defense.

CHAPTER 7

Military Health Care and Insurance

Sarah, a PFC at Fort Bragg in North Carolina, is happily married with three kids. Sarah has been healthy her entire life; in fact, just last year, she completed a triathlon and is training for another one this year. However, lately, Sarah's husband, Pat, has been having some back pain. Sarah and Pat know that he is covered by Sarah's service, but how exactly does that work? Does he have to call ahead to make sure he is covered? Does he have to go to a doctor on base? How much will that cost?

This chapter will provide you with an overall understanding of what military organization is responsible for your health care during and after periods of service; who may or may not be eligible for health care coverage by the military; and why it is important that you take a very active, responsible, and consistent role in your own health care and that of loved ones.

COMMON HEALTH INSURANCE TERMS

Understanding health insurance often involves learning a new language. Below are some of the more common terms that are used by health care providers and insurance companies. This list is by no means exhaustive; if you come across a term you don't understand, ask about it!

- **Premium:** The amount the policyholder or his sponsor (e.g. an employer) pays to the health insurance company to purchase health coverage.

- **Deductible:** The amount that the insured must pay out of pocket before the health insurer pays its share. For example, policyholders might have to pay a $500 deductible per year before any of their health care is covered by the insurer. It may take several doctors visits or prescription refills before the insured person reaches the deductible and the insurance company starts to pay for care; however, most policies do not apply co-pays for doctors visits or prescriptions against the deductible.

- **Copayment:** The amount that the insured person must pay out of pocket before the health insurer pays for a particular visit or service. For example, an insured person might pay a $45 copayment for a doctor's visit or to obtain a prescription. A copayment must be paid each time a particular service is obtained.

- **Coinsurance:** Instead of, or in addition to, paying a fixed amount up front (a copayment), the co-insurance is a percentage of the total cost that insured person may also pay. For example, the member might have to pay 20 percent of the cost of a surgery over and above a copayment, while the insurance company pays the other 80 percent. If there is an upper limit on coinsurance, the policyholder could end up owing very little, or a great deal, depending on the actual costs of the services they obtain.

- **Exclusions:** Those services or prescriptions not all covered by the policy. The insureds are generally expected to pay the full cost of noncovered services out of their own pockets.

- **Coverage limits:** Some health insurance policies pay for health care only up to a certain dollar amount, referred to as a coverage limit. The insured person may be expected to pay any charges in excess of the health plan's maximum payment for a specific service. In addition, some insurance company schemes have annual or lifetime coverage maximums. In these cases, the health plan will stop payment when they reach the benefit maximum, and the policyholder must pay all remaining costs.

- **Out-of-pocket maximums:** Similar to coverage limits, except that in this case, the insured person's payment obligation ends when he or she reaches the out-of-pocket maximum, and health insurance pays all further covered costs. Out-of-pocket maximums can be limited to a specific benefit category (such as prescription drugs) or can apply to all coverage provided during a specific benefit year.

- **In-Network Provider:** A health care provider on a list of providers preselected by the insurer. The insurer will offer discounted coinsurance or copayments, or additional benefits, to a plan member to see an in-network provider. Generally, in-network providers are providers who have a contract with the insurer to accept rates further discounted from the "usual and customary" charges the insurer pays to out-of-network providers.

- **Prior Authorization:** A certification or authorization that an insurer provides prior to medical service occurring. Obtaining an authorization means that the insurer is obligated to pay for the service, assuming it matches what was authorized. Many smaller, routine services do not require authorization.

- **Explanation of Benefits:** A document that may be sent by an insurer to a patient explaining what was covered for a medical service and how payment amount and patient responsibility amount were determined.

MILITARY HEALTH CARE COVERAGE (TRICARE) OVERVIEW

As a civilian, your health care or insurance provider may be Blue Cross/Blue Shield, United, or some other private insurance company. Once you enlist or are commissioned to serve in any branch of the United States military, your health care provider is known as TRICARE. TRICARE is the Department of Defense's health care program for members of the uniformed services and their families and survivors and retired members and their families.

Just as private insurance companies offer a variety of "packages" or service options, TRICARE also has a variety of combinations, and each comes with its own TRICARE designation. The TRICARE plans or packages are as follows:

- **TRICARE Standard:** A fee-for-service option that is the same as the former CHAMPUS benefit. Beneficiaries using this option have the greatest choice of civilian providers, but at a higher cost. The beneficiary is responsible for a deductible, plus copayments. Enrollment is not required to participate; coverage is automatic as long as your information is current in the Defense Enrollment Eligibility Reporting System (DEERS).

- **TRICARE Extra:** Similar to TRICARE Standard, but offers discounts to patients when they use TRICARE network providers. This option allows beneficiaries to receive their care from civilian network providers at a reduced cost compared to TRICARE Standard. There are no claim forms to file—just pay your reduced copayment after satisfying the deductible. You may use a combination of the TRICARE Extra and Standard programs at any time, depending on whether you choose providers inside or outside the network. Enrollment is not required to participate.

- **TRICARE Prime:** A managed care option offered by the Department of Defense. TRICARE Prime integrates military and civilian health care into a single health care system. Beneficiaries who choose this option agree to a one-year enrollment and select a primary care manager (PCM) to provide or arrange for their health care needs and offers additional wellness and preventive care services.

- **TRICARE Standard Overseas: International SOS** (www .internationalsos.com), a leading international health care, medical, and security assistance and concierge services company supports the TRICARE Overseas Program Office, TRICARE Area Offices and the Military Treatment Facility (MTF) commanders to deliver an integrated, global health care delivery system. Enrollment in TRICARE Overseas is not required; coverage is automatic as long as your information is current in DEERS.

- **TRICARE Reserve Select:** A premium-based health plan available worldwide for qualified Selected Reserve members of the Ready Reserve and their families. In order to be eligible for coverage, you must not be on active-duty orders, must not be covered under the Transitional Assistance Management Program, and not be eligible for or enrolled in the Federal Employees Health Benefit (FEHB) program.

- **TRICARE Retired Reserve:** A premium-based health plan for qualified retired Reserve members, their families, and survivors.

- **TRICARE for Life:** Secondary coverage to Medicare for all beneficiaries who have Medicare Parts A and B. TRICARE for Life applies worldwide.

- **TRICARE U.S. Family Health Plan:** An additional TRICARE Prime option available through networks of community-based, not-for-profit health care systems in six areas of the United States. See box on page 240 for more information.

- **TRICARE Young Adult:** Allows qualified adult children to purchase TRICARE coverage after eligibility for "regular" TRICARE coverage ends at age twenty-one (or twenty-three if enrolled in college). The Young Adult package has two options: Standard and Prime. All dependent adult children who qualify for TRICARE Young Adult can select the Standard Option. The TRICARE Young Adult Prime Option is based on your sponsor's military status and where you live.

- **VETERANS BENEFITS:** Veterans' health care issues are addressed in Chapter 7. Because the health care available to veterans is so significantly determined by time and/or events that occurred while in service time, it is important for veterans and their families to fully understand their eligibility for disability compensation and other services later in life.

▶ U.S. FAMILY HEALTH PLAN

U.S. Family Health Plan is an additional TRICARE Prime option, but it is only available in certain areas, including:

- *Johns Hopkins Medicine*—serving Maryland, Washington, D.C., and parts of Pennsylvania, Virginia, Delaware, and West Virginia; 1-800-808-7347

- *St. Vincent Catholic Medical Centers*—serving Long Island, southern Connecticut, New Jersey, Philadelphia, and area suburbs; 1-800-241-4848, www.usfhp.com

- *Martin's Point Health Care*—serving Maine, New Hampshire, Vermont, upstate and western New York and the northern tier of Pennsylvania; 1-888-241-4556

- *CHRISTUS Health*—serving southeast Texas and southwest Louisiana; 1-800-678-7347

- *Brighton Marine Health Center*—serving Massachusetts, including Cape Cod, Rhode Island, and northern Connecticut; 1-800-818-8589

- *Pacific Medical Centers*—serving the Puget Sound area of Washington state; 1-888-958-7347

You may enroll in U.S. Family Health Plan at any time during the year by completing an application for the plan in your area. After you enroll in the U.S. Family Health Plan, you will not access Medicare providers, military treatment facilities, or TRICARE network providers; instead, you will receive your care (including prescription drug coverage) from a primary care physician that you select from a network of private physicians affiliated with one of the not-for-profit health care systems offering the plan. If you need to see a specialist, your primary care physician will assists you in getting any necessary appointments and coordinate your care.

Military members may access their health benefits by scheduling an appointment with their assigned primary care manager. With TRICARE Prime, you have an assigned primary care manager (PCM), either at a military treatment facility (MTF) or from the TRICARE network, who provides most of your care. Your PCM will refer you to a specialist for care he or she cannot provide and coordinate with your regional contractor for authorization, find a specialist in the network, and file claims on your behalf.

Generally, active-duty service members and their families have no out-of-pocket costs for any type of care as long as care is received from the PCM or with a referral. All other TRICARE beneficiaries pay annual enrollment fees and network copayments as described above.

ELIGIBILITY FOR MILITARY HEALTH CARE

TRICARE beneficiaries can be divided into two main categories: sponsors and family members. Sponsors are usually active-duty service members, National Guard/Reserve members or retired service members. The term "sponsor" refers to the person who is serving or who has served on active duty or in the National Guard or Reserves. To use TRICARE, you must be listed in DEERS as being eligible for military health care benefits.

Eligibility for military health care seems simple enough at first glance. In reality, the issue can become more complicated depending upon certain circumstances. Some life events and categories of individuals that may impact eligibility include:

- **Divorce;**
- **Remarriage;**
- **Step-children;**
- **Children from previous or extramarital relationships;**

- The biological parent of a child who is eligible and the parent is not;
- Type(s) of discharge of the sponsor;
- Survivors;
- Victims of abuse;
- Family of sponsor missing in action; and more.

According to the TRICARE website, the following people are *not* eligible for TRICARE:

- People not enrolled in DEERS;
- People entitled to Medicare Part A who do not have Medicare Part B coverage, except for the following individuals:
  - Family members of active-duty service members: *Medicare Part B is not required until the sponsor retires,*
  - Beneficiaries enrolled in the *U.S. Family Health Plan: Medicare Part B is not required for U.S. Family Health Plan enrollment. But, if you disenroll from the U.S. Family Health Plan, you must have Medicare Part B to be eligible for any other TRICARE benefits.*
- People who are eligible for benefits under Civilian Health and Medical Program of the Department of Veterans Affairs (CHAMPVA).

What initially may seem like a very simple issue—who is covered—can and often does result in the need for the sponsor and family members to independently educate themselves and ask many important questions. The good news is the answers are easily available online and in military publications/pamphlets. Nongovernmental service organizations can often not only provide support and assistance but also direct you to military office(s)/official(s) who can be of further assistance. The end of this Chapter features a listing of a number of resources to help you navigate this system.

MAKING THE MOST OF YOUR HEALTH CARE COVERAGE

The most important thing to understand and incorporate into the concept of "health care" is that you are completely responsible for participating in your own care. What does this participation require? Generally, it requires you to become proactive, thoughtful, and prepared.

Compare the two scenarios below:

1. Routine patient visit with primary care physician. Patient complains of pain and discomfort in legs. Doctor asks how long the patient has noticed the pains. Patient cannot really recall, but "guesses" a few days. When asked to describe the pain, the patient replies, "It hurts really badly. I don't know how else to describe it."

   The doctor asks the patient what medications he is on and if he has noticed any other problems or discomfort. Patient is taking four or maybe more prescriptions, but he can't remember their names, much less their dosages.

2. Routine patient visit with primary care physician. Patient complains of pain and discomfort in legs. Doctor asks how long the patient has noticed the pains. Patient refers to his written notes and tells the doctor the date and general time he began noticing the pains. When asked to describe the pain, the patient replies, "It hurts really badly, it feels like pins and needles are poking through my skin from the inside out. On a scale of 1 to 10 (1=low, 10=want to die), I'd say the pain started off around a 3, but now it's closer to a 7 or 8."

   The doctor asks the patient what medications he is on and if he has noticed any other problems or discomfort. Patient refers to his written notes and hands a copy of the current list of medications he is taking, the dosage and frequency, and the condition for which the medication was prescribed and by what doctor. (The patient keeps his own copy of the same information for his file.)

Will there be a significant difference in the outcomes of the above scenarios? Perhaps. The point is that doctors, nurses, and medical professionals are not mind readers or able to feel your symptoms. The more and better information you can provide to your medical professional(s), the better the chances are you will be medically treated more accurately and with a deeper sense of concern from the staff.

Patients at military treatment facilities within the TRICARE system have a number of rights, including the right to:

- considerate and respectful services;
- current and complete information about your diagnosis, treatment, and the expected results;
- assessment and effective management of pain;
- knowledge of which doctor or health care provider has primary responsibility for your care;
- consent to or refuse medical treatment, as permitted by law;
- have an advance directive such as a living will, which expresses your desires about future care or names someone to speak for you when you cannot. You may provide this written document to the hospital or your doctor;
- privacy in your health care;
- confidentiality in your care and treatment records unless you consent or provide permission to release information about your care;
- to be told of realistic care and alternatives;
- initiate a complaint regarding the quality of your care and for you to have your complaint reviewed and resolved or explained. This includes the right to be informed of resources such as patient advocates, ethics committees, and other resources that can help you resolve problems or answer questions regarding your care; and

▶ KEEPING TRACK OF YOUR HEALTH HISTORY

SUGGESTIONS FOR SERVICEMEMBERS:

- Keep a small notepad/notebook. In the front cover, write your identification information, any allergies, blood type, and medications you are taking (prescribed or not). In the back cover, make some abbreviations for things you don't want to write out each day along with their meaning(s).

- If you have access and clearance to email, send yourself an email with the above information along with any other details you may want to express. Send it to a trusted friend or family member too, if possible.

- Have an injury/wound? Take pictures and date them. What might seem like nothing now could be the evidence you need as a veteran in forty years.

SUGGESTIONS FOR PARENTS, SPOUSES, AND OTHER FAMILY:

- Save every letter, email, and communication you receive from your soldier.

- Keep notes reflecting the tone, affect, and condition of your soldier during phone calls, and note the date/time/place if possible.

- Note the condition of his/her fellow soldiers. Did someone get injured? Who? How is morale? The VA currently allows "buddy" statements to support a veteran's claim for benefits. Not only could the notes help a fellow soldier later, they could clue you in to emotional conditions your family member doesn't want to talk about.

- Keep track of the medications and physicians treating your soldier.

- Maintain a family notebook, chart, electronic file, or other record.

- Identify the name, age, date, weight, height, blood type, allergies, doctors' appointments/surgeries, diagnoses, therapies prescribed, reactions, and general mood/affect on a monthly or more frequent basis.

- Contact information for emergencies.

- **be informed of hospital policies and regulations that affect you and your treatment and about charges and payment methods.**

The medical care you receive from the VA and elsewhere will be greatly dependent upon written documentation. Documentation concerning what occurred twenty, thirty, forty, and more years ago is often invaluable to not only your medical professionals, but also to other professionals advocating on your behalf. The military may or may not have kept good records regarding your health back then. Their documents may have been lost in a fire. The responsibility for maintaining complete health records is yours and yours alone.

Whether you are on the front lines and under constant attack or in a less dramatic situation, you must find a way to keep track of your health. Find a method that works for you—whether it's a notebook in which you jot down the date(s), events, your feelings, and physical status or a calendar containing the same information, that information can and will make a world of difference to you and maybe your loved ones.

Health Care Rights of the Wounded Warrior/ Injured Servicemember

Injured servicemembers may require prolonged treatment, time to heal, and rehabilitative care before a decision can be made on their medical ability to remain on active duty. The military health care system coordinates medical care for these individuals through military and civilian treatment facilities using the TRICARE health benefits system. Active duty servicemembers may get a priority in certain clinics if their service has given them a special designation as "wounded" and if the treatment facilities are actually giving priority. This varies from service to service and from installation to installation. Wounded warriors should make appointments with their PCMs and the specialty providers with referral or consult to the specialty clinic. There are generally no limits for life saving care for injured servicemembers; however, there are some limits for what is called

> ### ► UNDERSTANDING TRAUMATIC BRAIN INJURY
>
> To date, more than 200,000 servicemembers and veterans have sustained a traumatic brain injury (TBI), mostly from blast injuries; however, other military duties and recreational activities can increase their risk of suffering from TBIs.
>
> TBI occurs when a sudden trauma or head injury disrupts the function of the brain. Servicemembers and veterans are often diagnosed with TBI after involvement in combat exposures to improvised explosive devices (IEDs), artillery attacks (i.e. mortars, RPGs, etc.), vehicle crashes, and other similar incidents in combat or in training for combat. Servicemembers can also suffer TBIs in hand-to-hand combat training, parachute training, and other similar military training. The National Institute of Neurologic Disorders and Stroke has information on TBIs, including links to other resources and glossary of terms related to brain injury (www.ninds.nih.gov/disorders/tbi/detail_tbi.htm).

"medically optional" treatment, which is treatment that is beneficial but will not save the life of the patient, prevent loss of function, or return the patient to military duty status. Examples might include refractive eye surgery, bunionectomy, rhinoplasty, and vasectomy. If you have questions about your care or any treatment limits, talk to your PCM.

MENTAL HEALTH CONCERNS

A mental illness is a medical condition that disrupts a person's thinking, feeling, mood, ability to relate to others, and daily functioning. Just as diabetes is a disorder of the pancreas, mental illnesses are medical conditions that often result in a diminished capacity for coping with the ordinary demands of life.

Mental illnesses can affect people of any age, race, religion, or income. Mental illnesses are not the result of personal weakness, lack of character, or poor upbringing. Mental illnesses are treatable. Most people diagnosed with a serious mental illness can experience relief from their symptoms by actively participating in an individual treatment plan.

According to VA records collected through 2007, more than 100,000 combat veterans sought help through the VA for mental illness since the start of the war in Afghanistan in 2001. Almost one-half of those were post-traumatic stress disorder (PTSD) cases. Many of the veterans treated had two or more distinct mental health diagnoses.

Getting Mental Health Treatment

To receive care for any mental health concerns, active-duty personnel should contact the mental health, behavioral health, or clinic at your local military treatment facility. If you are currently deployed, contact the combat stress team or combat support medical team nearest you. Your chaplain can also help you get the care you need.

Family members and nonactive-duty members with TRI-CARE can go directly to a health provider in the TRICARE network without a referral or prior authorization for the first eight sessions.

If you have a mental health emergency (such as wanting to hurt yourself or someone else), go to the nearest hospital emergency room or call 911. If you are feeling suicidal, you can also call the National Suicide Prevention Lifeline 1-800-273-TALK (8255) and press 1 for the Veterans Suicide Prevention Hotline, or visit www.suicidepreventionlifeline.org and click on "More Help for Veterans." Mental health professionals are available to talk with you twenty-four hours per day.

If you have a mental health problem and have never been seen in a VA hospital or clinic, call the VA general information hotline at 1-800-827-1000, or visit VA's website at www.va.gov. You will be able to find the address and phone number of a VA hospital or clinic near you. Some veterans begin the process of

▶ HOMELESSNESS

Many homeless men and woman have served in the armed forces. Many other veterans are considered at risk for homelessness because of poverty, lack of support from family and friends, and precarious living conditions in overcrowded or substandard housing. Although the majority of homeless veterans are single males, the number of female veterans and veterans with dependent children who are homeless is increasing each year. Many homeless veterans suffer from mental illness and alcohol or drug abuse problems.

The Department of Veterans Affairs (VA) is the only federal agency that provides substantial hands-on assistance directly to homeless people. Although limited to veterans and their dependents, the VA's major homeless programs constitute the largest integrated network of homeless assistance programs in the country, offering a wide array of services and initiatives to help veterans recover from homelessness and live as self-sufficiently and independently as possible.

If you know a veteran who is homeless or at risk of homelessness, contact the VA's National Call Center for Homeless Veterans at 1-877-4AID-VET (1-877-424-3838) to access free VA services. The hotline is free and neither VA registration nor enrollment in VA health care is required to use this service.

finding mental health care through a Veterans Center. Homeless veterans can get help finding mental health care at a veterans drop-in center.

If you are already using VA medical services, ask your primary care provider to arrange for you to see a VA mental health provider.

There are many specific types of mental health issues and concerns that military families may deal with and there is simply no way a book like this can deal with all of them (or even deal with some in great detail). Below, we provide some basic information on PTSD and suicide concerns; by no means should this be seen as an exhaustive resource, but instead, as a jumping-off point to understand the basic issues and know where to start.

PTSD

After a trauma or life-threatening event, it is common to have reactions such as upsetting memories of the event, increased jumpiness, or trouble sleeping. If these reactions do not go away or get worse, you may have post-traumatic stress disorder (PTSD).

Most people who go through a trauma have some symptoms of PTSD immediately after the trauma. However, only some will develop full PTSD over time. It isn't clear why some people develop PTSD and others don't.

Whether or not you get PTSD depends on many things, including:

- **the intensity of the trauma;**
- **the length of the trauma;**
- **if you were injured or lost someone important to you;**
- **your proximity to the event;**
- **the strength of your reaction;**
- **the degree to which you felt in control of events; and**
- **how much help and support you got after the event.**

PTSD symptoms usually start soon after the traumatic event, but they also may not appear until months, or even years, later. The symptoms also may come and go over many years. If the symptoms last longer than weeks, cause you great distress, or interfere with your work or home life, you might have PTSD.

When you have PTSD, dealing with the past can be hard. Instead of telling others how you feel, you may keep your feelings bottled up. But treatment can help you get better. There are two main types of treatment: psychotherapy (sometimes called counseling) and medication. Sometimes people combine psychotherapy and medication. You should consult with a medical professional to assist you in determining which treatments are best for you. TRICARE covers most treatment for PTSD. You can schedule up to the first eight of your appointments without a referral for treatment from your primary care manager.

Suicide Concerns

People experience emotional and mental health crises in response to a wide range of situations—from difficulties in their personal relationships to the loss of a job. For servicemembers, these crises can be heightened by their experiences in military service. Sometimes a crisis may involve thoughts of suicide.

There are several warning signs that you should be aware of:

- hopelessness, feeling like there's no way out;
- anxiety, agitation, sleeplessness, or mood swings;
- feeling like there is no reason to live;
- rage or anger;
- engaging in risky activities without thinking;
- increasing alcohol or drug abuse; and
- withdrawing from family and friends.

The presence of the following signs requires immediate attention:

- thinking about hurting or killing yourself;
- looking for ways to kill yourself; or
- talking about death, dying or suicide.

If you or someone you know is experiencing any of these warning signs, the first thing to do is ask for help. There are many crisis lines staffed by trained professionals that are open 365 days per year, twenty-four hours per day. These professionals are available at no cost to you and can help you get the help you need. One such crisis hotline is the Veterans Crisis Line, which is available by calling 1-800-273-TALK (8255) and pressing Option 1.

RESOURCES

- **After Deployment** (http://afterdeployment.org): A mental wellness resource for service members, veterans, and military families.

- **America's Heroes at Work** (www.americasheroesatwork. gov): A U.S. Department of Labor project to help returning service members affected by traumatic brain injury (TBI) and/ or PTSD succeed in the workplace. Designed for employers and the workforce development system.

- **DoD Outreach Center for Psychological Health and Traumatic Brain Injury** (1-866-966-1020, or email resources@dcoeoutreach.org): Provides authoritative information and resources twenty-four hours, seven days a week to servicemembers, veterans, families, and those who support them.

- **Hooah4Health.com** (www.hooah4usa.com): The U.S. Army health promotion and wellness website.

- **TRICARE** (www.tricare.mil): The TRICARE website has a variety of information helpful for military families. The website includes information on the different "types" of TRICARE, determining who is eligible, and issues affecting eligibility.

- **International SOS** (www.internationalsos.com): A leading international health care, medical, and security assistance, and concierge services company that supports the TRICARE Overseas Program Office.

- **Institute of Medicine—Veterans Health** (www.iom.edu/ Global/Topics/Veterans-Health.aspx): The IOM website includes information about a variety of military-related health issues.

- **Veterans Suicide Prevention Hotline and Online Chat** (www.veteranscrisisline.net): If you are in crisis, you may call the hotline any time to speak with someone who can help: 1-800-273-TALK (1-800-273-8255) (en Español, 1-888-628-9454). Veterans, press one after you call. You can also chat live online with a crisis counselor at any time of day or night.

- **Department of Veterans Affairs** (http://www.va.gov): Features information on health care services and benefits for veterans and their dependents.

- **Wounded Warrior Project** (http://www.woundedwarrior project.org): Nonprofit organization with the mission of helping wounded veterans and their families.

CHAPTER 8

Military Service and Your Employment Rights

Sloan is a busy graphic designer for a local advertising agency, a mother of three, and an active member of her church. Sloan has also been a reservist in the Marine Corps for the past ten years. Lately, Sloan's boss has been complaining about the time off she needs for her annual training. Sloan is afraid she might lose her job. Is Sloan's job protected? Who can she talk to about her boss's comments? If she does get fired, what can she do?

Active-duty veterans usually enter the civilian workforce after completing their military obligation. National Guard and Reserve members balance civilian employment and military service. For Reserve component members, finding or maintaining a job and maintaining their military service is likely a concern that is front and center in their minds. The government takes their employment rights very seriously; a number of programs and laws exist to ensure that National Guard and Reserve members are not discriminated against due to their service obligations.

This chapter explores the employment-related rights of veterans and the obligations of employers under the Uniformed Services Employment and Reemployment Rights Act.

VETERANS' EMPLOYMENT OPPORTUNITIES

Many public and some private employers have preference point systems for veterans. Many other employers have hiring campaigns that specifically target military veterans. There are far too many employers and employment programs offering assistance or preference to current and former military personnel to publish here. The key to finding these employers is research. The VA website, VetSuccess (vetsuccess.gov), has a good listing of employment programs and resources for translating military skills into a nonmilitary work environment, as well as interview and application tips.

For federal jobs, there is a concrete set of preferences for veterans. When applying for jobs within the federal government, veterans can receive preference in hiring based upon their service or their disability. Veterans' preference gives qualified veterans an advantage in selection over many applicants. Veterans' preference is not guaranteed to all veterans; only those released from active duty under honorable conditions are eligible. Spouses and dependents of active-duty personnel can also receive preference for federal jobs under the Military Spouse Preference Program and the Family Member Preference Program.

There are two types of hiring in the federal system: external hires, for which veterans' preference applies, and internal hires, for which veterans' preference does not apply. The preference program does not apply to promotions, transfers, and reassignments. Internal hires are presumed to have used their veterans' preference in the initial hiring.

Veterans' preference eligibility is explained on the Office of Personnel Management website. On that site, you can find information on the Feds Hire Vets program (www.fedshirevets.gov) and the Veterans Guide (www.fedshirevets.gov/hire/hrp/vetguide/index.aspx).

Discrimination Against Servicemembers in Employment

There are federal and state laws that protect many "protected categories" of individuals from discrimination in the workplace. These categories frequently include race, gender, religion, and national origin. For servicemembers, particularly National Guard and Reserve component members, discrimination in the workplace can be an all too common occurrence. Federal statistics show that National Guard and Reserve component members have complained about employment discrimination in a number of different areas:

- **Initial employment decisions:** It is illegal for an employer to discriminate against an applicant because he or she is in the National Guard or Reserve.

- **Promotion opportunities:** It is illegal for an employer to refuse to promote an employee because he or she is in the National Guard or Reserve.

- **Pay, terms, and conditions of employment:** It is illegal for an employer to offer fewer opportunities to an employee because that employee is in the National Guard or Reserve.

- **Transferring, denying certain assignments, reducing hours:** It is illegal for an employer to offer fewer opportunities to an employee because that employee is in the National Guard or Reserve.

- **Denying leave for military duty:** It is illegal for an employer to deny an employee leave for military service. An employee is not required to get military leave "approved" by the employer.

- **Delay in returning the employee to work following military duty:** Employers are required to place an employee back to work as soon as reasonably possible. That length of time can vary depending upon the amount of time the employee is gone, but is always a short period of time.

- **Waiting periods for a return to the employee health plan:** There is no waiting period for the returning servicemember to get back into the employee health plan.

The tools you can use to enforce these rights are detailed in the following sections, but know that discrimination is a serious matter that your employer should (and the courts do) take very seriously.

UNIFORMED SERVICES EMPLOYMENT AND REEMPLOYMENT RIGHTS ACT

Congress enacted the Uniformed Services Employment and Reemployment Rights Act (USERRA) in 1994 in response to the issues that arose during the Gulf War. But don't think of this law as eighteen years old—think of it as seventy-two years old. USERRA was a long-overdue rewrite of the Veterans' Reemployment Rights Act (VRRA), which was originally enacted in 1940, as part of the Selective Training and Service Act (STSA). The STSA was the law that led to the drafting of millions of young men for World War II.

Although the VRRA was amended in 1941 to apply to voluntary enlistees as well as draftees, it remained part of the draft law until 1974. Almost from the very beginning, the reemployment statute has applied to voluntary as well as involuntary service, in peacetime as well as wartime, within our country and overseas.

With the military's heavy reliance on National Guard and Reserve members, it is important to know your rights under the USERRA law.

Determining USERRA Eligibility

USERRA covers all members of the National Guard and Reserve components in their civilian jobs when they are performing federal service. There are two types of service for National Guard members: federal service and state service. Federal service includes military training as well as deployments for Army missions. State service is for state-specific missions. For example: Deployment to Afghanistan is federal service, while responding to a natural disaster in the home state is probably state service. National Guard members who are activated solely for state service and are not covered by the USERRA law. However, many states have laws that protect National Guard members who are

▶ USERRA'S PURPOSE

According to USERRA, the law has three main purposes:

1. *To encourage service in the National Guard and Reserve by minimizing the disruption to the servicemember's civilian employment due to military service.*

    This purpose is pretty straightforward. National Guard and Reserve enlistment is vital to the strategic and operational needs of the military. People might be inclined not to enlist if they think that civilian employment cannot be protected while a citizen-soldier is performing military service. If people do not enlist in the National Guard and Reserve, then national security is possibly threatened because the military will lack manpower.

2. *To minimize disruption to the servicemember's employers, family, community, and coworkers by providing for prompt reemployment upon return.*

    This purpose is related to USERRA's first purpose. Military activation, annual training, and drill can cause a disruption in the home and workplace. USERRA is designed to reduce that disruption by introducing certainty to both the employer and the employee. Under USERRA and regulations, the obligations of both the employer and the citizen-soldier employee are laid out in detail. As discussed below, USERRA provides definite timeframes for return to work after activation, drill, and training.

3. *To prohibit discrimination in employment and reemployment against National Guard and Reserve members because of their military service.*

    National Guard and Reserve enlistment is vital to the military. If there is a perception that employers are discriminating against citizen-soldiers based upon membership in the National Guard or Reserve, then people might be inclined not to enlist. Congress extended workplace anti-discrimination protections to National Guard and Reserve members similar to other workplace protections for race, age, and disability-based discrimination.

performing state service. If there is a question about whether state service is protected service, refer to the website of your state's Veterans Department or attorney general.

USERRA applies to almost all employers in the United States, including the federal government, the states and their political subdivisions (counties, cities, school districts, etc.), and private employers. An employer needs to have only one employee to be an employer for purposes of USERRA. Only religious institutions, Indian tribes, and foreign embassies, consulates, and international organizations are excluded. USERRA also applies to U.S. companies abroad and to foreign companies that are controlled by U.S. companies.

USERRA applies to part-time, temporary, probationary, and at-will employment situations. You do not have rights under USERRA if you are a partner or an independent contractor. However, keep in mind that the mere fact that someone labels you a partner or independent contractor does not make you one. USERRA is to be liberally construed in finding coverage.

USERRA does not apply to the relationship between a student and a college or university, but other federal laws provide nearly the same protections to students whose educational careers are interrupted by voluntary or involuntary service.

Reemployment Rights Under USERRA

National Guard and Reserve members who leave to perform military service have a right to return to their civilian employment as if they never left. In order for USERRA to apply to a service-member's reemployment, the following five criteria must be met:

1. You must have left employment for the purpose of performing service in the uniformed service.
2. You must have given the employer proper notice of your upcoming service.
3. Your cumulative service must not have exceeded five years.
4. You must have been released from service without a disqualifying discharge.

5. **You must have made a timely application for reemployment after release from the period of service.**

1. Uniformed Service

To have the right to reemployment under USERRA, you must have left your position of civilian employment in order to perform voluntary or involuntary service in the uniformed services. For USERRA purposes, the uniformed services are the U.S. Army, Navy, Marine Corps, Air Force, and Coast Guard, as well as the commissioned corps of the Public Health Service. USERRA is not limited to National Guard and Reserve service. It applies equally to service in the regular component of the armed forces.

2. Notice of Military Service

The servicemember must provide advance notice of the military duty for USERRA to apply. The notice should be in writing and advise the employer of the type of duty, dates of duty, and anticipated date of return. Advanced notice might not be possible because of the nature of the duty—however, those instances are rare.

USERRA defines the term "service in the uniformed services" broadly, to include:

- active duty,
- initial active-duty training,
- active duty for training,
- fitness examinations, and
- funeral honors duty.

▶ **KEEP YOUR EMPLOYER IN THE KNOW**

Servicemembers are encouraged to keep their employers on notice about upcoming drills, training, and deployments. Reducing surprises to the employer is helpful in maintaining a good relationship.

Military leave takes precedence over an employer's leave policy. An employer cannot deny military leave and require an employee to get a military leave "approved" by the employer. If there is a benefit not guaranteed by USERRA, such as health care continuation for family members, the employer can require the employee to fill out the paperwork. However, an employer cannot deny military leave to an employee who does not complete the paperwork for that benefit— only the benefit tied to the paperwork can be denied if the paperwork is not completed.

3. Applying for Reemployment Within the Proper Time Frame

A servicemember must apply for reemployment in a timely manner for USERRA to apply. Filling out a formal application is not required—servicemembers are required to notify their employers only that they will be returning to work. Although written notice is not required, it is a good idea. The timeframe for reapplication depends upon the duration of military duty.

If military duty was less than thirty-one days:

The servicemember must report back to work at the beginning of the first full regularly scheduled work period following the period of service. An employee can take eight hours' rest after the trip from the place of service to home. Employees are not required to take the eight-hour rest period, but an employer cannot require them to return early. If reporting within the period is unreasonable or impossible, through no fault of the employee, the employee should report as soon as possible after the eight-hour period. An example of an impossibility would be return flight delays. However, regardless of the reason for the delay, if an employee cannot report at the beginning, the employer is not required to allow the employee a late start.

If military duty is greater than thirty days but less than 181 days:

The employee must submit his or her reemployment application no later than fourteen days following the completion of military service. This allows a servicemember some time to readjust before returning to work.

If military duty is greater than 180 days:

The employee must submit his or her reemployment application no later than ninety days following the completion of military duty. This allows a National Guard or Reserve member a significant amount of time to readjust before returning to work. In reality, a large percentage of employees do not use the full ninety days because they cannot afford it.

If a servicemember is injured during military service:

He or she should report back to work after hospitalization or convalescence is completed. An employee has up to two years to recover. As a practical matter, the employee should notify the employer that he or she is recovering from injury dur-

▶ **FAILING TO REPORT BACK TO WORK**

Failure to report back or re-apply in a timely manner does not automatically mean that employment is forfeited. Rather, a failure to timely report or re-apply means that an employer can start the process for disciplining and removing any AWOL employee. If you must be delayed in reporting back to work, notify your employer of the possible delay immediately.

ing military duty and keep the employer notified of the progress of recovery.

4. Cumulative Period of Military Service is Less Than Five Years

If a servicemember exceeds five years of cumulative military service, USERRA protections will not apply. The five-year limit is per employer and it starts anew when the servicemember changes employers. There are many exceptions to the five-year rule. *All* involuntary service and *some* voluntary service are exempted from the computation of the five-year limit. The following are not countable toward the five-year cumulative period of military service:

- the initial period of service;
- when the employee is unable to get orders releasing them from service—commonly referred to as "stop-loss";
- required training, such as drills, annual training, specialized training, advanced training, and military "schools";
- activation or retention because of national emergency or war;
- activation for "operational" or "critical" missions; and
- presidential order mobilizing the National Guard into federal service.

5. Qualifying Discharges for USERRA Protection

USERRA protections do not apply to employees discharged from the military for bad conduct discharges, dishonorable discharges, and certain types of other than honorable discharges. All other discharges qualify for USERRA protections.

An employer is required to presume that a discharge is a qualifying discharge if there is no available DD-214 or other documentation confirming the qualifying character of the discharge. However, an employer can request that an employee assist in obtaining the documentation and the employee is required to assist the employer.

Returning to the Workplace

When determining where a servicemember should be placed upon return to the workplace, the answer is: *where the servicemember would have been if he or she never left.* This means that longevity-based pay and benefits increase as if the employee had remained continuously in the service of the employer. For example, if an employee would have received a seniority or longevity-based raise had the employee not had to leave for military service, the employee will get that raise when he or she returns.

The application of the "as if they never left" concept can sometimes be confusing—the job of the returning employee depends upon factors such as how long the employee has been gone, whether the job still exists, and whether the employee is disabled to the point of not being able to return to the same job.

For periods of service less than ninety days, the servicemember returns to the same job he or she would have had as if the servicemember never left.

For periods of service more than ninety days, the servicemember returns to the same job—unless returning to that position is not possible. If return to the same position is not possible, then the employee should be placed in a substantially similar position of "like seniority, status and pay."

"Like seniority, status and pay" can be understood with USERRA's "escalator provision." The "escalator" means an employee who is absent for military service is treated like similarly situated employees who remained in the workplace. This theoretical "escalator" considers pay, status, seniority, and other aspects of employment. The returning servicemember gets on the escalator with the similarly situated employees. The escalator usually goes up. However, as we know from the current economy, the escalator can also go down; pay, hours, and ben-

> ## YOU CAN BE LAID OFF, EVEN IF YOU AREN'T THERE
>
> USERRA requires that employees be returned to where they would have been "as if they never left." However, the reality of the current economy can have a bad result for returning servicemembers; companies have been laying off employees and going out of business. Servicemembers who are gone for military service are to be treated the same as civilian employees. If the civilians go down the employment "escalator" by losing pay or benefits, servicemembers will join them at the same point. If servicemembers are among a group of employees getting laid off, the servicemember can be laid off, too.

efits have been cut for some employees. USERRA requires that the National Guard or Reserve member be treated the same as civilian employees. It does not require that a servicemember get more than his or her coworkers.

Job requirements can change while a servicemember is deployed. USERRA provides that if an employee is not qualified to return to the job he or she would have had but for military duty, the employer must make reasonable efforts for the employee to become qualified. For example, the employer must make training and education available if that would help the employee become qualified for the job. If the employee still does not become qualified, the employer still cannot terminate the employee. Rather, the employer must place the employee in a position of "like seniority, status, and pay" for the employee's qualifications.

USERRA recognizes that citizen-soldiers can become ill or injured during service. The USERRA law places more requirements on the employer than the Americans with Disabilities Act (the main federal law regulating the employment of disabled individuals). USERRA requires not just an accommodation for the disabled returning employee, but also that the employee be placed in a position consistent with his or her disability if the employee cannot go back to the job he or she would occupy if the employee never left.

The employer must make reasonable efforts to accommodate the returning disabled servicemember. What is reasonable will depend on the specific employer and the servicemember's disability; "reasonable" could mean modifying the facilities (adding a wheelchair ramp, for example), acquiring equipment such as a special telephone for an individual with hearing problems, or providing readers or interpreters. Again, what will be "reasonable" varies depending on the situation. In addition to what the employer must do, the VA has a Vocational Rehabilitation Program available. Vocational Rehabilitation is discussed on page 307.

USERRA's Anti-Discrimination Protections

There are state and federal laws that prohibit employment decisions based upon many factors such as race, religion, gender, ethnicity, disability, age, and pregnancy. USERRA is similar to those laws because the anti-discrimination provisions of USERRA prohibit employers from making decisions based upon whether the employee or prospective employee is in the National Guard or Reserve components. Simply, employers cannot consider National Guard or Reserve membership as the main or substantial reason when making employment decisions such as initial hiring, promoting, layoff/retention, promotion, and reemployment when returning from military service.

An employer cannot deny any benefit to an employee because that employee is in the National Guard or Reserve. For example, an employer cannot decide to exclude a reservist from a bonus program due to the reservist's military service. An employer also cannot retaliate against an employee because of membership in the National Guard or Reserve, performance of military service, or filing a USERRA complaint. This means, for example, that an employer could not deny an employee a promotion because of the employee's status as a reservist.

Federal courts have not agreed as to whether USERRA protections extend to an employee who is being subjected to workplace harassment because of his or her military obligation. If you are being harassed in the workplace due to your military service, you should talk to a lawyer in your area with experience in employment law issues; you may be able to make a claim under other anti-discrimination laws.

If Your Rights Are Violated

If you think your employment or reemployment rights have been violated, you have every right to take action. A servicemember can contact the Employer Support of the Guard and Reserve (www.esgr.mil) and register a complaint. ESGR will refer you to an ESGR volunteer ombudsman in your state. Upon your request, the ombudsman will contact the employer on your behalf and try to work out the problem. The ESGR process is nonconfrontational and quick. ESGR will normally resolve the matter within two weeks or tell you that it cannot resolve it and that you should consider your next step. ESGR has no enforcement authority; this means that the ESGR cannot penalize or fine an employer. You may also file a complaint with the U.S. Department of Labor. Details are at www.dol.gov/vets. The Department of Labor and the Department of Justice have an agreement for USERRA enforcement. The agencies enforce USERRA violations in "appropriate cases."

If you want free legal help from the U.S. government in asserting your USERRA claim, you must file a formal complaint with the Veterans' Employment and Training Service of the U.S. Department of Labor (DOL-VETS). That agency will investigate your complaint and try to persuade the employer to come into compliance if the DOL-VETS investigation indicates that your claim has merit. If the DOL-VETS investigation does not result in a satisfactory resolution, you can request (essentially insist) that DOL-VETS refer your case to the U.S. Department of Justice (DOJ), if the employer is a state, a political subdivision of a state, or a private employer. If your employer is a federal agency,

DOL-VETS will refer the case to the U.S. Office of Special Counsel (OSC).

If DOJ believes your case has merit, DOJ will file suit on your behalf, at no cost to you, in the appropriate U.S. District Court, and will represent you in your case. Similarly, if OSC finds your case to have merit, it will initiate a case on your behalf in the Merit Systems Protection Board (MSPB) and will represent you. In a typical year, the DOJ initiates fifteen to twenty-five cases in federal court against state and local governments and private employers, while OSC initiates a somewhat larger number of USERRA cases against federal agencies in their capacity as employers.

You also have the option of consulting with and hiring your own private attorney. Attorneys privately retained by USERRA plaintiffs bring the majority of cases against federal agencies (in the MSPB) and against private employers and local governments (in federal district courts). Unlike other federal employment laws, USERRA has no "exhaustion of remedies" rule that would require you to pursue your claim administratively before resorting to the courts. You also don't need a "right to sue letter" before you file suit in federal court or in the MSPB.

If you proceed with private counsel and prevail, the court or the MSPB can award you attorney fees in addition to other

▶ **AVOIDING PROBLEMS**

Servicemembers should be proactive and inform an employer of upcoming military obligations by supplying drill schedules, AT schedules, activation and return dates. Because the Guard and Reservists are such a small portion of the population, many employers have limited understanding of the USERRA law. Simply bringing a copy of the Employer Resource Guide (available at esgr.mil) to your human resources department can put the employer on notice of its obligations and the servicemember's rights.

relief. An award can be significant if you prevail. First, the court will order the employer to come into compliance. If you were fired unlawfully, or if you were unlawfully denied reemployment, the court will order the employer to reinstate you and to pay you back pay and other relief to make you whole for the violation. If the court finds that the employer violated USERRA willfully, the court will order the employer to pay you an amount equal to the actual damages, and in addition to those damages, an equal amount as *liquidated damages.* This effectively doubles the award if the court finds that the violation was willful. The MSPB will order similar relief, except that there is no provision for ordering a federal agency to pay liquidated (double) damages for willful violations.

RESOURCES

- **Servicemembers Law Center** (www.servicemembers -lawcenter.org): You will find more than 800 articles about USERRA and other laws that are especially pertinent to those who serve our country in uniform, along with a detailed subject index and a search function, to facilitate finding articles about very specific topics. Start with Law Review 0766, a primer on USERRA.

- **United States Department of Labor VETS Program** (www .dol.gov/vets): Includes resources and information to assist veterans and help prepare them for meaningful careers; also focuses on protecting veterans and servicemembers' employment rights.

- **Employer Support of the Guard and Reserve** (www.esgr .mil): An organization within the Department of Defense with the goal of promoting cooperation between Reserve component members and civilian employers; assists in the resolution of conflicts arising from an employee's military service.

- **American Bar Association HomeFront** (www.abahomefront .org): Includes information on USERRA rights and a state-by-state listing of legal service programs for veterans and their family members.

- **Feds Hire Vets** (www.fedshirevets.gov): Has more information about this program.

- **Vet Success** (vetsuccess.gov): Has a good listing of employment programs and resources.

CHAPTER 9

Discharge from the Military

George has been in the military for five years and has been deployed to a combat zone three times. As he nears the end of his first enlistment and begins to make decisions on whether to re-enlist or to separate and go to school, his military doctor informs George that injuries he suffered on his last deployment make him fall below retention standards and that he is being referred for a medical separation. George now wonders what he should do next and where he should go for advice.

Early release from the military, known as a discharge, for any reason can be difficult to understand due to the complicated and cumbersome separation process. Often the paperwork that informs a servicemember of the basis for his or her discharge is written in formal, old-fashioned language. It also uses military-specific language that may not be easily understood without reading the information multiple times or having a lawyer explain the separation in plain language.

This chapter provides an overview of the various types of discharges and provides basic information that will assist servicemembers and their families in evaluating their own situations.

Regardless of which discharge a servicemember receives, all administrative discharges from the military have one thing in common: The member is entitled to see a military attorney for free to have the discharge explained to him or her *before* signing any documents or actually separating from the military. The servicemember is also entitled to file an appeal of any separation following their specific service rules to see if the discharge can be avoided.

MEDICAL DISCHARGE AND MILITARY PHYSICAL DISABILITY EVALUATION SYSTEM

One of the most difficult administrative separations service-members may face comes from injuries or a medical conditions that impacts their ability to perform their military duties. Many of these situations result in a servicemember being evaluated for and receiving a medical separation through the Department of Defense Disability Evaluation System. The box below details two common examples of how a servicemember might become eligible for a Disability Evalution System.

▶ SCENARIO 1

Petty Officer Jones is a personnel specialist in the U.S. Navy. During a normal health screening, he is informed that his medical testing indicates he has developed Type 2 diabetes. Petty Officer Jones is referred into the Navy Physical Disability Evaluation System for a Medical Evaluation Board and is ultimately separated from the Navy through the Physical Evaluation Board process.

▶ SCENARIO 2

Staff Sergeant Smith is an infantryman in the U.S. Army. He is injured in an improvised explosive device attack while deployed to a combat zone. He suffers severe injuries to his left foot. These injuries leave him unable to stand or walk for long periods of time or carry more than thirty pounds. Staff Sergeant Smith is referred into the Army Physical Disability Evaluation System for a Medical Evaluation Board and is ultimately separated from the Army through the Physical Evaluation Board process.

Overview of Disability Evaluation System

The Department of Defense Disability Evaluation System, which is mandated under federal law, addresses medical conditions and injuries related to, or caused by, a servicemember's military service. The Disability Evaluation System consists of two parts:

1. **A medical evaluation by a Medical Evaluation Board; and**
2. **An evaluation of physical disability and fitness to perform military duty evaluation by a Physical Evaluation Board.**

Every branch of the military has its own Disability Evaluation System regulations. Although each military branch has its own regulations, all branches are required to follow Department of Defense rules regarding when a servicemember may be referred to the disability evaluation system if such a referral has the potential to make the member eligible for separation or a loss of benefits.

Additionally, all services must follow the Department of Veterans Affairs' Schedule for Rating Disabilities when determining a separation rating for each medical condition that makes a servicemember unfit to continue his or her military service.

Since 2011, all services have transitioned to a joint disability evaluation system, called the Integrated Disability Evaluation System. The Integrated Disability Evaluation System is administered jointly by the Departments of Defense and Veterans Affairs to make disability evaluations for servicemembers simpler and more efficient. The integrated system takes evaluation processes that the Department of Defense and the Veterans Affairs each performed separately and uses one combined evaluation process to determine whether a servicemember is able to continue to serve. For servicemembers unable to continue service, the integrated system determines the disability rating the member will receive.

▶ DISABILITY RATINGS

Your disability rating will be determined by the VA by using its disability guide, called the Schedule for Rating Disabilities. This schedule is used to help evaluate and assess the severity of a disability. It contains a very long list of medical conditions. The schedule consists of more than 700 diagnostic codes that are organized under a variety of body systems.

The VA schedule provides criteria for assigning a disability rating. Your rating will be given as a percentage. It can range from 0 percent all the way to 100 percent. The greater your disability, the higher the percentage will be. This in turn will allow you to collect a larger amount of disability compensation. More information on disability ratings can be found on page 308 or 340.

Counseling

Each servicemember who is referred for a Disability Evaluation is entitled to receive free legal assistance from a military lawyer. Counseling ensures that a servicemember undergoing evaluation is advised of the significant consequences that may result from the medical evaluation board and the physical evaluation board. The counseling also ensures that servicemembers are informed of the rights, benefits, and entitlements they may be eligible to receive.

The initial counseling is usually performed by a Physical Evaluation Board liaison officer, who is an administrative specialist with focused training in the Department of Defense Disability Evaluation System and in the specific service's rules for disability cases. Since the passage of the National Defense Authorization Act of 2008, servicemembers are entitled to receive information and counseling about the disability evaluation system from a military attorney, which is available at no cost to the servicemember. A servicemember is entitled to work with an attorney from the very beginning of the disability evaluation process. All servicemembers are also entitled to representation by a military attorney for free once their cases have been referred to a Physical Evaluation Board for a fitness determination. A servicemember may also hire a civilian attorney at his or her own expense to assist with the case. As of 2012, all services offer some level of free legal services or legal assistance at the beginning of the medical evaluation board process.

The Army has the most robust legal assistance program, with specially trained civilian and military attorneys available to represent servicemembers beginning with their initial referral into the disability evaluation system. The Soldier's Counsel are available at most large installations and can be contacted by calling the local installation legal office.

The Navy also has specialized representation for servicemembers in the disability evaluation system; such legal representation begins with the referral into the disability evaluation system. These services are generally available at larger installations that host significant populations of personnel processing through the disability evaluation system. The attorneys available to assist Navy personnel with their disability evaluation system can be contacted by calling your local installation legal office.

The Air Force has general information available through attorneys at local installations. Specialized representation and information is available to all Air Force personnel by contacting the Air Force's Disability Counsel Office, AFPC/JA, Air Force Formal PEB, or by phone, 1-210-671-4295. This office is located at Lackland Air Force Base in Texas; it handles all formal representation at the physical evaluation board for Air Force personnel.

▶ **FINDING LEGAL HELP**

Chapter 1, "Working with an Attorney," has more information about finding an attorney for your specific case and the various options for free or low-cost legal services.

Whether you have a military attorney, a Physical Evaluation Board liaison officer, or some other counselor assisting you during the disability process, that counselor should be adequately trained on such matters and should help you understand the sequence and nature of the steps in the disability process. The counselor should also assist you with determining what benefits might be available depending on which specific course of action you take; the counselor is there to help you make an informed choice regarding your future.

Medical Evaluation Boards

As the first step in the Department of Defense disability evaluation system, the medical evaluation board (MEB) process is probably the most important step. This is the earliest opportunity for servicemembers to evaluate their situations and decide the best outcome for them and their families; this step also gives members the chance to identify what documents are needed to achieve their desired outcome. It can make a huge difference in the entire process if servicemembers have a good understanding of how their injuries and medical conditions will be rated and how to ensure their conditions are properly documented in their medical records and the evaluation board files.

The medical evaluation board determines whether you have any injuries or medical conditions that disqualify you for continued retention in the military based on your service-specific regulations. The medical evaluation board *will not* make a fitness determination. The medical evaluation board's purpose is to accurately diagnose all of a servicemember's injuries and/or medical conditions and develop a written record—a narrative summary—of these injuries or medical conditions.

Using the service-specific regulations for a given servicemember, the MEB will document the medical status and duty limitations of the servicemember. These regulations generally identify what medical status is necessary to be retained within a particular service. These regulations also provide guidance on how to document physical limitations of a servicemember (i.e.

> ## SERVICE REGULATIONS GOVERNING RETENTION OF PERSONNEL WITH DISQUALIFYING CONDITIONS
>
> - Army: *AR 40–400, Patient Administration,* Chapter 7
> - Navy/USMC: *Manual of the Medical Department,* Chapter 18
> - Air Force: *AFI 41–210,* Chapter 10
> - Coast Guard: *COMDTINST M1850.2D*

profiles, LIMDU, etc.) and often identify specific medical or physical conditions that will cause a servicemember to fall below his or her service's retention standards. Each military service has slightly different requirements for its personnel due to the different missions performed by each, and you must look at your departmental regulations to determine if your service is following its published rules in your case.

Medical providers (i.e. medical doctors and physician assistants) conduct medical evaluation boards on any servicemembers who do not meet the standards outlined in departmental regulations regarding retention for continued military service. Each medical provider on a medical evaluation board receives special training on performing a medical examination and on documenting various medical conditions or duty-limiting injuries. Each service has specific regulations that outline retention standards and provide medical guidance on how to evaluate various medical conditions.

The medical evaluation board itself consists of an actual physical examination of the servicemember. The report of the board states whether each individual condition or injury forms a basis for referral into the disability evaluation system based on the service regulations applicable to the servicemember (i.e. Army Soldiers will be evaluated under Army Regulations, while Air Force Airmen are evaluated under Air Force Instructions). Clinical information (meaning the servicemember's medical records) must include a full medical history of the servicemem-

▶ **SERVICE REGULATIONS GOVERNING MEDICAL EVALUATION BOARD PROCESSING**

- Army: *AR 40–501*, Chapter 3
- Navy/USMC: *SECNAVINST 1850.4E*, Chapter 8
- Air Force: *AFI 48–123*
- Coast Guard: *Medical Manual*, Chapter 3, Section F

ber, appropriate physical examinations of any injuries or medical conditions that exist, medical tests and their results, medical and surgical consultations as necessary or indicated, diagnoses, treatment, and prognosis. Often, the servicemember's medical records will already contain medical tests, results, consultations, and other medical information, and these records will be used to conduct most of the examination. If this is not the case, the servicemember has the right to ask for any medical examination that he or she feels should be conducted to complete his or her medical records. The servicemember is also entitled to ask for second opinions and independent medical reviews (also called independent medical adviser reviews) to ensure that each injury or medical condition is fully documented for the Medical Evaluation Board.

The Medical Evaluation Board file should also contain various administrative documents to be used by the physical evaluation board in determining if a servicemember is fit to continue performing his or her military duties. These administrative documents should include: a copy of the line of duty determination made under the departmental service regulations; a statement from the servicemember's immediate commanding officer describing the impact of the servicemember's medical condition or injury on the servicemember's ability to perform his or her normal military duties and to deploy or mobilize; and pertinent personnel records, as required by the servicemember's service, to establish the servicemember's military history. These documents should include items such as performance evaluation reports, documentation of awards and decorations, promotion orders and promotion lists, and other similar historical documents.

As a servicemember, you are entitled to review the entire Medical Evaluation Board file and ensure that it contains all necessary medical documents, administrative documents, or other evidence that you feel is important for your service to make the right decision in your case. If you have conditions or injuries that the Medical Evaluation Board is not considering or that are not properly or adequately documented, you have the right to appeal the findings and recommendations of the Medical Evaluation Board. You should submit your appeal in writing to the Medical Evaluation Board and detail the errors you want corrected. You should include any medical documentation you have that supports your positions, including civilian medical records, medical journal articles, second opinions from other medical providers, and anything you feel will help persuade the reviewers to adopt your position.

As of 2007, the DoD and the VA have teamed up to work together on MEBs. This new program allows a servicemember to file a VA disability claim when he or she is referred for a MEB. The VA now performs a full medical exam on the servicemember and provides a disability rating for any condition found. A servicemember files a VA claim for any conditions that he or she believes may be disabling, not just those identified on the service profile. After all appropriate VA specialists have consulted with the servicemember, all reports will be forwarded to the MEB physician who drafts the narrative summary.

Physical Disability Evaluation Boards

The next step in the disability evaluation system is the physical disability evaluation; this step determines the fitness of servicemembers with medical impairments to perform their military duties. This evaluation is conducted by a physical evaluation board. Each service has a service-specific regulation for the physical evaluation board process.

▶ **SERVICE REGULATIONS GOVERNING PHYSICAL EVALUATION BOARD PROCESSING**

- Army: *AR 635–40*
- Navy/USMC: *SECNAVINST 1850.4E*
- Air Force: *AFI 36–3212*
- Coast Guard: *COMDTINST M1850.2D*

If a servicemember is found to be unfit to perform his or her assigned military duties under the service-specific regulation, the physical evaluation board also determines the servicemember's entitlement to benefits under Title 10, Chapter 61 of the U.S. Code. In short, such an evaluation determines whether you should be retired or separated with a severance payment based on the severity of your condition. Servicemembers can be rated by the physical evaluation board only for conditions that actually make them unable (i.e. unfit) to perform their essential military duties.

A servicemember's fitness is based on his or her individual ability to perform his or her military duties at his or her current pay grade and primary military job. For instance, a fairly new Airman (E-3) may have strenuous physical requirements in his or her position as an aircraft loadmaster while a senior Airman (E-7) is given primarily supervisory duties such as scheduling missions and checking load plans. Each Airman will be evaluated based on his or her individual pay grade and what is required to perform that specific job. The E-3 Airman may not be able to perform all of his or her duties with a serious physical injury due to the inability to lift, bend, or otherwise engage in physical activities required of a junior loadmaster. The E-7 Airman may have the exact same injury, but due to having more supervisory duties, may be able to perform more of his or her duties than the E-3 Airman and may have a greater fitness level.

The physical evaluation board happens in two stages. An

informal physical evaluation board is first conducted, during which all of the documentary evidence is reviewed; the service-member is not present during this review. This first review is conducted by a physician, a personnel officer, and another individual assigned to the physical evaluation board. The informal physical evaluation board provides the servicemember with the initial findings and recommendations of the physical evaluation board, including a determination of the servicemember's fitness to perform military duties. The servicemember must then review the packet and decide whether to accept the findings and recommendations or appeal the informal board's findings and request a formal physical evaluation board hearing.

Servicemembers should consider submitting a written rebuttal identifying the issues of disagreement with the informal physical evaluation board's findings and recommendations with any request for a formal board hearing.

If the informal physical evaluation board finds a service-member to be unfit, the member is automatically granted a formal hearing before the physical evaluation board upon request. Under federal law (Title 10, Chapter 61 of the U.S. Code), if a servicemember is being separated or retired for a physical disability, he or she has a legal right to a full and fair hearing. The formal hearing under the physical evaluation board fulfills this legal requirement. A servicemember may appear before the formal physical evaluation board in person, through a designated representative such as an attorney or another representative, or via video teleconferencing media.

During a formal hearing, you have the right to address any issues related to your military benefits or how your disability support will be characterized by the military (i.e. combat-related injuries or a slip and fall in the food court by your home), which affects how the Internal Revenue Services treats your separation or retired pay for tax purposes. Federal law protects your ability to ask about these issues. Final determination of your fitness to perform your military duties will comply with current service rules and regulations on fitness for duty and will include evaluations of whether you can perform the full range of military duties in your pay grade and military job, such as whether you can deploy to the harsh environments of a combat zone, whether you can carry and fire a weapon, and many other similar issues. Each service has its own criteria outlined in the service regulations to determine these answers.

At the formal physical evaluation board hearing, you have the following additional rights:

- **The right to the assistance of a detailed military counsel provided at no expense to you or a personal representative provided at no expense to the service.**

- **The right to make a sworn or an unsworn statement.**

- **The right to remain silent. However, if you exercise this right, you may not selectively respond and must remain silent throughout the hearing.**

- **The right to introduce witnesses, depositions, documents, sworn or unsworn statements (affidavits), or other evidence in your behalf and to question all witnesses who testify at the hearing. Witnesses who are not members or employees of the Department of Defense and members of the Department of Defense who are not deemed essential witnesses as determined by the physical evaluation board attend formal hearings at no expense to the government. (This means you or the witnesses themselves will have to cover travel-related costs.)**

- **The right of access to all records and information received by the physical evaluation board before, during, and after the formal hearing that may affect the findings of the physical evaluation board or appellate review authority.**

- **The right to appeal the findings and recommendations of the formal physical evaluation board.**

The physical evaluation board must make a written record of the proceedings, documenting its findings and recommendations, including the determination of fit or unfit and the rationale for such finding; the code and percentage of disability assigned to the physical disability in accordance with the Veterans Administration Schedule for the Ratings of Disabilities, and the reason any unfitting condition is not compensable.

Appealing Administrative Discharges

All of the military service regulations outline the administrative appeal options for the separations (including retirements) that occur under the physical disability evaluation system. You will receive written instructions about these administrative appeal options as part of written record of the proceedings documenting the findings and recommendations of the physical evaluation board.

After the administrative appeal process, it is not uncommon for servicemember to want or need to appeal their cases further. Often these appeals are not started until after the servicemember has actually separated from the military and returned to civilian life. In these instances, there are additional opportunities for appealing, including: the Board for Correction of Military Records, the Physical Disability Review Board, and the U.S. Court of Federal Claims. The Physical Disability Review Board, which is unique to physical discharges, is discussed in the following section. The other two avenues for appeals, which apply to more than just physical discharges are discussed starting on page 294.

▶ **FIRST COMES FIRST**

It is important to note that all of the avenues for appeal discussed in this section require that the servicemember first complete all other regulatory appeals that are available to him or her. This means that if your service's regulations make a certain avenue available for appealing, you must take those steps first before you can appeal to the Court of Federal Claims or other outside avenue.

Physical Disability Review Board

Veterans who have been medically separated from the U.S. military between September 11, 2001 and December 31, 2009, have the opportunity to have their disability ratings reviewed by the Physical Disability Board of Review (PDBR) to ensure fairness and accuracy. The PDBR was created by Congress to ensure the accuracy and fairness of disability ratings of 20 percent or less assigned to servicemembers discharged during this time. This additional board was created because all the services were not strictly following the VA Schedule for Ratings for Disabilities during this time period. Due to the variances the services were using, Congress determined that some veterans may have received lower ratings than they should have and may have been separated with disability severance pay instead of being retired.

The PDBR uses medical information provided by the Department of Veterans Affairs and the military department. Once a review is complete, the PDBR forwards a recommendation to the secretary of the respective branch of the armed services. It is up to the individual service branch to make the final determination on whether to change the original disability determination.

Army Disability Rating Review Board

If you were retired from the Army with a disability rating, the Army Disability Rating Review Board may consider your request to review the percentage of your rated disability. This board is established by Army regulation; none of the other military services has a comparable review board at this time.

If you are a soldier with a fully executed retirement order and think you should have a higher disability percentage, you may want to apply to this board. You will need to prove one of the following things is true in order for the board to review your case:

- The original retirement order was based on fraud or a mistake of law;

- You were not granted a full and fair hearing when a timely demand for such a hearing was made; or

- There is substantial new evidence that, by due diligence, you could not have presented before the retirement decision and such evidence would have warranted a higher percentage of disability.

The retired solider or his or her representative must present the written appeal within five years of the date of retirement.

Medical Discharges

The military may also discharge servicemembers for other physical and mental conditions that do not qualify for a disability discharge, but have the potential to interfere with the servicemember's assignment to or performance of duty. These conditions usually include chronic conditions such as seasickness, airsickness, enuresis, sleepwalking, claustrophobia, and other similar conditions. As with all administrative separation actions, the servicemember's service-specific regulations will govern what physical or mental conditions rise to the level of resulting in a disqualification. If any of these conditions is related to an injury or medical condition such as post-traumatic stress disorder that is related to a deployment to combat zone, the servicemember may be eligible for referral into the disability evaluation system for the condition.

DISCHARGES NOT FOR MEDICAL REASONS

Servicemembers may be discharged from the military before the normal expiration of their term of service (ETS) for reasons other than physical disability. Reasons for such discharge include misconduct and conviction by a civilian court.

All of these discharge types are personnel actions that cause a servicemember to be separated from military service.

Discharges for misconduct, conviction by a civilian court, and unsatisfactory performance are very similar to being fired from a civilian job, although the servicemember has many more rights and the opportunity to appeal.

The servicemember's time in service, rank, and the type of discharge the military wants to impose determine whether the servicemember will simply be given written notification of the intent to discharge or given the opportunity to appear in person before an administrative discharge board. A servicemember has certain due process rights during these discharges; those rights are outlined in the regulations that govern the administrative separation. Every branch of the military has its own service-specific discharge regulations, although the regulations have many similarities.

Before a servicemember can be separated for one of these reasons, the member's command must demonstrate, by a preponderance of the evidence, that:

- The servicemember did in fact commit the disqualifying act or have the disqualifying condition;
- As a result of this evidence, the servicemember should be discharged from the service; and
- As a result of all the evidence presented, the servicemember's discharge should be characterized as either honorable, general under honorable conditions, or under other than honorable conditions.

For most misconduct discharges, the servicemember will be entitled to a formal hearing before a panel of officers. The servicemember has the right to be present at the discharge hearing and to be represented by a military lawyer or a civilian military lawyer retained by the servicemember at his or her own expense. The hearing is a substantial evidentiary hearing, which means witnesses testify, documentary evidence is presented and both the military and the servicemember have the opportunity to make oral arguments regarding the evidence in the case. The servicemember has the right to challenge the government's evidence, cross-examine its witnesses, present his or her own witnesses and evidence, and testify on his or her own behalf. At each stage of the discharge process, the servicemember has the right to make a written response or appeal to any government documents and to any findings. If the board finds the servicemember did not commit the disqualifying act or have the disqualifying condition, then the case is normally closed and the servicemember is returned to duty.

Characterization of service at separation is based upon the quality of the veteran's service (how well he or she performed in his or her duties in the armed forces). There are five basic discharge statuses:

1. **Honorable Discharge (HD): issued at the end of a period of obligated service or as the result of administrative proceedings; appropriate when the service member's quality of service generally met the standards of acceptable conduct and performance of duty.**
2. **General Discharge (GD)/Discharge Under Honorable Conditions (DUHC): issued at the end of a period of obligated service or as a result of administrative proceedings or clemency after court-martial; servicemember had significant negative aspects in conduct or performance of duty that outweigh the positive performance.**
3. **Undesirable Discharge (UD)/Discharge Under Less Than Honorable Conditions (UOTHC): issued through administrative discharge proceedings, frequently as an option to avoid court-martial, and sometimes as form of clemency after a court-martial; servicemember's pattern of behavior significantly departs from the expected conduct.**
4. **Bad Conduct Discharge (BCD): issued only to enlisted personnel as a sentence of a special or general court-martial or, prior to 1951, some summary courts-martial.**
5. **Dishonorable Discharge (DD): issued as a sentence of a general court-martial (officers are issued "dismissals" by general courts-martial).**

UPGRADING YOUR DISCHARGE

The reasons for wanting to upgrade a discharge are numerous: eligibility for Department of Veterans Affairs benefits, improved employment opportunities, and increased self-esteem by removing the stigma of a bad discharge. This section describes the two most common ways of upgrading your less than honorable discharge or changing the reason for a discharge through each service's Discharge Review Board (DRB) and the Board of Correction for Military (or Naval) Records (BCMR).

Nature of Original Discharge

Determining the nature of a veteran's discharge is the first step in aiding a veteran who wishes to apply for a discharge upgrade. When a veteran is discharged, he or she receives discharge documents, the most important of which is the DD-214. There are two versions of the DD-214—a long form and a short form. The long form includes the following: the stated reason for the discharge, character of the discharge, reenlistment code, and a three-letter or -number code indicating the reason for the discharge. The short form does not contain most of the information included on the long form; here, you will mainly find the reason for discharge and characterization of service.

In addition to the character of discharge, veterans may want to change the reason (i.e. disability, hardship, personality disorder, etc.) for discharge (the "narrative" on the DD-214; the Army refers to this as "chapters").

Obtaining Service Records

Before applying for a discharge upgrade through either the DRB or the BCMR (unless a statute of limitations is close to running out, meaning that the legal time limit has expired), veterans should obtain and review their military records. In order to obtain your records from the National Personnel Records Center, you must fill out an SF-180—Request Pertaining to Military Records. The SF-180 is available at VA regional offices and online at www.archives.gov/research/order/standard-form-180.pdf. Send the SF-180 to National Personnel Records Center, Military Personnel Records, 9700 Page Avenue, St. Louis, MO 63132–5100.

Even if you have a copy of your records from when you were discharged, you still want to order an official copy to compare against your own records. Military records are notoriously known to somehow disappear from, or be lost from, your official record after you are discharged. Also, the personnel records centers tend to provide incomplete sets of records. If this is the case, you will need to make a follow-up request for the records that you believe should be there. You can also review the DRB's copy of your record at the DRB office or hearing site before the case is decided to check for any omissions or errors.

You should also get copies of other records (other than your service record), which the review boards will not normally see, but which you may want to submit to support your case. These "other" records include copies of your record of trial (if court-martialed) or any investigative records made or obtained by Army CID, NCIS, etc. It is up to you to submit these records to the board as they will not have access to them otherwise.

Unless proven to the contrary, your service records are the official version of the case and are accepted as containing all necessary factual information. Your personnel and medical

> ▶ **WATCH THE CLOCK**
>
> If you are close to the fifteen-year limitation for applying to the DRB, you may need to submit the SF-180 after filing your application to the DRB. The copies of your military records can be obtained after filing with the DRB. These time limits are discussed more on page 294.

records are the starting point in formulating your argument for discharge upgrade. These records will help you and your advocate decide what arguments will likely be successful as well as what additional evidence, if any, may be necessary to gather.

You must review the regulations that governed your discharge—those in effect at the time of the discharge—and compare them with the current version. If it has been a few years since you were discharged, the current regulations may be more to your advantage; this would mean that your advocate would argue that had you been discharged today under the current standards, you would have received a better discharge. The DRB considers this to be grounds for an upgrade.

Where to Apply

Typically, a veteran has two choices of where to apply for a discharge upgrade—the Decision Review Board or the Board of Correction for Military Records. However, if your main concern is to receive VA benefits, you can ask the VA to make a character of discharge determination, and if it is favorable, the VA will grant benefits. However, this is not a discharge upgrade and will not change your DD-214. Additionally, the VA also has a few legal bars to benefits that could completely prevent you from obtaining VA benefits no matter what type of discharge you received.

A major consideration in choosing where to apply (legally, this is called selecting your forum) is the different statutes of limitations (time limits) imposed by the DRB and the BCMR. The DRB statute of limitations is fifteen years from the date of discharge. This statute of limitations cannot be waived under any circumstances. This means that even if the government wants to make an exception for you (waive the statute of limitations), it cannot under the DRB. The BCMR has a three-year statute of limitations from the date of discovery of the error. However, this statute of limitation can and usually is waived upon request, if relief on the merits appears appropriate.

Typically, a veteran with either a compelling story or evidence should first apply to the DRB, since a personal appearance is guaranteed if requested. However, if a veteran has a BCD or DD issued by a general court-martial, those discharges may be reviewed only by a BCMR, and then only for clemency. Also, if a veteran applies first with the DRB and has his or her request denied, then the veteran can have BCMR review and act as an "appeals" court.

Applying

Applying for a discharge upgrade, through either the DRB or the BCMR, requires the veteran to fill out a form—DD Form 293 (DRB) or DD Form 149 (BCMR). Both forms are available from VA Regional Offices, VA Service Reps, or online from the BCMR websites. A family member or legal representative may apply on behalf of a veteran if the veteran is deceased or incompetent.

When applying to the BCMR, a veteran should write a letter to accompany his or her application requesting copies of all the materials the BCMR will consider in deciding his or her case. This letter should specifically request the following: any advisory opinions from any sources, staff briefs/memorandums, or military/civilian investigative reports.

Possible Outcomes

The DRB's power is limited to upgrading a discharge. On the other hand, the BCMR has multiple powers, including:

- **Removing the effect (i.e., bad discharge and forfeiture of pay) of a court-martial conviction (but cannot erase the conviction);**
- **Voiding a discharge by changing its date of issue;**
- **Reinstating a veteran into military duty;**
- **Removing disciplinary actions (except court-martial convictions that occurred before 1951) from a veteran's record;**

- Crediting a veteran with service time or changing a record to qualify a veteran for VA benefits;
- Upgrading any bad discharge, including a dishonorable discharge or bad conduct discharge issued by a general court-martial;
- Changing the reason for a discharge; and
- Correcting any other error in a vet's service record.

Proving Your Case—Who Has The Burden?

Many veterans have the misconception that his or her case starts on an even playing field, meaning that the boards will give the case a fair and objective review. However, the legal standards and presumptions in place make almost every case an uphill battle.

As the veteran, the burden is on you to prove that your discharge is either improper (illegal) or inequitable (unfair). The DRB and BCMR tend to view the discharge historically, meaning that if the discharge would be issued today under current, more liberal standards, and if it is fair to continue the stigma of a bad discharge. The DRBs, under federal law, consider discharge upgrade cases with a "presumption of regularity in the conduct of governmental affairs." This means that the boards presume that the discharge was fair and legal, that commands and discharge authorities acted properly, and that the military records given to the board provide an accurate statement of the necessary facts. Some boards want to look at the "whole person" and want to see how the discharge has affected the veteran. This approach tries to balance management of the military, maintenance of morale, interests of the veteran, discipline, equity, and public perception.

DRBs and BCMRs consider discharge upgrade cases on the basis of the fairness and the legality of the discharge at the time it was given. The DRBs call these issues equity (fairness) and propriety (legal and technical sufficiency), while the BCMRs use the terms injustice (unfairness) and error (legal error). Discharges given by court-martial are handled differently, though—here the boards consider only clemency, not fairness at the time of the discharge or legal error in the court-martial. Usually, the primary consideration in an upgrade case is rehabilitation and good conduct. Court-martials are beyond the scope of this book; talk to your military assistance office if this is your concern.

In recent years, the DRBs and BCMRs have not been favorable to veterans with "close" cases. Consequently, it is even more important to develop evidence to counter the evidence found in your military records, which is likely predominantly stacked against you.

There is one legal rule during this process that may benefit veterans: The normal rules of evidence do not apply. Almost any type of evidence, including second-hand information, testimony and statements that are not given under oath, and very informal evidence, can be submitted.

What Evidence Should You Submit?

In both DRBs and BCMRs, no formal rules of evidence apply. Therefore, you should present as much evidence as possible, including evidence that normally would not be admissible in a formal court proceeding. The following types of evidence may help your case:

- Evidence of impropriety during the discharge process
- Evidence that shows the unfair nature of your discharge and its impact on your life
- Awards showing your educational, work, and philanthropic achievements, during and after military service
- Any educational record
- Documentation of community service
- Employment history
- Information showing financial history
- Letters of reference/character

- Marriage license
- Dependent information
- Police report of good citizenship
- Letters of support from previous and current workers/servicemembers (any witness statements must be signed by a notary)

DISCHARGE REVIEW BOARD

Each service has their own discharge review board (DRB) composed of five active-duty officers (major or higher). The DRB presides over challenges to discharges issued within the past fifteen years. This fifteen-year limitation cannot be waived. If more than fifteen years have passed since discharge, the veteran must apply for an upgrade only through the Board of Corrections for Military Records (BCMR). The DRB hears cases in Washington, D.C. Some DRBs (currently, only the Air Force and Army) also travel to regional locations when there is a sufficient number of applicants.

A DRB has the ability to review most discharges, including bad conduct discharges (BCDs) issued by a special court-martial. However, there are some limits on the powers of a DRB: A DRB cannot review bad conduct or dishonorable discharges (DDs) issued by a general court-martial, nor can it change a re-enlistment code or modify a veteran's record beyond upgrading a discharge and the reason for discharge. A DRB hearing is an administrative hearing whose sole purpose is to determine whether a veteran's period of service was properly characterized. The burden of proof that the characterization was wrong lies with the veteran.

When filing an upgrade application, a veteran can choose either a personal appearance hearing before a review board or a nonpersonal appearance review (called a records review, which considers only the available medical and military records as well as any other evidence submitted by the veteran). Many veter-

▶ **YOU MUST SHOW UP**

Selecting a personal hearing and then failing to show up means you give up your right to a personal appearance, and only a records review will be performed. Of course, you can make a prior timely request for a continuance, postponement, or withdrawal of your application if you will be unable to make the personal hearing.

ans select the personal appearance option as they have a much higher rate of success when compared to a records review. A personal appearance lets the board hear what happened, allows the board members to judge the veteran by his or her words and demeanor, and lets the veteran call witnesses and make an argument to the board.

However, if you choose a records review and are denied an upgrade, you can ask for a personal appearance review, thus getting your records reviewed twice. Doing this requires planning ahead to ensure that enough time is available for the two reviews before the fifteen years is up.

When filling out the discharge upgrade request form (DD Form 293), the most important item, in terms of a veteran's success, is "item 6." Item 6 is where a veteran must list separately each specific issue supporting the upgrade request being considered. Each specific issue must show that the current discharge was either inequitable or improper. Before sending in your DD Form 293, ensure that all evidence you wish the DRB to review is attached to it.

The DRB is required to consider every issue or argument that you raise from "item 6" on the DD Form 293. Each argument should be listed separately and accompanied by a statement explaining why a discharge upgrade is necessary. Each argument must present an issue of "equity" or "propriety" or both. (Equity is a legal term meaning fairness and propriety generally means being proper or correct.) There is no set formula for presenting arguments and issues. For example, to request an upgrade for an OTH for going AWOL, a veteran may say something similar to:

"My discharge is inequitable, and should be upgraded to honorable and changed to discharge by reason of hardship/dependency in that serious family problems led to my AWOL and other than honorable discharge."

This is a process that can be complicated and time-consuming; do not hesitate to get legal advice if you think you need it.

After filing your application, if you requested a personal appearance, you will be notified of the time, date, and place of the hearing. Remember that all expenses incurred, including travel for you and any witnesses, as well as lodging and meals, will not be reimbursed; you will need to cover them.

DRB hearings are informal and nonadversarial. There is a "recorder" (usually the lowest ranking officer on the board) who explains the procedures to the veteran before the hearing and again when the hearing begins. This is done to ensure that veterans know their rights during their hearing. A DRB proceeding typically begins with opening remarks by the veteran or his or her counsel followed by the veteran's counsel asking questions of the veteran; the board members then ask the veteran a few questions. If a veteran is not represented by counsel, the veteran has a choice of making a sworn or unsworn statement to the board. A sworn statement allows the board to ask the veteran questions, while an unsworn statement does not allow for questions from the DRB.

If a veteran has any witnesses, he or she may call them after the initial questions. Finally, a closing statement is given by the veteran (or counsel). The government is not represented. The whole hearing usually takes about an hour, but there is no time limit. After the hearing, the DRB will not make a decision immediately. The members of the DRB discuss the case, each member then votes (majority rules), and the DRB sends the veteran a written decision, usually four to six weeks later. If the DRB agrees to upgrade a veteran's discharge, the veteran will receive a new discharge certificate, updated DD Form 214, and the decision certificate. If the veteran's case is denied, in whole or in part, the DRB will explain why it disagrees with each issue or why an upgrade is not required.

Occasionally a new issue may come up during a hearing. If this happens, the recorder should ask that any new issue(s) be written on a DD Form 293 for documentation. The veteran may ask for the DRB to defer its decision until new evidence or arguments can be submitted to address this new issue; however, this is a rarity.

Appealing a DRB Decision

If the DRB denies all or part of a veteran's request, the veteran has several options. If the veteran has only a records review, or had a hearing without any representation, the veteran can reapply by requesting a hearing at any time up to the fifteen-year deadline. After that, the next logical step would be to petition the BCMR. The BCMR can consider the case as you presented it to the DRB, along with any new evidence and arguments. The final avenue available is appealing to the federal courts. However, this step is very unlikely to result in success. Courts can address major issues of law, but rarely decide that the DRBs abused their rather broad discretion in deciding upgrade cases.

BOARD FOR CORRECTION OF MILITARY RECORDS

The Board for Correction of Military Records (BCMR) consists of three or five high ranking civilian employees of the same military branch and convenes in Washington, D.C. While the BCMR typically is concerned only with whether an error or injustice was made in a veteran's discharge, it has the ability to change, delete, modify, or add to the contents of military records when "necessary to correct an error or remove an injustice." In fact, the BCMR has the power to do anything to a veteran's record except overturn a court-martial conviction. However, even for

court-martials, the BCMR has some ability: It can order a correction to a record showing that the BCMR approved part of a
sentence, but not a punitive discharge. (Punitive is a legal term
that refers to something that is done as punishment.)

Similar to the DRB, the BCMR has a statute of limitations
on cases it can hear: A veteran's request must be made within
three years of the date of discovery of the error or injustice.
However, this three-year limit can be (and often is) waived if
the BCMR determines that a waiver is in the "best interest of
justice." The BCMR does have a strict requirement that the veteran must have exhausted all other options through government
agencies before the BCMR will hear the case; this requirement
cannot be waived. Unlike, the DRBs, BCMRs do not have written standards or guidelines for deciding cases. The BCMR rarely
grants personal appearances, but one can still be requested (and
it is probably a good idea to request one).

After the BCMR receives a veteran's upgrade application
packet, it will request an advisory opinion from the veteran's
service branch. If the advisory opinion does not recommend a
change, the veteran will be given a copy of the opinion and have
thirty days to make comments regarding the opinion. An additional thirty days to comment on the advisory opinion can be
given if requested, for a total of sixty days. However, the veteran
is not required to respond to the advisory opinion, as it is only
part of what the BCMR will use to make its final decision. Not
responding neither increases nor decreases your chances for a
favorable decision.

A veteran has three choices if the BCMR authorizes a personal hearing: appear without counsel, appear with counsel, or
have counsel appear for you. You can call witnesses to appear
on your behalf, but the BCMR does not have subpoena power
and cannot require any witness to appear and will not pay the
expenses of producing any witnesses. In order to save money,
consider videotaping any witnesses beforehand and using the
video at the hearing.

In evaluating an application for a discharge upgrade, the

BCMR will generally not concentrate on a single event or a single time period. Instead, it will look at many factors over many years. The BCMR will not only evaluate your military accomplishments and experiences but also your life before and after the military. The BCMR will weigh your positive achievements against the offense that led to the bad discharge. The BCMR will reach what it considers to be a fair result, taking special consideration that the veteran may have suffered for years due to the stigma of a bad discharge. In providing evidence to the BCMR, keep in mind that similar to DRBs, no formal rules of evidence apply for the BCMR.

Favorable BCMR decisions are subject to review by that military branch's secretary. In most instances, after denial of relief by either board or both boards (DRB and BCMR), federal district courts can review the cases by using the same standards of review that apply to other administrative agencies. If the BCMR denies the application, it will mail a brief statement of its reasons for the denial.

Appealing a BCMR Decision

There are two options if you wish to challenge a BCMR decision: resubmit your DD Form 149 with new evidence or court review.

A denial from a BCMR does not mean that a veteran's discharge will never be upgraded; it means that the veteran failed to provide enough evidence to show an error or injustice has occurred. If the veteran obtains new evidence, he or she can resubmit the DD Form 149 (along with previously submitted evidence) for consideration. If the BCMR reconsiders the case, it will be treated as a new application.

Veterans can also appeal their denials in the federal courts. Review is granted only in specific circumstances: denials of money claims (i.e. back pay) if the suit is file within six years of the date on which the error first existed or denials of "equitable relief" within six years of the denial by the BCMR.

GOING TO FEDERAL COURT

Once a servicemember or veteran has exhausted all administrative appeals for his or her specific service, the member may choose to appeal a separation or discharge upgrade to federal court. The first step is the U.S. Court of Federal Claims. The Court of Federal Claims is a *federal court* that hears monetary claims against the U.S. government (meaning any claims against the government where the individual is asking for money damages). Cases before the Court of Federal Claims must be filed within six years from the time the claim first accrued; for disability separation appeals, this means six years from the date the military made the last decision in your case. This limitation is strictly enforced by the court.

All trials at the court are bench trials, meaning they take place before judges and without juries. Because the court hears only cases against the government, the United States is always the defendant in cases before the Court of Federal Claims. Orders and judgments from the court are appealed to the U.S. Court of Appeals for the Federal Circuit.

RESOURCES

- **Veterans for America "The American Veterans and Servicemembers Survival Guide"** (www.nvlsp.org/images/Survival%20Guide-102309.pdf): Includes articles on upgrading your discharge and correcting military records.

- **GI Rights Network** (www.girightshotline.org): Offers counseling on a number of issues for veterans and servicemembers, including discharges.

- **National Veterans Legal Service Program: Lawyers Serving Warriors** (www.nvlsp.org): Provides free legal representation for servicemembers and veterans who served during Operation Iraqi Freedom and Operation Enduring

Freedom; representation includes disability, discharge, and benefits proceedings.

- **Military OneSource** (www.militaryonesource.org): Central clearinghouse for information and resources for active-duty servicemembers, National Guard and Reserve members, and their families.

- **Veterans Organizations:** There are a number of national veterans organizations that, through their local chapters, may be able to provide you guidance and assistance during your discharge proceeding and/or appeals:

  - The American Legion: www.legion.org/members/locators/posts

  - AMVETS: www.amvets.org/membership/find-your-post.html

  - Disabled American Veterans: http://dav.org/veterans/ContactUs.aspx

  - Iraq and Afghanistan Veterans of American: http://iava.org/

  - Student Veterans of American: www.studentveterans.org/

  - Veterans of Foreign Wars: www.vfw.org/oms/findpost.aspx

  - Vietnam Veterans of America: www.vva.org/chapters.html

- There are a few books that can help you understand the discharge process and articles:

  - Waddington, Michael. *Upgrade Your Army Discharge.* Evans: Michael Waddington, 2011.

  - "Obtaining Military Records and Information to Help Substantiate a Claim." *Veterans Benefits Manual.* Ed. Barton F. Stichman and Ronald B. Abrams. 2011 ed. Charlottesville, VA: LEXIS Law Pub, 2011. 1519–548. Print.

  - "Military Records Corrections Issues." *Veterans Benefits Manual.* Ed. Barton F. Stichman and Ronald B. Abrams. 2011 ed. Charlottesville, VA: LEXIS Law Pub, 2011. 1677–693. Print.

CHAPTER 10

Disability Issues

Howard has been in the Army for eight years as a combat engineer and is now retiring due to injuries from his last deployment to Iraq. He is concerned that his traumatic brain injury (TBI) and leg injuries from an IED blast will limit his ability to find employment and take care of his growing family. Although he has a slight limp and tires easily, his injuries are not readily apparent to someone who does not know him. As he transitions to civilian life, he wonders if he will ever be able to find a job that accommodates his new physical limitations.

For servicemembers and their families, disability and injury is often a real concern and worry. However, if you or a loved one becomes disabled during military service, don't despair; there is support available, including financial and training support that comes in many forms, including support payments, retraining, and accommodations at schools and on the job, just to name a few. Of course, like most government programs, these have specific guidelines and regulations. Educating yourself about these programs is the best way to ensure that you maintain your eligibility and take full advantage. This chapter looks at some of the more common types of disability programs for servicemembers and highlights important pitfalls.

EMPLOYMENT AND DISABLED VETERANS

A veteran who was discharged or released from the military because of a service-connected medical condition or a veteran who is rated for a disability by the Department of Veterans Affairs

(VA) at 30 percent or more may be considered a disabled veteran for employment purposes. (Disability ratings are discussed more on page 308 or 340.) A person rated at 10 to 20 percent by the VA but is deemed to have a serious employment handicap under Section 3016 of Title 38, U.S. Code, is also considered a disabled veteran. Veterans can still be considered disabled veterans years after their service has concluded if they are diagnosed with a medical condition that can be connected to their military service.

A disabled veteran who files an application with the VA is eligible to receive a variety of benefits. These benefits include financial assistance for education programs, vocational rehabilitation to gain new employment, VA-provided medical care for the service-connected medical conditions, home loan assistance, various dependent and survivor benefits, and a monthly disability pension for the veteran depending upon the extent of the disability.

Two federal laws provide important protections for veterans with disabilities when it comes to finding and maintaining employment. The first, the Uniformed Services Employment and Reemployment Rights Act (USERRA), is enforced by the U.S. Department of Labor and sets out the requirements for reemploying veterans with and without service-connected disabilities. Chapter 7 contains more information about USERRA and its application.

The other, Title I of the Americans with Disabilities Act (ADA), is enforced by the U.S. Equal Employment Opportunity Commission, and prohibits both private employers and state and local-government employers with fifteen or more employees from discriminating against individuals on the basis of disability. Under the Rehabilitation Act of 1968, ADA standards apply to federal agencies, including the armed services, and to the U.S. Postal Service.

Together, these laws help disabled servicemembers who seek or hope to maintain a job. This includes legally requiring certain changes, or accommodations, be made to assist a disabled person to complete a given task or by training and retraining disabled veterans for specific employment needs.

Accommodations

Title I of the ADA generally requires employers covered by the act to make reasonable accommodations for disabled employees. An employer makes an accommodation by making physical changes in the workplace or by changing the way work is completed to allow the disabled person to complete his or her assigned work.

Although both USERRA and the ADA include obligations to make reasonable accommodations for the disabled, USERRA goes further than the ADA by requiring employers to make reasonable efforts to assist a veteran who is returning to employment to actually become qualified for a job. The employer must help the veteran become qualified to perform the duties of the position whether or not the veteran has a service-connected disability requiring reasonable accommodation. This can include training or retraining for the position.

▶ **WHAT IS REASONABLE?**

A reasonable accommodation is any modification or adjustment to the work environment or how and when a job is performed. A reasonable accommodation removes workplace barriers that interfere with a disabled veteran's ability to perform the job required by the employer, such as making an existing structure accessible, modifying a work schedule, acquiring or modifying equipment, or other similar adjustments. Reasonable accommodations must allow the disabled veteran to perform the essential functions of the job position. Reasonable accommodations do not include changes to the work environment that cause the employer to incur excessive costs, that are unduly extensive, substantial, or disruptive, or changes that would fundamentally alter the nature or operation of the business. Employers must assess accommodation requests on a case-by-case basis to determine if the requested accommodation will cause undue hardship.

Reasonable accommodations in employment may be available under USERRA for veterans whose service-connected disabilities do not necessarily meet the ADA's definition of "disability." Unlike Title I of the ADA, USERRA also applies to all employers, regardless of size. Information on the reemployment rights of uniformed service personnel can be found on DOL's website at www.dol.gov/vets.

Accommodations will vary depending on the veteran's disability and the specific job. It is not uncommon for veterans with service-connected disabilities to need one or more of the following accommodations to apply for or perform a job:

- written materials in accessible formats, such as large print, Braille, or on computer disk;

- interviews, tests, and training and duty positions held in accessible locations;

- modified equipment or devices (for example, assistive technology that would allow a blind person to use a computer or someone who is deaf or hard of hearing to use a telephone, a glare guard for a computer monitor used by a person with a traumatic brain injury, or a one-handed keyboard for a person missing an arm or hand);

- physical modifications to the workplace (e.g., reconfiguring a workspace, including adjusting the height of a desk or shelves for a person in a wheelchair);

- permission to work from home (i.e. telecommuting to work);

- time off for treatment, recuperation, or training related to disability;

- modified or part-time work schedules;

- a job coach to assist a veteran with initial difficulty in learning or remembering job tasks; or

- reassignment to a new position where a disability prevents performance of the employee's current job, or where accommodating the employee in the current job would result in undue hardship.

The process of providing a reasonable accommodation usually begins with a request from the veteran with a service-connected disability. A family member, friend, health professional, rehabilitation counselor, or other representative also may request a reasonable accommodation on the veteran's behalf. The request does not have to mention the ADA or use the phrase "reasonable accommodation"; it can be a simple oral or written statement indicating that the veteran needs an adjustment or change in the application process or at work for a reason related to a medical condition. A request for a reasonable accommodation is the first step in an informal interactive process between the veteran and the employer.

The next step is to determine whether the veteran has a disability (where this is not obvious or already known) and identify possible accommodations. The employer should ask the veteran what is needed to do his or her job. There are extensive public and private resources to help employers identify reasonable accommodations for employees with particular disabilities. For example, the Job Accommodation Network (JAN) www.askjan .org, provides employers with a practical guide on reasonable accommodations, as well as information on accommodations for specific disabilities, including a section titled "Accommodating Service Members and Veterans with PTSD." After an employer has completed an assessment, the employer must implement the accommodation and ensure that the accommodation is effective.

Many veterans do not view their service-related injuries or medical conditions as disabilities. Thus, they may not ask, or know that they are entitled to ask, for a reasonable accommodation. As a result, employers should be mindful of a veteran's potential needs and initiate a conversation with any veteran who is experiencing work-related problems to determine an appropriate accommodation. Working together, the employer and veteran should identify what the veteran can and cannot do and then discuss ways to address any identified performance issue(s). If an employer refuses to provide a reasonable accommodation upon a request, the veteran may have to file a claim with the

Equal Employment Opportunity Commission or an equivalent state agency.

Many states also have employment laws covering veterans, disabled veterans, or disabled people in general. Many state laws mirror the federal requirements, although some have more protections for disabled employees. For more information, contact your state Veterans Employment Service, a department of the State Employment Service or your state's Department of Veterans Affairs. The agency is listed under state government agencies in the telephone directory.

Vocational Rehabilitation and Training

Vocational rehabilitation and training programs help people with disabilities prepare to return to the workplace. Such assistance can involve career retraining, going back to school, or learning how to continue doing what you've done before, only in a different way. The end goal for vocational rehabilitation and training programs is for the person with a disability to find meaningful employment.

A disabled veteran, (i.e. an individual who has applied for disability benefits from the VA and had his or her application approved) is often eligible for many federal and state-sponsored vocational rehabilitation programs. Such programs can be found by contacting the appropriate state or federal agency and applying for the vocational rehabilitation and training benefit. Often, such benefits are available even before the veteran is released or has separated from the military and state or federal compensation or pension claims are finalized. Accordingly, it is essential for you to explore these benefits as soon as possible before or immediately after separation from the military.

The VA supports a nationwide vocation rehabilitation program for qualified veterans with disabilities related to their service. There are fifty-six regional offices that administer this program. These offices are a good place for employers to recruit qualified disabled veterans. For the number of the nearest vocational rehabilitation office, call the VA's national toll-free num-

ber, 800-827-1000, or visit the VA website at www.vba.va.gov/
bln/vre/index.htm.

Most veterans with service-related disabilities are eligible
for the VA vocational rehabilitation program. Typically, veterans
must have a disability rating of 20 percent or higher, but veterans
with a 10 percent rating also qualify if their service-connected
disabilities pose a significant employment challenge. If a veteran is approved for vocational rehabilitation training, the VA
will pay for the veteran to attend college or a training program
that has a focus on employment. This program also includes
a subsistence stipend. Applications can be made directly to
the VA, but veterans can get help with the application from

WHAT IS A DISABILITY RATING?

If you are a veteran who was injured or developed a medical condition during your military service, you may be entitled to disability
compensation. Veteran benefits are usually provided by the Department of Veterans Affairs (VA).

To obtain these benefits, you must file a claim for disability compensation with the VA and receive a medical examination. The information from this examination will be used by the VA to determine
whether your earning capacity has been reduced by your disability,
and if so, by what percentage. This percentage is the veteran's disability rating. The percentage may range from zero, or no disability, to
100, or complete disability. The greater the disability, the higher the
percentage. In turn, a high percentage entitles a veteran to collect a
greater amount of disability compensation.

The VA uses a disability guide called the *Schedule for Rating Disabilities, www.warms.vba.va.gov/bookc.html* (book C is listed under
Title 38 Code of Federal Regulations), to determine a veteran's disability rating. This schedule provides criteria the VA uses to evaluate
and assess the severity of a disability. It contains a list of medical
conditions and more than 700 diagnostic codes organized under a
variety of body systems.

an accredited service officer. Applicants for the VA vocational rehabilitation program should contact the nearest VA regional office for insight into the job opportunities available in that area.

Many states also have programs to assist veterans or disabled veterans in finding employment and retraining for a new career. For more information on state-level vocational rehabilitation programs, contact your State Veterans Employment Service, a department of the State Employment Service. The agency is usually listed under state government agencies in the telephone directory. You can also search www.va.gov/statedva.htm for links to your state's Department of Veterans Affairs.

▶ EDUCATIONAL ASSISTANCE

The majority of education programs for veterans are administered by the VA, including the GI Bill. Veterans looking for information about how to continue their education must visit the VA GI Bill website located at www.gibill.va.gov. Veterans may also contact the VA regarding educational benefits at 888-442-4551.

Know that the GI Bill is not just for college; it also covers some trade schools that focus on skills such as welding and truck driving. Depending on which GI Bill you are eligible to receive, tuition assistance, book fees, and a monthly stipend may be available. Check your GI Bill eligibility status with the VA to determine which program you are eligible to receive.

In addition to VA education programs, many states offer veterans educational assistance programs. For instance, Illinois has the Illinois Veterans Grant and Texas has the Hazelwood Act; both provide some level of educational assistance to the veteran returning to or beginning college in the state. More information on the state-specific programs can be found at www.va.gov/statedva.htm and using the links to your state's Department of Veterans Affairs.

EDUCATIONAL ACCOMMODATIONS

Many veterans returning to college or entering college for the first time are not aware of how a newly acquired injury (physical or psychological) may impact their learning. This is especially true if the veteran had no learning difficulties prior to military experience. Additionally, a veteran may be discharged from the military without realizing that she or he may experience a significant learning or memory-related impairment, since a true diagnosis of an injury such as post-traumatic stress disorder (PTSD) or mild traumatic brain injury (TBI) can occur long after the veteran has separated from military service. All of this is often compounded by worries about identifying oneself as having a disability. Far too many veterans are unfamiliar with the phrase "reasonable accommodations" and do not know how to access appropriate resources. Therefore, it is all the more important for individuals and educational institutions to be aware of the potential need for accommodations.

Most colleges and universities have an Education Access Office or Department to assist veterans in developing reasonable accommodations in the educational environment. Common accommodations include, but are not limited to, priority registration (to allow extra time between classes, to allow the veteran to select classrooms with fewer distractions), extra time for taking exams, provisions for adaptive equipment, and audio books.

Colleges and other educational institutions turn to the American with Disabilities Act (ADA) and Section 504 of the Rehabilitation Act (Section 504) to defining a "disability" that requires reasonable accommodations. The definition of "disability" within the ADA and Section 504 is quite broad; any condition that affects "major life activities," such as concentration or thinking, may be a disability. However, although the definition of disability is broad, collecting the documentation to obtain a reasonable accommodation can be a challenge.

Delays frequently occur when colleges and other educational institutions ask, either the veteran or the VA, for documentation

▶ **UNDERSTANDING PTSD AND TBI**

PTSD and TBI have several symptoms in common: irritability, anxiety, concentration problems, memory problems, reduced cognitive processing, sleeping disturbances, reduced motivation, and fatigue. These symptoms make learning new things, particularly in a classroom environment, a challenge due to the difficulties in transferring information from the short-term memory to the long-term memory. It is essential that individuals relearn how to focus and problem-solve due to the difficulties with attention and concentration that PTSD and TBI can create.

If you or someone you know has service-connected PTSD or TBI symptoms, the VA has many resources for learning more about these medical condition and obtaining assistance for the condition. Additional resources may be found at:

- www.ptsd.va.gov
- www2.va.gov/directory/guide/ptsd.asp
- www.polytrauma.va.gov

to determine eligibility under the ADA or Section 504 as to what accommodations may be required. The VA and other medical providers often do not adequately document conditions such as impaired concentration or other cognitive difficulties since these concerns are usually a symptom of a medical condition, not necessarily a medical condition in and of themselves. If the medical condition causing impaired concentration or other learning difficulty is not adequately documented in your VA or military medical records, you should have your VA providers or civilian medical provider write a letter specifically describing your limitations and provide it to the educational institution. If the educational institution refuses to make reasonable accommodations after receiving the documentation about your impairment or limitation, you may have a claim with the Equal Employment Opportunity Commission or an equivalent state agency.

If you are a disabled veteran, it is important that you be your own advocate when it comes to obtaining educational assistance. Unlike students who received special education services in high school, veterans may not know what accommodations are necessary for them based on their disability. Additionally, veterans often subordinate personal issues for the good of the unit and it is commonplace for a veteran to still feel uncomfortable requesting special accommodations. However, programs exist for your benefit and because of your service. Take advantage of them.

DISABILITY INCOME AND YOUR DEBTS AND SUPPORT OBLIGATIONS

Don't be fooled into thinking that VA disability compensation payments are fully protected and may never be garnished or otherwise ordered used in the payment of debts. Although there are federal laws in place to protect a veteran's benefits from being seized by commercial creditors through garnishment proceedings, there are some situations when individuals or organizations may be able to collect from these payments.

If you owe the federal government, then the government may reduce your compensation benefits for repayment. For instance, compensation may be taken to repay a federally insured student loan or an overpayment of veteran's benefits or other federal debt. Disability benefits may also be reduced to satisfy unpaid federal taxes. VA-provided disability pensions are considered to be income in bankruptcy proceedings and will be used to calculate how much you can pay on a debt under Chapter 13 repayment plans.

Additionally, most states have determined that disability income from any source (i.e. Social Security benefits, disability insurance payments, workers' compensation, and even VA pension benefits) must be included in the calculations to establish child support obligation orders. This is true even if the veteran's disability benefits are the noncustodial parent's sole means of support.

If a garnishment order is entered against you and the VA is served, or presented, with the order (i.e. someone is trying to garnish your VA benefits), you have the right to appeal. Upon service, the VA will send you a notice that it proposes to reduce your compensation benefit and will provide you the necessary information to appeal the garnishment through VA channels. You will also have to appeal a court-ordered garnishment through the state court that ordered the garnishment in order to fully resolve the issue. If you choose to appeal a court-ordered garnishment, you should get a lawyer to assist you with your appeal. Legal representation ensures that you address all issues to the court regarding the garnishment order. Finding and hiring a civilian lawyer is explained on page 9.

RESOURCES

- **Veterans' Employment and Training Services** (www.dol
  .gov/vets): A Department of Labor agency that offers job-related assistance to veterans, employers, and service providers.

- **National Resource Directory** (www.nad.gov): Connects wounded warriors, servicemembers, veterans, and their families with services and resources at the national, state, and local levels. The employment section enables users to find a job, hire a veteran, and learn about employment laws and workplace support and accommodations.

- **Veterans Employment Resources** (http://askjan.org/ topics/veterans.htm): A list of resources related to veterans' employment issues provided by the Job Accommodation Network.

- **REALifelines** (www.dol.gov/elaws/realifelines.htm): A Department of Labor effort to help wounded and injured servicemembers and veterans access valuable online resources and contact information for one-on-one employment assistance to help them transition into the civilian workforce.

- **You Have a Lot to Offer: Ten Points for Veterans to Consider When Returning to Work With a Disability** (diversity.ucsc.edu/eeo-22/images/veterans_disabilities_work .pdf): A thorough fact sheet developed by Cornell University's Employment and Disability Institute highlighting items veterans should keep in mind as they re-enter the workforce. It contains links to many of the references listed above as well as many other Internet sources that may be useful to a veteran.

- **Job Accommodation Network** (askjan.org): Provides a practical guide for employers on reasonable accommodation, as well as information about accommodations for specific disabilities.

CHAPTER 11

Veterans Benefits

Henry is forty-three and served in the U.S. Army for fifteen years. During his service, Henry spent much of his time as a paratrooper in the 82 Airborne Division. Even after dozens of parachute jumps, Henry's knees felt fine. They did hurt now and again, but he wasn't going to complain to anyone. However, it's been three years since he left the Army and now he has intense, grinding pain in his knees. His doctors have diagnosed him with degenerative arthritis of the knees and are stunned at the disease's progression. The knees of an otherwise healthy forty-three-year-old man shouldn't look like Henry's. One doctor in particular is convinced that Henry's knee condition is related to years of parachuting in the military. Henry knows that the U.S. Department of Veterans Affairs offers disability compensation benefits, but he isn't sure whether or not he qualifies because he never complained about it in service. What documents does he need to submit to the VA? Does he need to gather any evidence himself? How does he go about filing a claim? These are the questions that this chapter will attempt to answer.

Veterans may be eligible for a variety of compensation schemes administered by the United States Department of Veterans Affairs (VA). Although the VA offers a range of services from health care to home loans, this chapter discusses only the service-connected disability and pension benefits. The VA claims and appeals process are also outlined. Information on other VA benefit programs, including education and vocational training, can be found at the VA's website: www.vba.va.gov/VBA/.

VA benefit programs are varied and different; your eligibility and benefits can vary greatly depending on the program and your situation. Veterans who are disabled due to a service-connected disease or injury are eligible for disability compensation. Pension benefits are available based on your need and provide a monthly payment to certain veterans based on income. Survivor benefits are for dependents of veterans whose death was due to a service-connected condition. Education benefits provide money to assist with educational expenses. Each VA benefit has certain eligibility requirements. These requirements largely derive from statutes, Title 38 of the U.S. Code, and VA regulations, Title 38 of the Code of Federal Regulations. Throughout this chapter, keep in mind that if you are requesting VA benefits, the burden of proving you are eligible falls on you. This means that you are responsible to provide the VA with all the evidence necessary to prove each and every legal requirement of your claim.

INITIAL ELIGIBILITY CONSIDERATIONS

Different VA benefits have different qualification requirements. However, in order to be considered a "veteran" in the eyes of the VA, certain service and discharge requirements must be met.

Qualifying Service

For the purposes of VA benefits, a veteran is most often a person who performed active service in the Army, Navy, Marines, Air Force, or Coast Guard and was discharged "under conditions other than dishonorable." Although this requirement seems simple, it can be rather complicated, considering the variety of discharges used by the services and service in the National Guard and Reserve.

Active Service in the Armed Forces Requirement

Service in the United States Armed Forces consists of "active-duty service" in the conventional branches of the military: the Army, Navy, Marines, Air Force, and Coast Guard. Additionally, Reservists who are "called up" to active duty count as having active-duty service equivalent to their time in active duty. Similarly, members of the National Guard who are activated for federal purposes are considered to have active-duty service for that time period. Guard members who are activated for state purposes cannot count that period of service as active-duty service for VA purposes.

Outside of either being called up or activated, National Guard and Reserve members have active service only in very specific circumstances. These circumstances are referred to as active duty for training. Active duty for training is when a Reservist is performing full-time duty for training purposes or when a National Guard member is performing full-time duty for training purposes, at the behest of the federal government. To be considered for VA benefits, the individual on active duty for training must be disabled or have died from a disease or injury that was incurred or aggravated during the training. The important distinction is that if an injury or disease does not occur during the active duty for training, and there is no other qualifying service, then that member is not considered a "veteran" in the eyes of the VA.

Character of Discharge

A veteran must have been discharged or released under conditions other than dishonorable. The various military branches use five types of discharges: honorable discharge, discharge under honorable conditions (or general discharge), discharge under other than honorable conditions, bad conduct discharge, and dishonorable discharge. Note that none of these discharges is specifically labeled as "under conditions other than dishonorable." Due to the difference between how the military and the VA define discharges, it must be determined whether a specific discharge is a discharge under other than dishonorable conditions.

Honorable discharges and discharges under honorable conditions are usually considered to be qualifying discharges. On the flip side, dishonorable discharges are not. It becomes more complicated when the discharge at issue is a discharge under other than honorable conditions or a bad conduct discharge.

> **UNDERSTANDING DISCHARGES**
>
> For more information on the various categories of discharges, and the notice and appeal process, please see page 285–290.

In the case of either a discharge under other than honorable conditions or a bad conduct discharge, the VA will first make a determination as to the character of service. This initial determination will decide whether or not the person's discharge was "under conditions other than dishonorable" or not. The VA will make the decision based on the specific facts of the individual's case and will likely take into account the record of the entire length of service.

Various laws and regulations also help define the types of conduct that will result in a non-qualifying discharge. This conduct includes: accepting an undesirable discharge to escape a trial by general court-martial, mutiny, spying, an offense involving moral turpitude, willful and persistent misconduct, sexual acts involving aggravating circumstances or affecting the performance of duty, and being absent without official leave for 180 continuous days. Any of these factors could increase the chances of a discharge being considered "non-qualifying" for VA benefit purposes.

In the event of being absent without leave, the former servicemember can argue that compelling circumstances caused the unauthorized absence. The VA must then make a factual determination about whether or not those circumstances should excuse the absence. This factual determination also takes into account the overall nature and character of a veteran's service. If the VA finds that compelling circumstances did exist, and the veteran had a good overall service record, then the absence will not prevent a former servicemember from receiving VA benefits. A classic example of a compelling circumstance is when a servicemember was an outstanding soldier, yet went absent in order to take care of a severely ill spouse or parent.

Insanity Exception

An important exception to the character of discharge requirement is the insanity exception. Even if a veteran has a discharge that would normally prevent him or her from receiving VA benefits, if that veteran was insane at the time of committing the acts leading to discharge, he or she may still qualify for benefits.

The term "insanity," legally, can often have different meanings when used in different contexts. In the context of this exception, the VA defines an insane person as:

> One who, while not mentally defective or constitutionally psychopathic . . . exhibits, due to disease a more or less prolonged deviation from his normal method of behavior; or who interferes with the peace of society; or who has so departed (become antisocial) from the accepted standards of the community to which by birth and education he belongs as to lack the adaptability to make further adjustment to the social customs of the community in which he resides.

This definition is very different from the common criminal definition of insanity, usually involving knowing the difference between right and wrong. In order to successfully use the insanity exception for VA benefits, the veteran should obtain a medical opinion, or other medical evidence, that uses the VA language defining insanity. This medical opinion should also specify that the veteran was suffering from the insanity at the time of the commission of the relevant acts. The evidence does not need to state that the insanity necessarily caused the acts, just that the insanity was present at the time.

Wartime and Peacetime Service

Some, but not all, VA benefits require that the veteran have served during a period of war. Most importantly, wartime service is a requirement in order to receive VA pension. Congress passed statutes that define periods of war. In the relevant part, the periods of war are as follows:

- **World War II:** December 7, 1941–December 31, 1946;
- **Korean Conflict:** June 27, 1950–January 31, 1955;
- **Vietnam Era:** August 5, 1964–May 7, 1975; and
- **Persian Gulf War:** August 2, 1990–a date to be prescribed by presidential proclamation or law.

It is important to note that since 1990, the United States has been in a period of war. This obviously includes the wars in Iraq and Afghanistan, as well as the global war on terror at large since 1990.

The actual location of service does not matter in determining wartime service. The veteran need not have been deployed to a combat zone. All that needs to be shown is that the veteran's time in service coincided with one of the above periods of war.

Length of Service

Length of service normally does not factor into eligibility for the most used VA benefits. Technically, a veteran must have served for either twenty-four months of continuous active duty or the full period for which the veteran was called to active duty.

Most of the time, a veteran whose service did not last for a full twenty-four months would still meet the length of service requirement because he or she served the full period for which he or she was called. This would include National Guard members and Reservists who were called to active duty, served their full period, and then were subsequently deactivated. Similarly, veterans who were discharged or retired due to a service-connected disability meet the length of service requirement. Although the length of service requirement is usually easy to meet, veterans who were discharged before twenty-four months of service or their full period of enlistment due to a reduction of forces would be ineligible to receive other VA benefits aside from service-connected disability benefits.

A major exception to the length of service requirement is that entitlement to service-connected disability compensation in general does not require twenty-four months of active-duty service. If a servicemember is injured or gets a disabling disease during active duty, that injury or disease will be eligible for service connection no matter the overall length of service.

Willful Misconduct

A VA finding that a disability was the result of willful misconduct will disqualify that disability as the basis for a host of benefits. The VA defines willful misconduct as "an act involving conscious wrongdoing or known prohibited action." The VA applies a presumption that injuries or death suffered while on active duty are not due to willful misconduct. However, if the VA can show that willful misconduct did take place and caused the disability, then benefits regarding that disability can be denied. Due to the powerful nature of a finding of willful misconduct, the rules regarding such misconduct are part of the initial consideration for most VA benefits. Just like other reasons the VA denies a claim, a finding of willful misconduct can be appealed to a Decision Review Officer or the Board of Veterans Appeals, which will be discussed later in this chapter.

A disability that results from willful misconduct cannot be considered when determining: service connection, non-service–connected pension, service-connected death, vocational rehabilitation, and extending the deadline for use of education or vocational rehabilitation benefits.

Common examples of willful misconduct include alcohol and drug abuse. The VA has established specific rules for each of these types of misconduct. Regarding alcohol: If the disability results from the use of alcohol to "enjoy its intoxicating effects," then any injuries resulting from the use of alcohol would be considered the result of willful misconduct. This means that if the VA can show that an injury was caused by drunkenness, either directly or indirectly, then that injury probably could not be the basis for VA benefits.

The use of illegal drugs is treated much like the use of alcohol. If drugs are used to "enjoy or experience their effects" and

> ▶ **USING DRUGS OR ALCOHOL TO COPE WITH A DISABILITY**
>
> There is a special exception when considering a drug or alcohol use or addiction stemming from a service-connected disability. If a member is using drugs or alcohol as a result of such a disability, any injury resulting from that use or addiction is not considered willful misconduct.

such use results in injury or death, the injury or death will be considered due to willful misconduct. This includes both the resultant conduct from a single use, and the effects of drug use to the point of addiction. The definition of illegal drugs include prescription drugs that are not used for their medical purposes or are illegally obtained. Willful misconduct cannot result from drugs that are taken legally, such as prescribed painkillers. This is true even when the use of the legal drugs develops into an addiction.

Another important point regarding both alcohol and drug use is that a veteran can still receive compensation for alcohol- and drug-related disabilities that occur as a direct result of a service-connected disability. This means that if an alcohol or drug addiction is directly connected to a service-connected disability, the veteran can still receive benefits. This is seen most often in the context of service-connected mental disorders. Veterans who abuse drugs or alcohol due to self-medication of a mental disorder or other disability can receive compensation for any resulting disabilities. Any death resulting from secondarily connected drug or alcohol use could also be considered service connected. This would have a tremendous impact on the benefits for a veteran's survivors because major survivor benefits, most notably dependency and indemnity compensation (known as DIC) depend on whether or not the veteran's death was service-connected. More information on survivor's benefits can be found on page 231 or by visiting benefits.va.gov/persona/ dependent_survivor.asp.

The Fugitive Felon Rule and Incarceration

Even if a veteran fully qualifies for VA benefits, the fugitive felon rule may still present a hurdle. The rule prohibits the payment of benefits to a veteran who is considered a fugitive felon. According to the VA, a veteran is a fugitive felon if he or she is avoiding prosecution or confinement for a crime that is a felony in the state from which he or she is fleeing. A veteran who has violated a condition of probation and parole connected to the commission of a felony is also considered a fugitive felon. Significantly, the VA can recoup any benefit payments paid to a fugitive felon.

There is also a statutory bar for veterans who are incarcerated. When convicted of a felony, benefits will be terminated upon the sixty-first day of incarceration and remain precluded until the end of the incarceration. Like payments made to fugitive felons, any payments made after the sixty-first day of incarceration will be later recouped by the VA.

SERVICE-CONNECTED DISABILITY BENEFITS

The Veterans Benefits Administration's mission statement reads, "The mission of the Disability Compensation program is to provide monthly payments to veterans in recognition of the effects of disabilities, diseases, or injuries incurred or aggravated during active military service, and to provide access to other VA benefits. The Compensation Program also provides monthly payments, as specified by law, to surviving spouses, dependent children and dependent parents in recognition of the economic loss caused by the veteran's death during active military service or, subsequent to discharge from military service, as a result of a service-connected disability."

Service-connected disability payments make up the largest category of benefits paid out by the VA and consist of fixed monthly payments based on the level of the veteran's disability. These types of benefits are available only for disabilities, injuries,

QUESTIONS FOR ESTABLISHING ELIGIBILITY FOR VA BENEFITS

Does veteran have qualifying service?

Was service during wartime or peacetime?

Was the veteran's service at least 24-months long?

Note that this does apply to service-connected benefits.

Was the veteran's service active?

What type of discharge did the veteran receive?

Does the veteran meet the fugitive felon and incarceration rules?

or diseases that were incurred or aggravated during service. This means that nearly every claim regarding a service-connected disability should somehow relate to events that occurred during a veteran's service. The various legal requirements all reflect the idea that the VA is compensating a veteran for something that happened in service and is now affecting the veteran's life.

Proving Service Connection and the Benefit of the Doubt Doctrine

Every VA claimant has the ultimate burden of proving to the VA each and every requirement for his or her claim. However, the VA must apply the "benefit of the doubt" doctrine in deciding whether or not to grant a claim. If the VA is deciding a claim and the evidence is roughly balanced by law, the VA must give the benefit of the doubt to the veteran. For example, in order to prove service connection, a veteran will have to meet many different requirements and prove a number of individual facts; the benefit of the doubt doctrine will apply to each individual requirement and fact. This doctrine differs greatly from that of other administrative benefits schemes, like the Social Security Administration, which requires claimants to prove entitlement by the "preponderance of the evidence" and does not apply any benefit of the doubt. Due to the powerful nature of this doctrine, it should be argued whenever there is evidence both in favor of and against granting a claim. It is important to keep the impact of the burden of doubt doctrine in mind when examining the elements of service connection outlined below.

Elements of Service Connection

Establishing service connection for any given disability requires medical evidence of a current disability, evidence of an in-service incurrence or aggravation of a disease or injury and medical evidence of a nexus between the current disability and the in-service incurrence or aggravation. In other words, a veteran must prove to the VA that he or she suffers from a disability and that more likely than not, the disability is related to an event that happened in service.

As these requirements are very fact intensive, different types of evidence are often necessary. Because the requirements focus on medical issues, much of the evidence will be from a medical expert or professional. This type of evidence, usually a doctor's letter or opinion, is what is referred to by the term "medical evidence." "Lay evidence," on the other hand, is evidence submitted by someone who is not a medical professional, such as statements made by family members or other people who served with the veteran. Each of the sections below details whether lay evidence is accepted for a given requirement and how such evidence is valued.

Current Disability

If a veteran is seeking disability compensation, he or she must currently be suffering from that disability. Although medical evidence is nearly always required to establish a current disability, lay evidence may also be enough to establish a diagnosis of a condition when a layperson is competent to identify the medical condition, the layperson is reporting a contemporaneous medical diagnosis or lay testimony describing symptoms at the time supports a later diagnosis by a medical professional.

The VA has a duty to provide a medical examination or opinion when it is "necessary to make a decision on the claim." Often, when a claim for benefits is made, the VA will schedule the veteran for a compensation and pension exam (C&P) at the VA hospital used by the veteran. This means that when a veteran files a claim simply listing symptoms of a condition that could be related to service, a C&P is scheduled. The C&P will provide the actual medical record, which the VA counts as evidence of a current disability. Of course, a veteran could submit evidence of a diagnosis obtained from his or her own physician to satisfy this requirement or challenge the C&P exam results.

In-Service Incurrence or Aggravation

An in-service incurrence or aggravation of a disease or injury can be established by both lay and medical evidence. Oftentimes, a veteran's service records will be enough to prove that a condition occurred or was aggravated during service. Such records may indicate that the veteran received treatment for an injury, was diagnosed with a disease or disorder, or may include other information that may tend to prove an in-service incurrence or aggravation. A veteran's personal service records can be obtained by completing and submitting Form SF-180. Often, veterans may remember an injury or event from service but never reported the event or received treatment for the injury. Unless the veteran is a combat veteran, as discussed below, simple statements years after service about something that happened in service will generally not be accepted by the VA, and this is where lay evidence becomes important. It is important to get treated for a disease or injury while in service. Such treatment will create a record that

▶ WHAT COUNTS AS BEING IN SERVICE?

For active-duty veterans, any circumstances leading to any injury or disease can qualify for service connection. There is no requirement that the injury or disease be related to military duties or even that the injury occurred while on a military installation. All that has to happen is that the injury or disease first occurs after the time the servicemember enters service and before the servicemember is discharged. In this sense, there is no difference between a gunshot wound in combat and a sprained ankle from a stateside volleyball game, as long as the injury occurred during active-duty service. This is also true for National Guard members activated to federal duty. As long as the injury occurs between the date of activation and the date of deactivation, it will count as being in service for the purpose of veteran's benefits. Guard members who are activated should receive a DD-214 record listing the dates of the activation.

can later be used to substantiate a claim for service-connected benefits.

In the event that there is no mention of the incident in the service records, alternative evidence must be gathered in order to prove to the VA that the in-service incident happened. Alter-

▶ AN IMPORTANT NOTE: PRE-EXISTING CONDITIONS AND THE PRESUMPTION OF SOUNDNESS

Some veterans may have suffered from an injury or disease before entering service, which was aggravated after an in-service event. The VA takes a special approach to these conditions, which are referred to as pre-existing conditions. The VA will not consider a pre-existing condition to be connected to a veteran's service unless there is aggravation of the injury or condition during service. Aggravation is essentially an event, or series of events, which causes a pre-existing condition to get worse. The worsening of the pre-existing condition must be beyond the natural progression of the specific condition. This needs to be shown by medical evidence. For example, a doctor's letter stating that a thirty-five-year-old veteran's degenerative joint disease has progressed beyond what the doctor would normally expect in a thirty-five-year-old who hadn't suffered an injury would be evidence of the aggravation of injury during service.

Federal law states that veterans are presumed to have entered the military in sound condition: "[E]very veteran shall be taken to have been in sound condition when examined, accepted, and enrolled for service, except as to defects, infirmities, or disorders noted at the time of the examination, acceptance, and enrollment, or where clear and unmistakable evidence demonstrates that the injury or disease existed before acceptance and enrollment and was not aggravated by such service" (38 U.S. Code Section 1111). To rebut, or disprove, this presumption of soundness, the VA must show by clear and unmistakable evidence both that the condition existed before entering service and that it was not aggravated by service.

native evidence can include newspaper articles, letters home describing the event sent during service, and statements of friends and family members. Another key piece of alternative evidence is a buddy statement. This is a statement by a veteran or servicemember who, for whatever reason, was present during the incident. If the veteran has no direct contacts with other veterans who might have been present, often the Internet can be used to locate other servicemembers and veterans who may have witnessed the incident.

Certain categories of veterans are treated more generously: combat veterans' lay statements must be "accepted as sufficient proof of service connection if the evidence is consistent with the circumstances, conditions or hardships of such service even though there is no official record of such incurrence or aggravation." The VA allows lay statements from these veterans because records aren't often created during combat situations and seemingly minor injuries can create major problems in the veteran's future. However, the incident must have occurred while the veteran was "engaged in combat." For former prisoners of war, omission of history or findings from clinical records made upon returning is not determinative of service connection.

Nexus Between the Current Disability and the In-Service Event

The final step in proving a service-connected disability is showing a causative link between the current disability and the in-service occurrence. This link is referred to as the nexus. A nexus between the claimed in-service disease or injury and the present disease or injury can be shown through a variety of ways: direct service connection, aggravation of pre-service disability, by way of statutory or regulatory presumption, and conditions that are proximately due to, or aggravated by, a service-connected disease or injury ("secondary service connection"). Additionally, compensation may also be awarded to individuals who become disabled due to VA treatment or vocational rehabilitation.

> ## ▶ GETTING ASSISTANCE FOR CLAIMS INVOLVING THE PRESUMPTION OF SOUNDNESS
>
> Claims that involve the presumption of soundness are often very technical in nature. "Clear and unmistakable evidence" is a very specific legal term referring to a specific level of evidence. Furthermore, the evidence required changes depending on whether or not the VA can properly rebut the presumption. Due to this complexity, it may be especially helpful to seek the advice of a lawyer or veterans service organization representative for assistance in navigating these issues.

In determining whether a nexus exists, the VA considers the circumstances of the veteran's service as shown by service records, medical records, and all other pertinent medical and lay evidence. This determination must be made based upon the entire record and a broad and liberal interpretation of the facts of each individual case. Different rules apply to each theory when attempting to prove the requisite nexus.

No matter which method is used to show a nexus, you will want to have medical evidence to demonstrate the nexus. Many claims are denied because there is no medical evidence in the file linking the injury to the in-service event. The VA will not take a veteran's word that a current condition is related to something that happened in service. Even if the connection seems relatively easy to comprehend, such as an ankle disability due to a severe ankle injury in service, the VA will not connect the disability to service without medical evidence specifying that the disability is related to service. The importance of medical evidence is paramount, regardless of the method used.

There are a number of ways to show a nexus, including a direct service connection, a pre-existing condition, statutory presumptions, or a secondary service-connection injury or disability. These methods are detailed below.

> ## THE "AS LIKELY AS NOT" STANDARD

Throughout the discussion of the different methods of relating a disability to service, the phrase "as likely as not" is frequently used. "As likely as not" refers to the likelihood, in the opinion of a medical professional, that the disability is related to the in-service event. Under this standard, the medical professional must, in his or her judgment, determine that there is at least a 50 percent chance that the disability is related to service. This phrase often comes as a surprise to medical professionals, who are used to the phrase "medical certainty" when making medical determinations. When seeking out medical evidence from a medical professional, make sure the professional understands that he or she needs only to determine that the disability "as likely as not" relates to service and that the relationship does not need to be within a medical certainty.

Direct Service Connection

A direct service connection means that the particular disability or injury happened during active-duty service. A direct service connection is considered the traditional method of obtaining a service connection finding. A nexus is established through direct service connection if medical evidence shows the current disability is "as likely as not" linked to the in-service injury, disease, or event.

A direct service connection can also be established for chronic conditions (whose symptoms may come and go despite the condition being permanent) and conditions that have a continuing symptomology. Although these methods typically make use of statutory presumptions (discussed on page 333), the VA considers the theories of chronicity and continuing symptomology as a subset of direct service connection. By statute, Congress established certain conditions as chronic and authorized the VA to expand the list as needed in the future. Establishing chronicity, the term used for service-connecting a chronic disease, is made easier if the veteran suffers from a disease recognized by the VA. If a veteran can show that one of the listed chronic diseases first manifested during service and continues to exist, the condition will be considered directly service connected. If a disease is not on the list of presumptively chronic conditions, medical reference materials or a physician's statement can be used to show that the disease is, in fact, chronic.

A veteran with an acute condition, a condition that has only lasts for a short time, during service, which then manifests again later in life may make a direct service connection through the theory of continuity of symptomology. The term "continuity of symptomology" means that even though the condition isn't recognized as chronic by the medical community, the veteran is still suffering from symptoms due to the condition's first appearance in service. Service connection through this theory can be established by showing evidence that a condition was "noted" during service or within one year of service, evidence showing post-service continuity of symptomology, and/or medical or lay evidence of a nexus between the present disability and the post-service symptomology. All of the requirements must be satisfied or the claim will be denied as being unrelated to the veteran's service. In determining whether or not a condition was "noted" during service, the VA will focus on the symptoms found in the veteran's file and not the exact diagnosis. Often, both lay evidence and supporting medical opinions are used to verify both the post-service continuity of symptomology and the nexus between that symptomology and the current disability.

Aggravation of a Pre-existing Condition

As discussed briefly on page 328, compensation may be awarded for a condition that started before a veteran entered service but where there is an increase in disability due to the condition becoming aggravated during service. Proving aggravation requires medical evidence of a permanent increase in severity of the condition that took place while the veteran was in service. Compensation will not be awarded for an increase shown by clear and unmistakable evidence to be due to the natural progression of the disease. Furthermore, service connection will be denied for the usual effects of medical and surgical treatment where a condition manifests itself during service and surgery or treatment is used to address the condition.

Statutory Presumptions

A nexus can still be shown even if there is no record of evidence during military service by way of any number of statutory presumptions. Statutory presumptions essentially allow veterans to qualify for service connection without needing to show that their current disability is "as likely as not" related to a specific in-service event. Instead, where the veteran's service meets specific time, place, and manner of service requirements and the veteran has certain medical conditions, those conditions are presumed to have occurred during active-duty service.

Secondary Service Connection

A secondary condition that is the result of a primary service-connected condition may be enough to show a nexus between an in-service incident and the current condition. For example, a veteran who has a service-connected finding for a right leg injury can obtain secondary service connection for a problem with his left leg caused by having to limp as a result of the first injury. Again, the veteran must show through medical evidence that the secondary condition was "as likely as not" proximately due to or the result of the primary condition.

▶ UNDERSTANDING A PRESUMPTION

In legal discussions, a presumption is a very specific term. A presumption creates an assumption, legally, that a certain fact exists. This means that if a presumption is in your favor, it will be assumed that a fact that helps your position exists, and the other party (in the cases discussed here, the VA) will have the burden of proving the opposite.

QUESTIONS FOR DETERMINING THAT A VETERAN'S DISABILITY IS SERVICE CONNECTED

Is the disability current?

Was there an in-service occurrence or aggravation?

Is there a nexus between the current disability and the in-service event?

This can be shown through:

Direct service connection

A secondary service connection

Aggravation of a pre-existing condition

Statutory presumptions

POST-TRAUMATIC STRESS DISORDER AND YOUR BENEFITS

Although most mental disorders follow the rules detailed in the previous section for proving a service connection, post-traumatic stress disorder (PTSD) follows a slightly different set of requirements. Establishing a service connection for PTSD can be complicated, as there are numerous regulations, cases, and manual provisions that can apply. Generally, a veteran must show three things: a medical diagnosis of PTSD, credible supporting evidence of an in-service stressor, and a link, shown by medical evidence, between the symptoms of PTSD and the in-service stressor.

Diagnosis of PTSD

A veteran's diagnosis of PTSD must be made by an expert who is competent to diagnose PTSD and must also follow the guidelines of the DSM-IV. Although a diagnosis of PTSD that occurs during service would simplify the claim, a diagnosis of PTSD can still be made years after service. Similar to other disability claims, the diagnosis must merely support the fact that the veteran "as likely as not" suffers from the disorder.

Once a diagnosis of PTSD is submitted, the VA cannot reject the diagnosis of a proper expert unless it can list adequate reasons for rejecting the opinion and cite medical evidence in the record to support those reasons. If there is a mix of positive and negative evidence, the VA may weigh the conflicting evidence and conclude whether or not a veteran has PTSD. Regardless, the VA must still follow the benefit of the doubt doctrine when weighing the evidence.

The In-Service Stressor

The second requirement for a PTSD claim is proof that a stressor "as likely as not" occurred in service. Any extreme traumatic event that satisfies the diagnostic criteria of the DSM-IV

▶ **FINDING A MEDICAL EXPERT**

Fortunately, PTSD now has a heightened awareness among the military's health care providers. As a result, more servicemembers are properly diagnosed with PTSD. However, service connection for PTSD can still be obtained even if diagnosed long after service. Most of the time, these diagnoses are obtained by VA psychiatrists and psychologists; however, private mental health professionals can also provide a diagnosis. Professional counselors and other licensed clinical professionals can also make a diagnosis of PTSD, as long as the diagnosis comports to the DSM-IV.

can be accepted as a stressor. Although combat experience is often the claimed stressor, such experience is not required for a veteran with PTSD to be eligible for benefits. However, when the claimed stressor is based on combat experience or fear of hostile military or terrorist activity, the evidence requirements are significantly liberalized.

The requirement that a stressor be corroborated by evidence is significantly relaxed for combat veterans. The VA PTSD regulations allow a combat veteran's lay testimony to establish the occurrence of the in-service stressor where that stressor is consistent with the "circumstances, conditions, or hardships of the veteran's service." The evidence still must establish that the veteran was engaged in combat with the enemy and that the stressor, by the veteran's own statement, was related to that combat. Evidence of combat experience includes the veteran's military occupational specialty, military decorations, awards, and citations. Buddy statements or letters home to family and friends can also be evidence of combat experience.

In 2010, the VA amended its PTSD regulation to eliminate the need for corroborating evidence of a stressor if it "is related to the veteran's fear of hostile military or terrorist activity." This revision was made in direct response to the nature of the conflicts in Iraq and Afghanistan. The definition of "hostile military or terrorist activity" includes: "a veteran experienced, witnessed, or was confronted with an event or circumstance that involved actual or threatened death or serious injury, or a threat to the physical integrity of the veteran or others, such as from an actual or potential improvised explosive device; vehicle-imbedded explosive device; incoming artillery, rocket, or mortar fire; grenade; small arms fire, including suspected sniper fire; or attack upon friendly military aircraft, and the veteran's response to the event or circumstance involved a psychological or psycho-physiological state of fear, helplessness, or horror." Although mainly aimed at veterans who served in Iraq and Afghanistan, the regulation does not specify that the stressor need have taken place in those theaters.

In cases where the requirement for corroborating evidence has not been eased, the veteran must provide "credible support-ing evidence that the claimed in-service stressor occurred." This evidence is often found in the veteran's service record. Although the service record need not corroborate every detail of the veter-

> ### WHAT TO DO IF YOUR CLAIM FOR PTSD IS DENIED
>
> The first thing to do if a claim for PTSD is denied is to find out why the claim was denied by the VA. Read the rating decision carefully. The reason for the denial will usually be that there is no evidence to support one of the requirements for PTSD service connection. Is there no diagnosis? Work with a VA or private medical professional to determine whether or not a PTSD diagnosis is appropriate in your case. No evidence of the in-service stressor? Request your in-service records using Form SF-180 or work to obtain alternative evidence of the event such as buddy statements. In either case, a lawyer or vet-erans service organization representative can help determine what needs to be done in order to substantiate your claim.

an's claimed stressor, there still must be evidence that indicates a stressful event that the veteran actually experienced. Other sources of evidence that may satisfy this requirement include "buddy" statements, which are lay statements of veterans who personally observed the event and can corroborate the occurrence of that event. Note that a medical opinion recounting the in-service stressor is not relevant toward the requirement of proving that a stressor occurred. Lay evidence is best submitted by those who have personal knowledge of the stressful event. Remember, the "benefit of the doubt" doctrine applies when the VA is deciding whether the in-service stressor occurred.

Link Between In-Service Stressor and Symptoms of PTSD

The last step in proving eligibility for PTSD is to provide evidence from a medical expert that demonstrates a link between the veteran's diagnosis of PTSD and the in-service stressor. Oftentimes, the diagnosis of PTSD will contain the link between the stressor and the current symptoms. If the veteran has a current diagnosis of PTSD, this requirement is usually easy to satisfy. Because the VA recognizes that PTSD can develop years after service, the passage of time between the in-service stressor and the current symptoms will not discount a link between the two that is backed by medical evidence.

ESTABLISHING THE PERCENTAGE OF DISABILITY

Once a service connection has been established for any disability, the VA then determines a disability rating. A disability rating reflects, on average, the extent to which the earning potential of a veteran with that given injury or disability will be effected. After a service connection has been established, the VA assigns a disability rating percentage according to the Schedule for

PROVING A SERVICE CONNECTION FOR POST-TRAUMATIC STRESS DISORDER REQUIRES:

An expert diagnosis of PTSD

Evidence of an in-service stressor

A link between the in-service stressor and the PTSD symptoms

Rating Disabilities (Rating Schedule). Disability rating percentages are set in increments of ten. However, a determination of service connection does not necessarily warrant a compensable disability rating. A veteran can have a service-connected injury or disease, but could be rated at a noncompensable zero percent.

The disability rating percentage corresponds to a monthly payment made by the VA. The higher the percentage, the higher the payment made to the veteran. The actual amount of the payments is set by statute and can be found on the VA's website at www.benefits.va.gov/compensation/rates-index.asp.

Using the Rating Schedule

The Rating Schedule is a series of tables that contains the disabilities recognized by the VA. The tables are organized by the systems of the body, e.g. musculoskeletal, endocrine, gastrointestinal, etc. Each table contains a series of diagnostic codes made up of five numbers. The diagnosis of each disability should relate to one or more diagnostic codes. The diagnostic code lists several sets of symptoms for that diagnosis. These symptoms then relate to a specific disability rating. As the severity of the symptoms increases, the percentage of disability rating generally increases.

When evaluating a disability claim, the VA examines the veteran's medical records to determine the appropriate medical diagnosis and corresponding diagnostic code. The VA then determines the degree of disability that corresponds with the veteran's symptoms.

Special Rules Regarding Disability Percentages

In addition to using the Rating Schedule, the VA has special rules that further complicate the issue of finding an appropriate disability percentage. Each of these complications is outlined below.

Multiple Disabilities

Many veterans are confused as to why, when, for example, they have multiple service-connected disabilities rated at 30 percent, 20 percent, and 10 percent, their disability rating is only fifty percent, instead of sixty percent. This is because when a veteran has multiple disabilities, the VA does not simply add up the ratings. Instead, the VA combines the disabilities together using the Combined Ratings Table to prevent a veteran from receiving more than 100 percent disability. Without going too far into the reasoning behind the table, the VA considers each veteran possessing a maximum of 100 percent "disability." After taking into account the disability with the greatest rating, the VA then calculates any subsequent ratings against any remaining portions of disability that have yet to be awarded. All percentages ending in "5" or greater are rounded up to the nearest multiple of ten. Percentages ending in "1" through "4" are rounded down.

The math to combine ratings can get rather complex quickly.

Therefore, the VA simply uses the table to do the math for it. The table can be found at www.benefits.va.gov/compensation/resources_comp01.asp.

Rule Against Pyramiding

The Rule Against Pyramiding prohibits a veteran from being doubly compensated for the same symptoms through two different disabilities. For example, if a veteran was experiencing a depressed mood and the inability to maintain social relationships due to both PTSD and a separate anxiety disorder, the VA would rate the veteran only for the disability predominately causing the symptoms, and not for both. However, if both mental conditions were causing different symptoms—for example, if the depressed mood was from PTSD and the inability to maintain social relationships was due to the anxiety disorder—then the VA should still assign the veteran a rating for both.

Analogous Ratings

Although the Rating Schedule contains codes for many disabilities, it does not contain all of them. If a veteran has a disability

▶ **COMBINED RATINGS TABLE IN ACTION**

Let's look at an example of the Combined Ratings Table in action. As an example, combining 30 percent and 20 percent would result in a 40 percent rating. After taking 30 percent from a total possible 100 percent, a veteran is left with 70 percent of un-awarded disability. Twenty percent, the next established rating, is then taken from the remaining 70 percent, resulting in 14 percent for that disability. Thirty percent, the original, largest rating, is then added to the 14 percent, to result in 44 percent. This is rounded down to 40 percent.

not listed in the Rating Schedule, the VA must find a closely related disability to use as a basis for a rating. The closely related disability should largely mirror the location of the real condition, the effect on the body of the real condition, and the symptoms of the real condition. A veteran can argue that the VA should have used a different rating than the analogous rating assigned using the same appeals process as for any other claim (more information on this can be found on page 353).

The Bilateral Factor

When a certain disability affects both sides of the body, an additional 10 percent is added to the combined rating for the two disabilities. This additional percentage is referred to as the bilateral factor. For example, service-connected neuropathy affecting both legs would result in each leg being rated separately and then an additional 10 percent added to the combined rating of both legs.

The Amputation Rule

The amputation rule limits the ratings veterans can receive for certain types of injuries. Under the rule, the combined ratings for an extremity or digit cannot exceed the rating that would be assigned if the entire extremity had been amputated. Therefore, disabilities for knee, ankle, and foot cannot have a combined rating greater than what would be received if the whole leg was amputated.

Increasing a Service-Connected Disability Rating

Once a disability is service connected and assigned a rating, the rating can be increased at any time if the disability worsens. A formal application for benefits is not required; a letter to the VA is enough to request a rating change. The letter should describe the service-connected disability and state how the disability has gotten worse. It is important to describe every symptom in as much detail as possible. For example, if the veteran suffers from nightmares or flashbacks, describe how many times per week or month they happen. Often, the VA will schedule an exam upon receipt of the claim for an increase. Much like the letter, describe your symptoms to the VA physician in as much detail as possible. Finally, other private medical evidence can be submitted as well.

Total Disability Based on Individual Unemployability

Total disability based on individual unemployability (TDIU) allows a veteran with a disability rating of less than 100 percent to receive the same amount of money per month as someone with a 100 percent disability rating. In order to qualify, the veteran must meet certain service-connected disability requirements and be unable to secure a substantially gainful occupation due to his or her service-connected disabilities.

First, the veteran must have one service-connected disability rated above 60 percent, or two or more service-connected disabilities, one of at least 40 percent, which combine to a rating of at least 70 percent. Second, the veteran must be unable to secure a substantially gainful occupation as a result of the service-connected disabilities. When making this determination, the VA will consider evidence of the veteran's education and occupational history. For example, if the veteran's education and work history was in carpentry and the veteran lost the use of his hands due to a service-connected disability, the veteran would be able to argue that his disability prevents him from working and the veteran is entitled to TDIU. There is no basis in the law for the VA to expect any sort of retraining once TDIU is established. However, evidence that retraining would be insufficient, impractical, or impossible would be convincing evidence that TDIU should be granted in the first place.

Non-Service–Connected Pension

Non-service–connected pension is another major category of benefits provided by the VA. Similar to service-connected benefits, if a veteran can prove that he or she is entitled to a pension, he or she will receive a monthly payment. Unlike service-connected benefits, pension payments are limited by the veteran's income. This is because a pension is a needs-based benefit designed to assist veterans who have served during a period of war and who are disabled, for any reason, such that they cannot work. Even though a veteran need not be disabled due to a service-connected disease, there are still strict requirements in order to be entitled to a pension.

Pension Requirements

The three main requirements to establish eligibility for pension are service during a period of war, permanent and total disability, and yearly income below the maximum annual pension rate (MAPR).

▶ SUBSTANTIALLY GAINFUL OCCUPATION

The Court of Appeals for Veterans Claims has defined a substantially gainful occupation as "an occupation that provides the veteran with an annual income that exceeds the poverty threshold for one person, irrespective of the number of hours or days that the veteran actually works." The poverty threshold is established by the U.S. Department of Commerce Bureau of the Census. Currently, the poverty threshold for one person under age 65 is $11,702 per year (www.census.gov/hhes/www/poverty/data/threshld/index.html). If the veteran makes less than this amount per year, he or she is not necessarily disqualified from TDIU. The VA can still evaluate the veteran's marginal employment and determine whether or not it is evidence that a substantially gainful occupation can be maintained.

Service During a Period of War

The veteran must have served a total of ninety days during one or more periods of war; ninety or more consecutive days, one of which is during a period of war; or at least one day of wartime service that results in a discharge for a service-connected disability. All veterans who have served since August 2, 1990, are considered to have served during the Persian Gulf/Global War on Terror era and consequently have wartime service. The other periods of war are listed on page 320.

Permanent and Total Disability

The second requirement is that the veteran is permanently and totally disabled. Remember, the disabilities that render a veteran permanently and totally disabled do not need to be service connected. However, the VA still uses the Rating Schedule to rate the non-service–connected disabilities. Total disability generally refers to a finding that the veteran is 100 percent non-service–connected. The way the VA goes about this finding is exactly the same as with service-connected benefits (see page 338 on establishing disability percentages). With submitted medical evidence, the VA identifies the different conditions the veteran is

▶ **NONMILITARY BENEFITS: SUPPLEMENTAL SECURITY INCOME**

Another common needs-based disability benefit is supplemental security income (SSI) provided by the U.S. Social Security Administration. SSI pays benefits to disabled adults and children who have a limited or no income. Visit www.socialsecurity.gov/pgm/ssi.htm for more information, or contact a lawyer who specializes in obtaining SSI benefits. Often, VA pension and SSI are applied for at the same time. As discussed in this section, SSI will not count toward income when calculating the amount of VA pension benefits.

QUALIFYING FOR A NON-SERVICE CONNECTED PENSION REQUIRES:

Service during a period of war

Meeting income requirements

Permanent and total disability

suffering from and examines the symptoms of those conditions. The VA then applies the Rating Schedule to those symptoms to arrive at disability ratings for those conditions. The ratings are then combined with the Combined Ratings Table. Remember, the conditions need not be service-connected; any condition the veteran is suffering from counts toward the total rating for pension purposes.

Fortunately, there are two easier ways to prove permanent and total disability; if a veteran is over age sixty-five or a patient in a nursing home, the VA will consider that veteran permanently and totally disabled.

Income Requirement

In order to be eligible for a VA pension, the veteran and his or her dependents must have a yearly income that does not exceed the MAPR. As of the publishing of this book, the base MAPR for a single veteran with no dependents is $12,256 per year. The MAPR for a married veteran, or a single veteran with one dependent, is $16,051 per year. Additional dependents further add to this amount. To find MAPR amounts for veterans with dependents and updated MAPR numbers, visit http://benefits .va.gov/pensionandfiduciary/pension/rates_veteran_pen12.asp.

To calculate the monthly payment, the veteran's income during a year is subtracted from the MAPR. This amount is then divided by twelve to determine the monthly payment. All income should be reported in the initial application for benefits. Additionally, the veteran's spouse's and dependents' incomes should also be reported, regardless of the source. After reporting annual income on the initial application, income earned by the veteran must be reported to the VA in an eligibility verification report (EVR). Even one-time payments such as gifts and inheritances can count as income. Reporting income is important because if the VA eventually discovers income that was not reported, the veteran may be required to pay any overpayments back to the VA. There are two special considerations when calculating your income: allowable exclusions and medical expenses.

Income Exclusions

Some income will not count toward a veteran's income for pension purposes. Most notably, "welfare" will be excluded from income. This includes Supplemental Security Income. However, in order to avoid any problems or allegations of overpayment, all income, including welfare, should be reported regardless. The VA will exclude income it deems appropriate under the law.

A veteran may be able to draft an estate plan that transfers assets out of his or her name. For example, before applying for a pension, a veteran could transfer assets to a valid irrevocable trust. Those assets would then not be considered when determining whether or not the veteran is entitled to a VA pension. Such a plan would reduce the veteran's income for VA pension purposes. Other benefit programs, such as Medicaid, have lookback periods that will recapture such transfers and count them against eligibility. However, the VA does not have a look-back period in order to police these types of transfers. Nevertheless, it is important to consult with an elder law attorney before taking steps to transfer assets, and any such plans should be carefully reviewed.

Unreimbursed Medical Expenses

Unreimbursed medical expenses can be taken out of a veteran's income calculation when reporting income for pension purposes. However, to be deducted, the medical expenses must exceed five percent of the MAPR ($612 for a single veteran with no dependents). Unreimbursed medical expenses include doctor's visits, prescription drugs, and other medical services and products. The costs of a nursing home can also qualify as medical expenses. Consequently, pensions can play an important role in helping elderly veterans cover the cost of nursing home care.

How the VA Adjudicates Claims and Appeals

The VA is an incredibly large federal agency that must process thousands upon thousands of claims every year. The adjudication of claims, during which the VA decides whether or not to grant a claim, can take place at several levels. All new claims begin at the regional office (RO). If the claimed benefits are not granted in full, the veteran can appeal the denial to the Board of Veterans Appeals (BVA). Further appeals can be taken to the Court of Appeals for Veterans Claims (CAVC), the U.S. Court of Appeals for the Federal Circuit, and finally, the U.S. Supreme Court.

ADJUDICATION OF NEW CLAIMS AT THE REGIONAL OFFICE

The most common type of "new" claims are initial applications for benefits. Initial applications are for benefits that have never been applied for in the past. Each individual disability or benefit sought is a separate claim, regardless if multiple claims are filed together. A claim for an increase for a service-connected disability rating is another type of new claim.

Filing a New Claim

To begin a new claim for benefits, a veteran must file the claim at his or her local RO. The easiest way to file an initial claim is to use VA Form 21–256, Veterans Application for Compensation or Pension (www.vba.va.gov/pubs/forms/vba-21–256-are.pdf). The VA will adjudicate claims that are substantially complete. This means that a veteran needs to have all of the necessary information during the initial filing. Filling out the required fields on the Form 21–256 guarantees that the application is substantially complete; however, a claim need not be made on the form and can be started in other ways. The VA will evaluate any sort of written claim as long as it includes the claimant's name (and relationship to the veteran if the claimant is a survivor), the benefit claimed, and the veteran's signature. Although the VA will adjudicate claims containing relatively little information, your best bet is to make sure the initial claim is as clear as possible and that you present the available evidence according to the requirements of each claim you are making. Putting together a clear, logical initial claim will save you a lot of time down the road if you eventually have to go through a lengthy appeal process.

Reopening a Claim

There are a number of deadlines a veteran must meet if he or she is appealing any part of the claims process (these are discussed more in depth on the following pages). If a veteran misses any of these deadlines, his or her rating decision will become final. A final decision cannot be appealed, but instead must be reopened. In order to reopen a claim, the veteran must have new and material evidence.

Before a claim can be reopened, the VA will first determine whether or not a veteran has submitted new and material evidence. If new and material evidence has been submitted, then the claim will be reopened and adjudicated on the merits. If not, then the claim is simply denied outright for lack of new and material evidence. Whether or not a piece of evidence is new and material is an issue that can be appealed in its own right.

Remember, even if new and material evidence is submitted, the VA can still deny the claim on the merits after the evidence has been considered.

Claims Processing at the RO

At the RO level, claims are processed by separate types of processing teams, each of which has a distinct function. The triage team reviews all incoming mail and establishes new claims folders or initiates transfers and works all fast action claims. The predetermination team prepares administrative decisions con-

> ### ▶ NEW AND MATERIAL
>
> The terms "new" and "material" have specific meaning during the VA appellate process. Evidence is "new" if it was not before the RO at the time of the original decision and is not cumulative. An example of cumulative evidence would be a new doctor's letter, which simply restates the conclusion of a previous doctor's letter. A doctor's letter that includes new reasoning or indicates new evidence reviewed would be considered new.
>
> Evidence is "material" if it tends to prove one of the requirements for a benefit the VA found was not met in the original denial. For instance, assume an original denial for service-connected benefits admitted that there was both a current disability and an in-service incurrence, but argued there was no nexus between the two. In that case, evidence that proved a current disability or an in-service incurrence would not be considered "material." Only evidence that proves the nexus requirement would be considered "material."

cerning eligibility for VA benefits and develops claims when a rating decision is needed. The rating team considers and makes decisions regarding whether an injury is connected to service, the amount of injury suffered, and the total level of disability. The post-determination team develops and processes rating decisions and prepares the letters advising veterans of the RO's decisions. The appeals team prepares "Statements of the Case" and processes appeals. Lastly, the public contact team answers routine correspondence.

VA Duties When Adjudicating Claims

If a veteran submits a substantially complete application, the VA has both a duty to notify the veteran of what is needed to support the claim and a duty to make reasonable efforts to locate the necessary evidence. The duty to notify is generally satisfied when the VA sends form letters in response to initial claims. These letters will often indicate the legal requirements necessary to prove the claim and indicate what type of evidence is needed. Although the form letters do lay out the legal requirements, they may not necessarily be helpful to veterans as they aren't specifically tailored to an individual veteran's case.

The duty to assist is generally satisfied when the VA attempts to retrieve medical records from various locations. It is relatively simple for VA adjudicators to obtain records from VA health care facilities. If the veteran indicates in the application the location of private medical records, the VA will attempt to obtain those records as well. However, the duty to assist only requires the VA to make "reasonable efforts" in obtaining evidence. If the VA cannot obtain the relevant records, then it has a duty to notify the veteran that such attempts have failed. In that case, it is the veteran's responsibility to submit the necessary evidence.

The VA can also satisfy its duty to assist by scheduling a compensation and pension exam (C&P) if the evidence in the initial application is not enough to prove the claim. These exams are generally carried out at a VA health care facility; the doctor conducting the exam will determine a medical opinion that will be included in the veteran's file.

Deciding Claims and the Benefit of the Doubt Rule

When reviewing a veteran's claims, the RO must consider all information, evidence, and testimony obtained by the VA and provided by the veteran. After reviewing all the evidence, the law requires the VA to give the benefit of the doubt to the veteran when deciding the claim. This means that if there is an approximate balance of evidence both in favor (positive evidence) and against (negative evidence) granting a claim, the VA must decide in favor of the veteran. Therefore, the VA would have to prove that the negative evidence outweighed the positive in order to deny a claim. The simple fact that negative evidence exists in a veteran's claim is not, by itself, sufficient to deny a claim.

It can take several months for the VA to decide an initial claim. Waiting periods of up to eighteen months are not unheard of. Such delays will vary from RO to RO and claim to claim, but length of time is a major issue when dealing with VA claims.

CHECKING THE STATUS OF YOUR CLAIM

Writing the VA to check on the status of a claim rarely garners much of a response. However, veterans check on the status of their claim either through the phone or online. The VA has established a relatively new eBenefits website that allows veterans to track the status of their claims. To create an account or log in, visit www.ebenefits .va.gov. If requesting a status by phone, the phone number for VA benefits assistance is 1-800-827-1000.

Decision Letters

Once the VA has made a decision on a claim, it will mail a letter to the veteran and the veteran's representative indicating whether or not the claim has been granted. The letter will also be accompanied by a rating decision. The rating decision describes the issues presented, the decision on each issue, the reasoning for the decision, and the evidence used to reach the decision. The letter will also include a description of the veteran's right to appeal.

ADMINISTRATIVE APPEALS AT THE REGIONAL OFFICE

After the VA denies a claim, the veteran may indicate that he or she wishes to appeal by filing a notice of disagreement (NOD). The NOD is an extremely important filing in every appeal. Although there is no specific form or language required, the NOD should indicate which rating decision and claims are being appealed. A simple statement that the veteran disagrees with an unspecific decision or claim is likely not enough to meet the NOD requirements. The NOD should be filed with the specific RO that decided the rating decision being appealed. The NOD must be filed within one year of the date on the decision letter. If the NOD is not filed within the one-year time frame, then the RO decision becomes final. A final decision cannot be appealed; after a decision becomes final, the veteran's only option is to reopen the claim with new and material evidence.

Once a NOD is filed, the RO will send the veteran a letter asking the veteran to make a choice about how he or she wants the appeal to proceed. The options are: a review by a decision review officer (DRO) or proceeding directly to the Board of Veterans Appeals (BVA). The veteran has sixty days to respond to the letter. The veteran need not wait until the VA sends the notice letter; in the NOD, a veteran may indicate his or her preference for the DRO or BVA route.

Decision Review Officer Review

The DRO will review the veteran's case with what is called a de novo standard. De novo is a legal term meaning the claim will be reviewed without regard or deference to any earlier decisions. Although the DRO may make the same findings as the earlier decision-maker, the DRO will not give any weight to those earlier findings. The review is carried out by a DRO or other VA employee who took no part in the original decision. The DRO may conduct an informal conference or hearing before making a final decision. The veteran can submit new evidence either before or during the hearing for the DRO's consideration. The DRO may uphold, revise, or reverse the initial RO decision. Decision review officers cannot settle with claimants; however, DROs can discuss the particular case with the claimant and encourage the claimant to withdraw a meritless appeal. In addition, nothing prevents the DRO from telling an advocate exactly what is needed to satisfy the appeal. If the DRO again denies the claim, the traditional appellate process proceeds as usual. Therefore, selecting a DRO hearing will not prevent the veteran from then seeking review by the BVA. This can be particularly helpful when a veteran submits new evidence after an initial denial. The DRO can review the evidence and grant the claim without going before the BVA. Even if the DRO denies the claim, an appeal before the BVA is still an option.

Statement of the Case and the
VA Form 9 Appeal

The statement of the case (SOC) is another document produced by the RO in response to a NOD. The SOC is a much longer document as compared to a rating decision and is supposed to contain a clear description of the reasons for the denial and the law supporting such a decision. In practice, much of the SOC is simply the statutes and regulations listed verbatim, followed by a brief reiteration of why the claim was denied. Although this is often little additional help to a veteran, the purpose of the SOC is to make clear what the veteran must argue before the BVA.

The SOC includes the VA Form 9 Substantive Appeal. This form is extremely important as it must be submitted to the VA within sixty days of the date of the SOC. Technically, this form is the veteran's argument to the BVA. As such, it should be carefully drafted to address all of the issues outlined in the SOC. Any legal or factual errors made by the RO should be pointed out. The veteran can raise new issues in the Form 9 that were not addressed in the SOC; however, if new issues or benefits are raised in the Form 9, the VA may decide to issue a new rating decision or a supplemental statement of the case. If you are about to fill out a VA Form 9, you should consult an attorney if you have any questions or need any guidance.

Additional evidence and arguments can be submitted for the BVA's consideration up until the record is "certified" to the BVA. A record is "certified" to the BVA when the physical file is physically transferred to the BVA in Washington, D.C. Normally, the physical file remains with the RO at all other times.

▶ FINDING AN ATTORNEY

The appeals process can be complicated and confusing. If you are unsure about how to fill out a certain form or how to present your case to the BVA or DRO, it may be helpful to contact an attorney to assist you. In order to practice before the VA, an attorney must be accredited through the VA's Office of the General Counsel. Veterans service organization representatives are also trained in VA benefits law and have been accredited with the VA. The VA's Office of the General Counsel's website provides a search engine to locate accredited attorneys and veterans service organization representatives at www.va.gov/ogc/apps/accreditation/index.asp.

STEPS TO A VA CLAIMS AND APPEALS

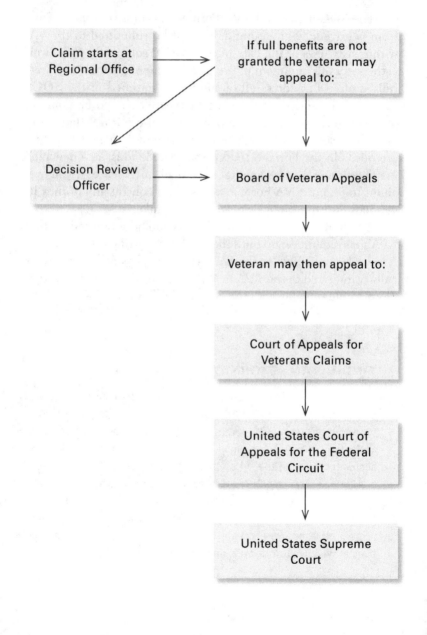

BOARD OF VETERANS APPEALS

After the record is certified to the BVA, the BVA will then make a decision. Before the BVA makes a decision, the veteran has a right to a hearing if he or she so chooses. This hearing can take place in Washington, D.C., or at the veteran's local RO in front of a traveling board member or via videoconference. Because most veterans are unable to travel to Washington, the RO options are usually selected. However, the backlog at the BVA is so great that it is possible for long delays before a hearing is scheduled. It is not unheard of for veterans to wait years before a hearing can be given.

Compared with regular court proceedings, BVA hearings are fairly informal. Most often, the only witness is the veteran. There is no standard of evidence or complicated courtroom procedure. Most often, the BVA member will ask the veteran a series of questions and then allow the veteran's advocate to ask questions as well. Representation is allowed at the hearings. You can get legal representation during the BVA process from various veterans service organizations or an attorney who is experienced in VA benefits law.

A hearing can be useful as it gives the claim a face, as opposed to just a stack of paperwork, which the BVA will consider in making its determination. It allows the veteran to tell his or her story. Some advocates put great value on this personal touch. In some cases, however, the delay caused by scheduling a hearing outweighs any type of advantage a personal impression could give a decision. An attorney or veterans service organization representative could help in deciding whether a hearing is necessary.

When making a decision, the BVA has a couple of options: grant the benefits, affirm a denial, or remand the claim to the RO for correction of a defect or for developing new facts. The BVA can also combine these options depending on the claims and issues in front of the BVA. If a claim is remanded, the vet-

DEADLINES DURING A VA APPEAL

STEP	APPLICABLE TIMELINE OR DEADLINE
BVA mails notice to the veteran of decision	
Veteran files notice of appeal	Within 120 days of receiving BVA notice
VA submits record of case	Within 60 days of case being put on docket
Veteran may file motion to challenge an issue in the record	Within 14 days of veteran having received the record
Veteran files brief	Within 60 days of the end of the 14-day period for the motion to challenge the record
VA submits its brief	Within 60 days of veteran's brief being filed
Veteran submits reply brief (if he or she decides to)	Within 60 days of VA submitting its brief
Court issues its decision	
Losing party (veteran or VA) may file a motion for reconsideration	Within 21 days of decision being issued
Judgment is entered	
Losing party can file notice of appeal to the Federal Circuit	Within 60 days of the judgment being entered

eran should expect additional information and notices from the RO indicating what the veteran needs to do in order to help carry out the remand. If the BVA denies the benefits, the veteran's next appellate option is the Court of Appeals for Veterans Claims.

COURT OF APPEALS FOR VETERANS CLAIMS

The Court of Appeals for Veterans Claims (CAVC) is a court created specifically to review decisions of the BVA. If a veteran chooses, he or she has a legal right to take an appeal before the CAVC. In order to appeal to the CAVC, the veteran must file a notice of appeal with the CAVC within 120 days of the date of the BVA decision.

Unlike the previous steps in the VA appeals process, the CAVC is much more formal and adversarial. The CAVC has a set of rules that, for the most part, need to be strictly followed. The process largely consists of the veteran filing a legal, written document called a brief, which outlines his or her main arguments; the VA filing a response brief; and then, finally, the veteran has a chance to file a response to the VA's response. During the CAVC process, the VA will be represented by a government attorney.

Although it is possible to take a claim before the CAVC pro se, or without an attorney, it is highly recommended that an experienced attorney be retained to assist with the appeal. There are many attorneys in the Washington area who practice before the CAVC. The CAVC's website (www.uscourts.cavc.gov) contains valuable information on attorneys admitted to practice before the CAVC, court rules and procedures, and how to file an appeal pro se.

For veterans who are unable to pay an attorney to represent them before the VA, the National Veterans Legal Service Program sponsors a Veterans Consortium Pro Bono Program. The

Pro Bono Program is a group of veterans law attorneys who represent veterans of limited means before the VA free of charge. To find out if your claim qualifies for Pro Bono Program representation, visit the website at www.vetsprobono.org.

U.S. COURT OF APPEALS FOR THE FEDERAL CIRCUIT

Veterans have a right to appeal CAVC decisions to the Federal Circuit. This step almost always requires the assistance of an attorney, as the Federal Circuit is forbidden by law to review issues of fact and issues of the application of the law to the facts. The Federal Circuit can review only issues of law. This distinction can become very technical, and an attorney is highly recommended. However, pro se litigants, meaning parties not represented by attorneys, are allowed. A pro se guide is located on the Federal Circuit's website at www.cafc.uscourts .gov/images/stories/rules-of-practice/pro%20se.pdf. In order to appeal a CAVC decision, a notice of appeal must be filed with CAVC within sixty days of the date on the CAVC decision.

RESOURCES

- **Veterans Benefits Administration** (www.vba.va.gov/VBA): Includes summaries on veterans benefit programs, eligibility rules, vocational training, and compensation and pension programs.

- **US Census Bureau—Information on Poverty Thresholds** (www.census.gov/hhes/www/poverty/data/threshld/index.html)

- **Social Security Administration** (www.socialsecurity.gov/ pgm/ssi.htm): Details on supplemental security income and instructions on applying.

- **eBenefits** (www.ebenefits.va.gov/ebenefits-portal/ebenefits
  .portal): VA online portal that allows veterans to track the
  status of their claims.

- **U.S. Court of Appeals for Veterans Claims** (www.uscourts
  .cavc.gov): National court for review of Board of Veterans
  Appeals decisions; website includes information on appealing
  and filing.

- **Veterans Consortium Pro Bono Program** (www.vetsprobono.
  org): Hosted by the National Veterans Legal Service Program;
  includes a group of veterans law attorneys who represent
  veterans of limited means before the VA free of charge.

- **Veterans Clinics:** Various law schools throughout the
  country have veterans clinics that offer free or low-cost legal
  services for veterans and can also provide you with assistance
  in determining where to get additional help. (This list is not
  extensive and more clinics are popping up each year.)

- **Widener University School of Law** (http://law.widener.edu/
  vetclinic/)

- **William and Mary School of Law** (http://law.wm.edu/
  academics/programs/jd/electives/clinics/veterans/index.php)

- **John Marshall School of Law** (www.jmls.edu/veterans/)

- **Yale Law School** (www.law.yale.edu/academics/
  veteranslegalservicesclinic.htm)

- **Thomas Jefferson School of Law San Diego** (www.tjsl.edu/
  clinics/veterans-clinic)

- **Phoenix School of Law** (www.phoenixlaw.edu/clinics/)

- **North Carolina Central University School of Law** (http://
  law.nccu.edu/clinics/veterans-law)

- **University of Detroit Mercy School of Law** (www.law
  .udmercy.edu/index.php/projectsalute)

INDEX